HEART

Previous Books by Lance Morrow:

Safari (with Neil Leifer)
Fishing in the Tiber
America: A Rediscovery
The Chief: A Memoir of Fathers & Sons

HEART

A MEMOIR

LANCE MORROW

WARNER BOOKS

A Time Warner Company

Some names have been changed to protect the privacy of individuals.

Warner Books, Inc., 1271 Avenue of the Americas, New York, NY 10020

 A Time Warner Company

Printed in the United States of America
First Printing: September 1995

10   9   8   7   6   5   4   3   2   1

Library of Congress Cataloging-in-Publication Data

Morrow, Lance.
    Heart: a memoir / Lance Morrow.
       p. cm.
    ISBN 0-446-51870-0
    1. Morrow, Lance. 2. Journalists—United States—Biography.
I. Title.
PN4874.M5865A3   1995
070'.92—dc20
    [B]   95–7566
                                                               CIP

For Susan

HEART

1

Placido Domingo is singing "Danny Boy" on the compact disc. I am seized by an impulse to burn down the house.

But it occurs to me that it is raining for the first time in days, and the house is less flammable than it ought to be. The kindling is wet. Conditions are not ideal.

I am off the hook. The apocalypse will wait.

I walk out of the house that I have reprieved.

I cross the fields at dusk, toward the coyotes' mouse-hunting grounds. The thick mown hayfield is wet, and it soaks my trousers. I startle deer on my left that bound off single-file at an angle to the right, flourishing their extravagant white tails upright. One doe stops when she is thirty yards off and drops her tail and looks back at me. I stop as well, and the two of us stare at one another a long time across the darkening field.

I left the house in a rage, but now, looking at the doe, I am distracted, and the anger blanks out into an alert animal curiosity. I wonder how long the doe will stay, whether she can smell me, why she is so evidently unconcerned by my presence. Wonder too if the coyotes are around, just inside the tree line, watching me as well.

The coyotes (the eastern kind, with much wolf blood, the size of German shepherds) do not run in packs in summer, but hunt singly now, or live on roadkill, which is ample, the roadsides strewn with raccoons and groundhogs and occasional deer in attitudes of car-whacked and tire-flattened death. Sometimes by the road I see the guts torn out of a deer: That would not be tires, but coyotes' teeth.

My son James and I were up on the white rocks yesterday, carrying shotgun and .22 rifle (we had been shooting in the woods below), looking down into the bowl of fields and woods where the farm and farmhouse lie. In the winter the coyotes hunt in packs: brittle clear winter nights, moonlight hunts on the ridge where the white-rock perch looks across the fields. But the deer on such moonlit nights would be in the thickest cover. In the morning, under the canopy pines, we would find their droppings close-grouped, small piles of shiny black shot.

The depression that is said to settle over someone who has had heart surgery has reorganized itself in my case, for some reason, as blazing anger. I passed through a violent storm of it this afternoon. (Placido Domingo is now sobbing Rachmaninoff—Pushkin's "Oh, Cease Thy Singing, Maiden Fair"—long silvery Slavic plaints, attenuated and shining in that stagy, appealingly false way.)

Susan met my train at the station in Dover Plains and drove us back toward the farm in rain. We quarreled. I shot up in a blaze of blindside irrational rage—like a bucket of gasoline thrown on a campfire. It sucked the oxygen from the air. My lungs might collapse, a violent implosion. I opened the door on the passenger side and was within an instant of jumping out at fifty miles an hour.

My heart raced, pounded.

Susan has gone out now. I walked through the pastures for an hour and came back to the farmhouse, trouser legs soaking, mind stilled somewhat, but thinking of suicide now and then (the shotgun, the shells in the center drawer of the dresser, hidden behind the bathing suits) and then indignantly chasing the thought, as if it were an animal. It would retreat a little way, cringing hyena-like, and wait to see if I would tolerate it again betimes.

Which I do when letting the attention drift, and back it comes with its yellow eyes, its pointed ears.

This is not an intelligent way to get well.

I could kill someone else or kill myself—either would do. I have the enraged, smoking heart of a postal sorter snapping somewhere anonymous in America, a parking lot, a McDonald's, and blazing away—to make life stop its intolerable self, to break up the days and throw away the pieces so that they can never be reassembled, never even be found. I give brief but serious thought to the possibility that I am going crazy.

Why would a man who has just been rescued from death by surgeons now find himself murderous and suicidal? A mystery.

From Domingo, I hear a Sigmund Romberg bombast, the Student Prince, serenading. How shapely and bogus he is tonight, Itzhak Perlman's violin weeping all around him, the air dense with groan and vibrato.

What am I to do? My heart is bursting with rage, and I cannot comprehend it. My heart is a house on fire, flame shooting from the windows. Shhh, shhh.

* * *

It is morning, a cool fog lies on the valley, a drizzle. The sound of crows now and then through heavy air. A Yugoslavian morning.

Emerson thought that we are mostly moping dogs. Every now and then we may sing like angels, remembering some music that we once heard in heaven . . . And then we return to our usual state, that of sullen dogs—brainless, surly. I am deep in the dog state.

A hawk comes down and challenges an enormously fat groundhog by the barn. Ambitious hawk.

The groundhog stands fast in a way suggesting her young are near. The hawk alights in a chestnut tree and watches, the two staring at one another. This seems to be country for rural standoffs—between men and deer, groundhogs and hawks, men and women, staring at one another across a distance with various kinds of interspecies curiosity and intent: murder sometimes, or arson, or suicide.

The rain has helped the grass a little, but it has been a dry summer, sere, the grass and hay stubble bristling underfoot and sticking the flesh.

August chirring. A breeze, light as a ghost, then a dog-day stillness again, the humid heaviness of the air that is suggestive of violence, the eye of the storm.

I drive miles this morning on the back roads of the South Taconics, trying to talk down the anger, to give it some air and scenery. The fields still have some of the clinging mist on them—the sun gets into the mist and makes it luminous. In this part of Dutchess County are dozens of opulent horse farms, rich-guy spreads owned by what the locals call "citiots," from New York. Millions of dollars gone to landscaping and fencing—an American city-boy idea of English hunt country.

Thoroughbreds graze in the close-hanging mist and

look up to see me as I fire past in my black-red dudgeon, sore aggrieved.

Beside a drying swamp bottom in the Shekomeko Valley, I see a dozen wild turkeys feeding. Quiet, quiet. They belong to the sane universe. I feel ashamed.

* * *

Is this the inevitable atmosphere?

It feels familiar, from long ago.

I swerve around the litter of dead raccoons and moles (Toad's friends murdered by the weasel mafia and dumped along the road).

Rabies is epidemic in our part of the country. One of the signs: A normally nocturnal animal wanders around at midday in the open. If a coyote eats a rabid raccoon, the coyote becomes rabid.

Now I see, in an open space beside the road, a raccoon staggering as if drunk, oblivious to the world around him. I slow the car, almost to a stop. The raccoon sees me — swivels his head dreamily and woozes toward me on six-martini legs.

Just a drop of saliva in an open wound, and after that: irrational furies and fears, muscle spasms, foaming at the mouth, then death.

I do not wait for my raccoon to bite the tires, but drive away in a spray of gravel.

Now my chainsawed chest bone has begun to ache. And the numbed novocaine sensation where the mammary artery was cut, on the left side, develops a centering pain. And it begins to occur to me that while a tantrum is recreational, it may exact a price.

I tell myself I must go still and Buddhist.

Is it possible that ranting is genetic? My mother, otherwise admirable, was a little atom bomb of ranting, a city-flattening genius of rage that (like Fat Man and Little Boy) left an aftermath of radiation in the air.

Well, Mother, Saint Joan, King Lear, let me pass over the ranting, stop my ears, not dwell on the troubles of your childhood (those troubles that were, so to speak, your plutonium). You suffered them, you paid for them, and you transmitted them, in that infallible chain reaction, falling dominoes of infliction, from parent to child to child's child—anger and injury refracted through time. I sympathize with you. I admire you abundantly. I forgive you, if forgiveness is called for. I have tried, with modest but imperfect success (we'll know more later), to interrupt the transmission, from myself to my children. I quote Oliver Wendell Holmes in his decision to allow a severely retarded woman in Virginia to be sterilized: "Three generations of imbeciles are enough!" My sons smile indulgently (right, Dad), for they have heard the line before.

Perhaps anger is an old habit that can be unlearned. I am not so sure. Maybe it is more like rabies: the fatal drop of ranter's spittle.

I must make this anger subside—if only for the sake of my heart, which is not (I know now) endlessly tolerant of me.

2

Lingza Chokyi did not understand that she was dead. She floated out of her body. When she looked down from midair at her bed, she saw a pig lying in it, wearing her clothes. She saw her children weeping and her family preparing for her funeral. She grew angry. No one paid attention to her. They did not see or hear her. They would not bring her her plate. They behaved as if she did not exist.

In Tibet, a delok is a person who apparently dies and then departs the body and hovers nearby, and after a time, returns to life. Lingza Chokyi was a famous sixteenth-century delok who, as Buddhists say, "arrived in the bardo realm"—that is, in the stage of transition between life and death—but eventually was sent back to the world, "as there had been an error concerning her name and family." (Metaphysical bureaucracy.)

The Zen master Sogyal Rinpoche, from whom I am quoting, reports that the phenomenon of the delok continues in Tibet today, despite Chinese occupiers and a prevailing demystification.

A delok may leave the body for as long as a week, sometimes to carry messages from the living to the dead. To prevent fraud (a pseudodelok setting up practice, claiming to carry messages to the dead that never arrive), Tibetans have devised validating tests: While the delok is supposedly out on a mission, the body's orifices are stopped with butter, and the face covered with a mask made of barley flour. If the butter does not run, and the mask does not crack, then the delok is pronounced to be genuine.

Today in the Himalayas, according to Sogyal Rinpoche, deloks still practice. "These deloks are quite ordinary people, often women, who are very devoted and have great faith. They 'die' on special days in the Buddhist calendar, for a number of hours, and their major function is to act as messengers between the living and the dead."

But the mind is always a delok. For years I have practiced some casual, secular version of the delok's floating. My spirit spends most of its time drifting fecklessly, miles and years away from my body, and returns only when required for emergencies and special occasions.

A journalist, of course, is a delok by profession.

But I have lately reversed the delok's pattern. When I approached death not long ago—or death approached me, a near-miss during a heart attack (my second) and a coronary bypass operation (my second)—I abandoned out-of-body wandering and descended for the most focused in-body experience of my life.

A heart attack, like the prospect of the noose in the morning—or, more closely, like the rope itself that morning, tightening up hard and starting to cut the neck—concentrates the mind.

* * *

I concentrated. The great elephant descended and left the indentation of its foot upon my chest.

And look here, Mother, what a precociously drooling geezer I've become, a Frankenstein's monster of zipper scars and pirated body parts. Two heart attacks and two bypass operations—six grafts in all, loops of hosing jury-rigged around my jalopy of a heart. Two major crashes, but the motor still runs. I am fifty-three years old.

Self-pity is detestable. I do not feel sorry for myself. I run to the other extreme. I blame myself. I rant at myself.

Still, all of this damage seems premature. I have a head of hair as full as a Kennedy's, and all my own-grown teeth but two, and strong muscles, and the kind of peasant packhorse energy that can carry a piano up four flights of stairs. But here I am with the medical résumé of a veteran of the Spanish-American War, the white-whiskery wraith you used to see at the head of the Memorial Day parade.

After my heart attack this time, Bob Hughes, *Time*'s art critic, called and started cheering me up in booming Australian. He said, "Well, mate, I don't guess you'd want to repeat this. . . . Reminds me of Voltaire. . . . Someone asked if he'd ever had a homosexual experience. Voltaire said, yes, once. He was asked if he'd been tempted to repeat it. Voltair said, oh, no. Once a philosopher; twice, a pervert."

I am a repeater—a recidivist pervert of chest implosions.

Another man with a fresh heart attack—there seem so many, I meet them everywhere now, the freemasonry of the cabbage (doctor slang for Coronary Artery Bypass)—told me the wonderful current phrase to describe the chief risk factor: not family history, not smoking, not bad diet, but "joyless striving."

Oh, woe, Little Father Time treadmilling grimly, I think I managed to pack a great deal of aging into a small container of birthdays. I became a compacter of time and life stages, like the *Thresher* at a terrible depth. By the age of six, I was a full-grown pseudo-adult, a prodigy in Mickey Rooney's long-ago freckleface.

By the time I arrived at my midthirties, I had the bad habits of two or three grown-ups: a journalist in my parents' trade, with the trade's behaviors, smoking and drinking; like a chimney, and like a fish. I got ahead of myself in wear and tear, leaping the decades by dog years. Hence the perfectly natural heart attack at thirty-six. By the time I reached the age of fifty, scurrying ahead, frisking round my father toward the finish line, trying to pass him on the outside, I must have been well on the way to eighty, hence the second heart attack.

But I exaggerate. I do not believe it was the bad habits, really. I had cut them out years before the second attack. Nor was it family history, for there was little premature heart disease in the genes. It was not even the "joyless striving," although the phrase has a ring of truth, a clinical poetry.

It would be self-important to think that God has been trying to teach me something. But if he were: what? His methods of instruction have been sharp; he does not come to me painlessly in dreams, after all. A myocardial infarction—the literal death of expanses of heart muscle—is a harder lesson to absorb than a warning vision slipped into an afternoon nap.

What must I learn? I know about cholesterol.

I played with the thesis that the past itself is evil. Emerson was getting at it when he wrote: "Why drag about this monstrous corpse of your memory?" The black sack of shadows, the irrecoverable.

The simple thesis is this: The past (traumas, golden ages, irretrievable horrors and treasures) may become so transfixing that it ends by ruining and thwarting the present—occludes the present moment, which is alive, as a clot blocks the heart, and makes the muscle (the life) die.

I have seen this at odd moments as a journalist, in the West Bank and Gaza (the indignant memories exhaled in Palestinians' living rooms, ghosting round in dense clouds of Marlboro smoke: the village, the well, the fig, the olive, the goats, the *nakba* [disaster] in 1948, or 1967, when the Jews came and, the Arabs say, ruined Eden, the clogging, enduring hatred), and in Bosnia (among the flourished tribal atrocity pictures, the old wrongs set glowing with slivovitz), and I have come upon it in the recurring dreams that I have of my father's ruined house (always a variation on the same dream, desolate and humiliating).

I mean that the subjective motifs share something; the Balkan tribal tragedies and my family's dream life fuse at a deeper level of my mind, like subterranean streams connecting. In the upper air, they have nothing like the same tragic proportions. They belong to different orders of importance. But down in the dark, they sound the same, and the sound envelopes me: savage anger and depression, concentrates of toxic myth, indignant hopelessness. Despairing, desolate, lashing.

The rage that I speak of is never merely political. It is too deep for that. It is in part a nostalgia for the scene of the crime. Deep word, *nostalgia*: the *nostos algos*, the agony to return home.

Anger jumps out of the body. It is an obsessive, time-traveling delok. It produces an unwholesome metaphysics (the kind that Emerson suggested: "the corpse of memory").

It traps the mind in metastable states, like rail sidings, like cul-de-sac Balkan dreams of outraged innocence and glory: nightmares of the irrecoverable, the unresolved. The delok is Hamlet's father's ghost, up in bad weather in the middle of the night, ruined but unable to sleep. Memory. And revenge.

During the periods I lay in the coronary care unit waiting for the second heart surgery, my mind went wandering about, out of body, working as a kind of journalist of memory and anger. I sought to connect my inner world and my dilemma (the rage that gave me this blocked heart) to outer catastrophes. I sailed off to Bosnia and Hiroshima—big objective correlatives.

I worry about something that has size. It is easier to absorb the large exterior events, and make sense of them, than to grasp the inner disasters, which are hidden from me (until too late, until implosion) by my evanescent but thousand-times impenetrable armoring of flesh and bone.

My parents were journalists. My father stood with the rest of the White House press at Franklin Roosevelt's desk in the Oval Office during the war and enjoyed the presidential performance, the cigarette holder clenched in the teeth, the patrician joshing, the smoke screens. And later, when he was an associate editor of the *Saturday Evening Post* in Washington, young senators on the make would come round, fresh from battle in the Pacific, which taught them something about the killer instinct and the way of the world, fresh to Washington, looking for an issue, a ticket to power. Joe McCarthy of Wisconsin would come to my father's office on Jackson Place, just across the way from the White House, and ask his advice: What's a good issue? What would work? What would sell? My parents would have dinner with Lyndon Johnson (who liked the fact that my mother cussed—"Bird, come meet this pretty little thing") or Richard Nixon, who liked my father and hated my mother for the evening at the Shoreham when she told him to get out of public life because he did not understand people. Nixon called my father the next day at his office and complained, in an oblique way, suggesting but not quite asking: "Can't you control your wife?"

The cast of characters who were the public center of my parents' lives (McCarthy, Johnson, Nixon, the Kennedy boys—word was good on Jack and scathing on Bobby, "that squirt, that little shit") played out their dramas in the early course of my professional career. I felt that I inherited them from my parents, taking on these public personalities and their stories the way the child of the butler and the cook might pass naturally into similar work in a noble household. It was a problematic inheritance, like having my parents resign from the tragedy at the end of the third act, while I took up the story for the fourth and fifth, which were the sixties, and, in Nixon's case, the early seventies, ending in Watergate. Joe McCarthy, of course, drank himself to death midway through the third act (in the mid-fifties). The royal houses of American politics fared in a Greek or a Shakespearean way, Jack and Bobby down in blood, Lyndon (for whom I fetched vanilla ice cream in the fifties when I was a Senate pageboy and he was Majority leader) driven back to the heath in the hill country of Texas.

* * *

So public events and private events were intertwined in even my earliest memories. The largest exterior events in the world reverberated inside the house, in the chambers of the mind and body—like my mother's scream in the instant she learned that Franklin Roosevelt had died, and I was going under ether in Children's Hospital to have my tonsils out, a piercing scream at the edge of my darkening consciousness.

All truths—large truths, small truths—ultimately must be connected in the heart, or they are useless. The heart either makes sense of them or does not (in which case they cease to exist), or else breaks down and stops, if the truths are too terrible. All memories of injury hurt the heart the same. There, catastrophes great or small are indistinguishable from one another.

For this I read Herodotus, who is surely the patron saint of journalists. One of his commentators, David Grene, explained Herodotus's mind this way: "It is the beliefs that people maintain, not their necessary truth, that concerns him. His *History* is as much about what people believe and think as it is about events that happen—and less about whether events *did* happen than that people thought they did. Because history, for him, is the total fabric of a moment and an era and a civilization, where thought is as important as acts or events."

The heart, traveling through time, becomes a part of "the total fabric of a moment and an era and a civilization."

Thucydides and Herodotus argue about this. Thucydides, somewhat the younger of the two, laments that "most of the events of the past, through lapse of time, have fought their way, past credence, into the country of myth." But Herodotus understands the country of myth as Thucydides does not.

Herodotus does not insist, as Thucydides does, upon that literal-minded "credence." The heart, the imagination, turns all facts universal. Public deeds and private dreams interpenetrate, and become interchangeable.

The proportions and physics that govern the objective world are not as stately as they seem, but partake, we know, of the fantastic and subjective, just as the Newtonian certi-

tudes melt betimes into chaos theory, or the subtle irra-
tionalities of fractals. Or, equally, into the absurd, lovably
imprecise metaphors that scientists now use to try to describe the universe and its origins—beer suds, strings. The
banality, the intimacy, of Being itself.

It is a dangerous principle for a journalist, of course. If
I were an editor with a reporter who reported only the
hearsay running through the crowds outside and not the
murder itself, I might have to fire him. This is an old journalist argument. Herodotus, in any case, was a journalist/
historian of ideas and beliefs, a cultural reporter. His city-
desk-legman's matter-of-factness mingled with a kind of
hallucinatory wonder, a tabloid sensationalism working up
the profoundest myths.

Herodotus reports:

> There is a place in Arabia just about the city of
> Buto, and to this place I went to inquire about the
> winged serpents; and when I came there, I saw the bones
> and backbones of serpents past all telling for numbers;
> there were heaps of backbones, great heaps and
> lesser. . . . Now this place where the backbones are
> strewn about is where there is a pass, from narrow moun-
> tains into a great plain, and this plain neighbors the
> plain of Egypt. There is a story that with the coming of
> spring the winged serpents fly from Arabia into Egypt,
> and the ibis birds meet the serpents at this pass and will
> not suffer the snakes to come through, but kill them. It
> is for this deed that the Arabians say the Egyptians have
> held the bird in great honor. And the Egyptians them-
> selves agree that they honor the ibis on these grounds.

I thought I found some mythy version of something—
to me—profoundly familiar in Herodotus speaking of another bird, the phoenix.

"I never saw one myself," Herodotus admits (he is fastidious about recording what he himself actually saw and what he merely heard about from others), "except in pictures." The people of Heliopolis say the phoenix comes but rarely, once every five hundred years. "He comes at the time his father dies."

When the father phoenix dies, Herodotus has heard, the son forms an egg of myrrh, of a weight that he is able to carry while flying. He hollows out the egg and places his father's corpse inside it, and "with more myrrh he plasters over the place he had hollowed out and stowed his father within . . . and so, having plastered it over, he sets out from Arabia and carries his father to the shrine of the Sun in Egypt."

It is a ridiculous fancy. But I myself have done something like what the phoenix did, using an egg of words.

* * *

Being an observer by birth and profession, but held to a hospital bed amid tubes and needles, I lie quite still and dematerialize. And drift on a sort of memory's jetstream. The delok's trajectory makes a throughline overhead.

I turn myself into a pale kite, translucent, the kind I watched some Arab boys flying over the Damascus Gate to the old city of Jerusalem just after the Intifada began. They were of the age to be throwing rocks at Jews, and probably had been. But now at the hour when the beautiful stone of Jerusalem turns its golden evening color, the boys flew a kite that found a breeze and lifted on its string high above the fortress walls. The kite leaped and jittered and jumped in the clear evening air, as if it were alive and happy.

I hover and hover and hover here. Dr. Krieger (Dr. War-Man, Dr. War-Maker) will presently crash through my chest with a chain saw, and with his perfect rubbered fingers begin to cut my heart expertly, like a sushi chef.

It has been a big year for the outside-inside melodrama. I toured an objective correlative, Sarajevo, and I somehow internalized it. I swallowed it, took it—or something like it, just as bad—into my body, into (literally) my heart, where it became just as dangerous to me.

I dabble in Buddhism to calm myself. Urgently dabble—speed-reading.

I say that all of the agitated past is tossed about in the Buddhists' "Sea of samsara," the terrible repetitions of lives given over to anger, revenge, selfishness. To escape that sea, the cycles of exhausting inevitability, Sogyal Rinpoche says that what must be learned is reflected in "the mirror of death." He quotes Montaigne: "Let us deprive death of its strangeness, let us frequent it, let us get used to it. . . . To practice death is to practice freedom."

I do not entirely believe it. We shall see.

3

Not death, for now.

Susan and I have made our way up to the farm in Dutchess County, at last, and I sit on the open porch, with my feet up, looking out past our barn, across the rolling pasture and into the woods in the distance, where they rise to the top of the ridge.

Deer come to water in the stream just beyond the barn. This morning by the house, a fawn. Five minutes ago, two fat groundhogs hurried across the grass below me— their furry fat rolling in smooth undulations as they went, their haste undignified—and into a thicket. A mocking bird imitates a cardinal in the tree above. (What is the mocking bird's motive? Why this elaborate mimicry? The bird has no ideas of its own?)

Susan has seen a coyote up in the far pasture—bigger than a western coyote, dark fur. I try to see, at a distance, I sweep the field with binoculars.

I wonder if it is simply a dog—a German shepherd even—on an outing, but Susan is convinced it is not.

I return to reading. I look over my shoulder every so often and sweep my eyes over the far field, lining up my sight on the birch tree that rises out of the bottom from the creek.

I advise Susan to start carrying a heavy stick, one of the Scottish ash canes, when she walks in the woods.

Susan sees him again. Now, peering through the field glasses, I make him out, standing at the end of the pasture by the tree line: not as dark as Susan said, but grayish, with some yellowing, I think, long ears. He moves, walking in profile to me, then trots, the springy, bouncing gait of the wild—distinctly not a dog—and, alarmingly, gaily (rabidly?), jumps twice, a bouncing-and-looping water-smooth arc, hard to decipher. He has that slouchy-springy but surreptitious look that hyenas and other such opportunists have. Susan says he is hunting field mice, although I cannot see why leaping would be part of that, unless it gives him some brief aerial perspective. He does pay minute attention to the hayfield, snuffling in the stubble.

He sees us, and looks in our direction for long seconds, then resumes his work and play. He seems in high spirits.

I try to calculate whether I could shoot him at this distance. Probably not, and certainly not without a .30-30 or some such. The coyote makes me nervous. It would be stupid to go trying to shoot it without knowing better whether it is rabid. Still, Susan walks in the woods out beyond the pastures.

* * *

I am glad to be alive. I take as my text a story that was told to me about Clare Booth Luce. She sat at the bedside of

a younger woman who was dying of cancer. The woman
kept repeating, "Why me? Why me?" Finally Clare Luce
said to her quietly, "But, dear, why *not* you?"

I love the story and turn it over in my mind. Good
medicine for the reclusive pastoral whiner.

I have not yet lapsed into taking life for granted. I remind myself not to do so, although it is human nature. The
healing makes me irritable (all that bone knitting itself
back together, the muscles trying to forget the insult), and
that irritability creates a background buzz of complaint in
the mind that sometimes obscures the overall miraculous.

Irritability and real exhaustion. I spend a lot of time
sleeping. The overpowering need to sleep descends
abruptly, as if someone had thrown a master switch in the
system. My heart seems to be mending and performing
well, back at its old stand.

I have stopped listening to it as carefully and anxiously as I did before. For a long time in the hospital, after
the heart attack, my heart felt as wild and irregular as a car
bouncing at high speed over bad road, or like an animal
straining and trying to bolt, as if it were lashing to get out
of the skin. I could see it thumping through the skin,
which had been shaved smooth and seemed too tenuous a
membrane to contain the animal.

Odd how porous—how overt and virtually public—
the body becomes in the hospital. Its private business
(what's in the veins, the bladder, and so on) becomes objectified, all measured and analyzed, the veins punctured with
needles and drips, the heart monitored by half a dozen tabs
on the chest that send signals through wires (sometimes
through the air) and turn the heartbeat into an EKG signature on a screen. I was amused to see that my EKG looked
very much like Lyndon Johnson's signature as I recalled it
from the sixties: the high, bold initial strokes of the *L* and *J*

being the big beats of the heart, and the ensuing squiggles being an illegible elaboration of the heart's distinctive electricities.

The heart's signature had that hurried negligence of the fortieth traveler's check you have signed while standing at the bank counter.

In one hospital my roommate was a Hispanic junk dealer from the Bronx. The room was so arranged that the two monitors tracking his heartbeat and mine were just above my bed, and I spent hours idly watching our two very different cardiac signatures on the monitor screens.

The junk dealer had come into the hospital because of severe heart irregularity. The signature of his beat was the wildest fandango I have ever seen in an EKG: great loops and swooping flourishes of the heart, extravagant orbits and descents. Sometimes the lines were densely and jaggedly shimmering, like an aurora borealis, and sometimes they stretched and woozed out drunkenly, and I wondered if the leash of life could hold the junk dealer, whose name was Hector, or if he would go too far on one of these orbits and not come down again.

My eye would study the EKG monitor for some time, and then I would become conscious of the actual Hector in the bed next to mine. He was a mountainously fleshy man who emitted loud animal honks and snorts and wheezes as he slept. The line of the EKG was more romantic and elegant, I thought, than the man himself, who was his own outward Caliban. I watched his heart dreaming while the beast slept. Who knew the great hulk concealed such an extravagant artist in his heart?

When he woke, Hector, who, I suspected, had been rendered sweet-natured by fear, told me about an opportunity he had to buy a second junkyard in the Bronx. But his partner was timid and could not do any of the big thinking necessary to clinch the deal. Hector himself signed the papers from his bed. He had to do everything, he said, or it did not get done. The burdens of office and power.

Then he talked about New York. He said that he'd been released from the hospital some months before after treatment for the same problem; he felt anxious leaving the hospital. He took a cab up First Avenue toward the Bronx, got as far as Eighty-sixth Street, where, right beside the cab window, he saw one man knife another one, in the middle of the afternoon. Hector told the cab driver to return to the hospital. His heart was screaming.

* * *

The birds are more subdued but still singing. Susan has returned from the Grand Union. She has brought a steak. The doctors have told me to eat anything I want, in the first month or so, in order to regain my strength. I think that I shall arrange a grand tour of every dish I love that is horrible for my heart. I shall say good-bye to each in turn—*Grande Bouffe*. The farewell glutton tour. My son James has promised me he knows where the best eggs Benedict in New York can be had, and I shall save those for last, one Sunday morning.

A heat wave has settled over the East, the weather locked and motionless for days and days. Over the Midwest, storms and tornadoes. The Mississippi and all its tributaries have flooded, whole towns underwater, vast farmland inundated. The storms bring no catharsis, but linger unnaturally.

Here, we sit day after day under airless haze, no winds, the clouds white cumulus on top but eliding down into a vague margin of dark and thunder that will not quite coalesce, a smear of menace in the lower air. But never rain, always the premonition of it, a Bangkok heat over pastures and pond and the wooded ridge beyond, just to the west where the sun will go down hours from now, big and red, its sinking being the only motion.

We swam yesterday in the neighbor's swimming pool across the road. The neighbor is a wealthy Wall Street man who comes on weekends and invited us to use the pool anytime. We drove up the long steep driveway through landscaped banks of flowers and trees and found the swimming pool, motionless and silent, with that haunted quality that such places have (most dramatically in southern California, canyon houses with empty pools, a menacing Didion silence)—a few children's pool toys floating on the water, a pair of swim goggles staring up from the pool bottom.

We were alone at the pool. Someone had left a pair of shorts on a glass-topped table, and three cherries discolored by the sun. The lounges and tables were luxurious, a forlorn rich man's pool. We swam all afternoon—or Justin did. My chest ached and I could not manage a swimming stroke because of the bone-pains in my chest and the rearranged muscles, but held a float in my arms and kicked lazily around the pool. Justin put on sunblock but got a bad sunburn anyway.

The neighbor's gardeners are Latin Americans. Two of their children—brown and very Indian looking and remarkably self-confident, speaking good English breezily—came to the pool and slipped into the water. Their mother, dressed in blouse and shorts, slid into the water beside a pool ladder without looking at us or acknowledging us and, clinging to the ladder, curled her legs to the side of the pool and closed her eyes and scooped handfuls of water onto her head and face, her eyes closed. Before long Justin made friends with the children, in that miraculous way that children have, that quick molding of selves to the common play.

Now on our own farmhouse porch, Justin's shoulders are flaming. He reads a Stephen King book (*The Stand*), his morale slowly returning as the sun-poisoning fades. All still. Flies, subdued bird chatter.

At night it is still difficult to find a position in which to sleep—if on my side, the knitting bone strains and aches. If on my back, I cannot sleep. Eternities of ceiling time—staring, thinking. In New York Hospital, I lay hour after hour in the passive patient's twilight, learning to accept the needles and tubes and noises and light.

4

A heart attack feels like this:

A sickness suddenly surrounds the lungs, a sort of toxic interior glow—fleeting at first, lightly slithering, but returning a moment later, more insistent.

Not the crush this time, but an alien something at the core of the body. Something dangerous has come inside and will not leave. It clings to ribs and lungs and surrounds the heart, like tentacles of green gas. Something wrong, close in, say the body's alerts, a serpent something in the dark.

And sweat shoots from forehead and coats palms before the conscious brain has entirely gotten the picture.

Body walks around, walks around quickly, to and fro, evaluating and denying—sweats and panics, calms, panics again. It will pass.

The sick green pressure tightens, not pain precisely, but a kind of terrible foretaste, a message that something is about to change.

Sit, clutch chest, rock forward and back as at the Wailing Wall, stare sidelong, listen: all the instruments turned inward to judge whatever dangerous business has come inside, into the familiar dark.

A minute passes. Four. Reach for the telephone. Wait. Listen. The wisping menace becomes definite pressure, and hardens into pain.

The stakes in the calculations mount abruptly, and mind calculates odds. The risks of waiting, the likelihoods—mind gone surprisingly rational and cool, the war room, making decisions.

It was 6:25 A.M. Heart attacks seem to happen in the morning. The sleeping bag—which I had borrowed from Justin, my eleven-year-old son—still lay spread on my office sofa.

I had spent the night there, having flown up from Washington and worked late the night before. I had not wanted to pay for a hotel room merely to sleep a few hours before getting up to take a taxi to Justin's school, St. David's, and see him perform in the school play (*Our Town*—he played the omniscient narrator) and then fly back to Washington, where I was on an extended assignment.

So I slept on the office sofa, rose, feeling well, normal. Took a shower in the shower room just off the men's room, made a cup of coffee in the automatic coffee machine, drank it as I watched the early news on television.

Then felt the toxic inner glow, and began, after a little time, to understand clearly that a part of my heart muscle was dying, and that if I wanted to save the rest of myself from dying, I must do something now. If my mind was a lucid war room, it was also detached, abstracted, in a sort of disinterested dream state.

I telephoned the building's security guards. After a long five minutes, two of them appeared at my office, moving slowly, sauntering like cops on the beat. They would decide what was urgent, not I. One of them asked, with a knowing sarcasm, "Now, what makes you think you are having a heart attack?"

I explained.

In half an hour (the world had gone into slow motion, except for me), the security guards handed me over to two EMS ambulance drivers. I lay down on their stretcher with an unwilling, overwhelming sense of resignation—of giving up all other freedom, for I had no choice, and going down the road with them.

The two paramedics were only slightly less casual than the security guards. I was amused for an instant, through my chest pain, to see that both were short, round Irishmen, with pug noses. They worked together with a symbiotic ease, giving me a condescending banter as they moved briskly to hook me to an IV that dripped streptokinase, a clot-buster, and a blood thinner, and some Valium, I think.

The two men, I realized, reminded me of the two paramedics who came for my father the morning he died in Spring Valley, New York. Those two dispatched to collect my dead father had been kind and discreet, bustling, efficient, very Irish. I almost thought now that my paramedics were the same pair—the angels of death as a matched set of quietly bubbling Micks. When my stepmother and I had left the bedroom, the boys got my father off his deathbed and into a body bag and trundled him out to their ambulance, and they said to us, "We're sorry for your trouble."

Was my father hovering then, delok? And had he sent his boys over for me now?

The memory of that flickered at the margins. I was intent upon my chest, through which dark waves succeeded one another—viscous, slow-motion surges, like clotty black oil pulsing in a sea cave.

A heart attack is one of the most unwelcome sensations, I suspect, that the body may entertain. I take it back. Perhaps delirium fevers are worse, brought on by terrible infections. Surely cancers are worse. And rabies.

The heart attack did not affect my mind, which kept a clammy, anxious clarity. The heart muscle, dying, sent apocalyptic last distress signals—SOS, SOS—that the brain at its great distance from the disaster could only helplessly receive.

The heart attack teaches an exquisitely focused attention to detail, or to the phantoms of detail, which must be sorted out: Which premonitions are real, which are only imagined symptoms? The future telescopes down to the next few minutes, even to the next thirty seconds—all future time gone dark, hypothetical, to be doled out, revealed, in the tiniest portions.

The Heisenberg Uncertainty Principle, demonstrated in the struggling heart: A person cannot observe his own heart attack in progress without his awareness of the event—his panic—pumping adrenaline into the overagitated organ, like pouring gasoline on the fire.

Now the pain would moderate, and grow still, and then would surge again. Like labor pains. I thought (a flicker of memory) of Lamaze classes years ago, before my sons were born: the ritualized and faintly ridiculous breathing and blowing to control the mother's pain as the contractions intensified, the huffing and puffing, all in a good cause, the best cause, the father/"coach" breathing and blowing along in (pain-free) moral support. I felt now that the heart contractions meant to squeeze life out of me. I would be the mother of my own death.

The Irish twins got me to the service elevator. No one was in the office yet. We waited a month or two for the elevator, and then descended.

In the ambulance, I tried to persuade the twins to take

me to New York Hospital, where my cardiologist was waiting (I had telephoned him) but one of them said, "Fella, it's
rush hour. We're talkin' about your life here. We got to
take you to the nearest place. And that's St. Monica's."
Since we were talking about my life, I said all right.

But then the same twin remembered that he had left
his jacket behind in my office—he had taken it off and put
it on my desk when he went to work on me. He now pro-
posed to go back upstairs to fetch it, an errand that, given
the elevator service, would have meant another month or so.

"Look," I said, "we are talking here about your jacket
and about my life. You can get your jacket later. I'll buy
you another jacket."

He saw that he had been done in by his own rhetoric
about my life and going to the nearest hospital, and he reluctantly started up the ambulance, not because it was the
medically correct thing to do, but because I had beaten him
on debating points. I wondered if, like me, he had gone to
school with the Jesuits.

Early rush-hour traffic going west on Fiftieth Street
(wrong way on a one-way street, it being early morning) in
the fancy rolling box of an emergency room, the siren doing
a slow listless moan, as if it were low on batteries, the twins
passing the time with chatter, the clear plastic IV line dangling and swinging with the rough streets.

The heart pain did not stop for many hours. Through
the day and late into the night, I passed through layers of
clarity and blur.

The emergency room at St. Monica's was staffed entirely by women this morning. They set about trying to
break the clot in my heart with potions dripped into artery
and vein. I began to retch, violent heavings unrequited except by evil-looking biles.

The pain surfed through my chest and began to be a

kind of routine, predictable and even lulling in a sinister way. Once I had survived a series of these waves, my body came to expect that though the waves were painful, they could be survived again.

The emergency-room doctor was a woman whose body English proclaimed a kind of coiled, fierce alarm. She bent over me, her face sharpened to a beam of concentration, boring into my chest and trying to read the events therein. She was young, in her late twenties or early thirties, and wore her brown hair in a braided rope that reminded me of my sister Cathy's. Cathy is also a doctor.

The cast of characters swirled about me, all women, each with a specialized role. The team moved in a kind of intense choreography, and my detached third eye was impressed to watch it.

I had gone in the space of an hour or an hour and a half from autonomy to the hospital mode: abject passivity saturated in anxiety. And medical object: permeable patient, problem, life to be saved.

They dosed the anxiety with Valium; they forced the creature back beneath the surface of the pond, where it swam quiet for a while, but menacing still.

The passivity felt like infancy, a shocking rapid trip back into a state of supine helplessness. But no kicking and screaming this time. Rather, a gingerly, fragile acceptance of the terms. When you have a heart attack, the last thing you want to do is make it worse by protesting, by getting angry. The mood becomes propitiatory, accommodating, polite, emotionally efficient: no unnecessary roughness now, no bravado or banging the furniture. Something in the center goes still, and listens, sensitive to the least signals in the dark, the slightest stirring of the attacker.

(I wonder if my anger later, all the ranting and rabies and depression, the wanting to kill myself, is only a deferred rage that was overaccumulated during the hospital time, as if the heart attack had upset the emotional ecology.)

Flat on your back, you become accustomed to a new angle of sight, looking at ceilings, overhanging lights, a distorted perspective on faces, which swim in and out of vision overhead, peering down—big, busy, intelligent fish. When they moved me from the emergency room, the perspective went into surreal motion: The rolling IV pole jolts alive, dangling gin-clear juices in tubed bladder-sacks; ceilings of corridors speed by; flapping doors; other schools of fish of different colors (light blue surgeon fish, white docs, green helpers) dart this way and that. Chrome box of elevator closing and rising; black-faced Jamaica-voiced elevator man-fish working lighted buttons, bored, then silver doors slide back and rush down corridors again; flap doors, and many Third World voices surf and break over me. The aquarium has become a spaceship with a crew of aliens from many planets.

I was settled at last in the coronary care unit. I retched from time to time into a banana-curved plastic bowl for that purpose, and when I made the retching sounds, a nurse glanced the Glance at me that I had seen before: the This-Guy-May-Die glance.

I had seen it seventeen years before in St. Mary's Hospital in Kansas City, where I had my first heart attack. A nurse there was giving me nitro pills—one, then pause, then another, then pause, then another—and when the chest pains did not diminish, she gave me the Glance, a complex signal of detachment and professional disclaimer mingled with pity and alarm. The Glance is a locking into place of comprehension (*ah, so*), a way of preparing, of turning a last corner and seeing an outcome. The mind behind the Glance projects the strong probability of your death, accepts the fact, regrets it minutely, and then discounts it and moves on—all of that achieved in the interval of an instant.

Now in St. Monica's as I retched into the banana-bowl—vomiting is not a good sign, the heart is heaving—the nurse with the Irish accent administered the Glance.

I hate the hospital sounds, the moaning, wretched, rasping, hawking, croaking swamp noises of near-death and terminal woe. Now my retching was the loudest hospital noise in the CCU. The unshaved geezers with angled knees and lolling, spiky heads arrayed in beds to my left and right would listen to me now, with pity and disgust and a slow-rolling desire not to hear me.

The dimension of sound in a hospital is an enveloping aural chaos that contradicts the measured, the precise, the scientific and premeditated dimensions of medicine. The EKG machines may beep sometimes like clever robots. The doctors'-nurses' voices keep up their campaign of rational matter-of-factness. But the swamp of hospital sound is given over mostly to the beasts of misery, to wild dogs howling in the middle of the night, and toads from the lungs and throat, with all their sick, slow inflations, their unearthly greens and eyes like evil jewels.

I think it is because of the noises, the patients' terrible muffled sick sounds, that the nurses and aides in the middle of the night grow louder, even hilarious. I studied the noise patterns and found that in the middle of the night, from ten o'clock until around two in the morning, the level of laughter, always female and sometimes hilarious, dramatically increased. The nurses loitered, told one another jokes, socialized. The doctors had gone, had turned the night business over to interns, and the nurses and their aides were then free to relax, out of the range of authority.

Did I detect, as well, something simpler and nastier, a current of punitive, slightly spiteful overmastery: the staff

disturbing the patients' misery for no reason more complicated than casual malice—a vaguely satisfying indifference
to the weak?

It would be unreasonable to think that a hospital and
its staff could be so saintly that they could tend intimately
to so much disgusting mortality without expressing at
some point (the middle of the night) a token of anger at
having to do the dirty job and without also asserting a
gloating radiant superiority of healthy life over the diseased
and dying. Human nature.

I came to believe, further, that the middle-of-the-
night noises were like the bonfire that Africans build to
keep off the lion and leopard in the dark. The hilarity of the
night staff was a big flame to scare away the dangerous animals loose on the floor.

At night in the midst of the whooping I thought of a
night when I lay in a tent on the edge of the Matthews
Range in northern Kenya. We had been walking for six or
seven days through the range and came upon an encamp-
ment of Samburu herdsmen. They were relatives of some of
the men who were walking with us, managing the pack-
donkeys. The herdsmen told us that lions had taken two of
their cows (an outrage to the wealth of nations, an act of
piracy). And so this night the men kept their cattle close,
and built an enormous bonfire, the largest I have ever seen:
whole uprooted trees dragged to the flames and heaved on.

I pitched my tent at some distance, but even so, the
heat reached me. Sparks flew skyward in an undulating
stream, and glowing twigs hovered, suspended, dancing
and side-slipping on the layers of heat. The men stayed
close to the fire, sweating and talking, and singing now and
then about the events of the day and about the cow-killing
lion, the narrative line of the song delivered in rapid-flow

falsetto of Masai, atop the menacing resonant basso
Hunnnnh! Hunnnnh! of the chorus.

As I drifted to sleep I thought of the thing I feared far
more than I feared the lion: a cobra I had seen just at dusk,
sliding along the riverbank nearby, a snake the size of a fire
hose, the size of an immense constrictor. It moved slowly
through the bushes beside the water and took a long time
to pass, like a long freight train never-endingly rolling
through the middle of a town in Iowa.

Then I woke to find a Jamaican woman coiling a
blood-pressure cuff around my left arm and pumping,
pumping at the rubber squish-ball, then releasing the constriction with a hiss and watching the gauge out of sight
above my head to read my pressure. Then vanishing again
on her slippers in the hospital twilight, an enormously fat
woman with a ham-waddle under her hospital uniform.

The retching stopped, and the surfing chest pains subsided in an almost imperceptible fade until gone, leaving
behind them a vast gray exhaustion.

And the exhaustion is punctured with needles. One
tribe of blood visitors are those with needles. They come at
all hours, unpredictably at first.

Some are gifted: You know instantly, by the skill of
the puncture. The best of them can find the vein by sure instinct and slip a needle in almost unnoticed; to do it well
requires just the right firm push to slide into skin, not a
lingering pseudohumane point-on-flesh with no conviction
behind it, and not the incompetent overjab either, that
awful approximation-stabbing, almost-got-it-almost-got-it
while the patient (me, I) writhes and deep-breathes. Then,
once the needle's in, the painless gradual tube-suck of dark,
dark blood (mine, but abstracted from me), then the test
tube shaken with a flicked wrist and the slick outslip of

needle—the droplet of red where the needle had been and the quick wad of cotton to hold it back.

The worst needles came to stay, in the array of IV tubes and "Hep Locks"—those permanent needles inserted and taped in place, just in case they might be needed later to dump in drugs or blood or God knows what admixtures. One needle went into my carotid artery.

It was at the end of the first day's attack, as my pain subsided, that the staff at the CCU built its biggest bonfire. Around midnight, the staff had a party.

They seemed to be celebrating something, but I could not make out from the sounds exactly what it was. I lay back, tried to sleep, listened. They laughed—male laughs mixed with female this time—and their conversation had many accents, the Indian subcontinent eliding with Caribbean lilts, some Irish and English, gutturals and long vowels twining and storytelling, and then bursting in midair in laughter like fireworks. Great bonfire. I was amazed that the natives would build it so high and pagan. It was Hawthorne's Young Goodman Brown in the middle of the night, in the forest. Here was a pagan abdication of medicine, the patients back in the shadows in awe and misery, and the docs and nurses given over to some hilarious mysterious business (boozing in intensive care, sneering at the heart monitors) so inappropriate and reckless as to be fascinating and to hint of contact with some immense, imminent disorder. The enemy was on the outskirts of the city. It would fall at dawn.

* * *

This was serious. My heart had been hit hard enough—we did not yet know how hard—and for the second time. I was not the anomalously youthful resilient thirty-six of my first attack. The first time had been surprising in one so young, but for that reason, obscurely cute: Look what a grown-up thing the boy has done! It was existentially novel. In some perverse way, it became for me a source of power, a way to gain respect, and a little dashing, like an eye patch.

When I was a child, making my way in the bad weather of my parents' brilliance and negligence and their dreamy narcissism, I became, as children do in such households, a little adult. My parents' dangerous veerings had so sensitized me to the adult world and its workings that I had near-perfect pitch for it and could navigate upon its waters. I had that weather eye a child develops the hard way. And lo, whatever praise I gained as a child would come from that precocious adult-seeming faculty, the adorable child speaking in adult tongues, performing grown-up tricks—a neat effect.

And so my first heart attack seemed to me a variation on that precocious child's vaudeville. What a stunt, to have a heart attack and bypass operation at thirty-six! When I returned from the hospital after that one, I looked thin and youthful: The contrast between that old man's coronary danger and the youthful victim produced a subliminal poignance, however brief. And as a thirty-six-year-old man I achieved something of the same effect I attained at seven or ten by performing grown-up stunts.

I am allergic to the rhetoric that urges the neurotic and wounded to "get in touch with the inner child." If given power and legitimacy, the inner child hiding in adult bosoms becomes a corrupt little tyrant—a sniveler and a bully. I know my inner child: a stunted, memory-crazed brat (young Mickey Rooney going on Mussolini) who—instead of holding his breath 'til he turns blue—has heart attacks to get attention. The intelligent thing to do, after getting in touch with the inner child, is to throw him out of the house. Before he burns it down.

The heart attack, normally an old man's business, has a perversely infantilizing aspect. Last time, and again this time. But different now. In this transaction, there would be something of both comeuppance and rebirth—provided the danger could be navigated, the pain endured, the old self left behind and a new one launched through this dark, jagged passage.

How much danger? There would be an angiogram: The catheter would enter the femoral artery just at the groin—I had done this before, seventeen years ago—and snake up, sneaking to the heart like a submarine (*run silent, run deep*), and make pictures there; the alien thump-flubbing heart, my own, but seen from within, on the TV monitor there above me if I craned my head.

A friend died on this table, or one like it, just the other day, for the submarine catheter cut loose a clot that lodged upstream in a bad intersection. Or else the catheter itself so irritated the heart it could not keep its electrical signals in order. I have not gotten the right version yet. They tried to perform emergency surgery but Frank died within the hour. *Beep, beep, beep . . . beeeep:* cold cessation on the EKG.

Noises on the floor again: One afternoon we heard a suddenly terrible shriek and wailing, not the usual moaning because of pain, but a grief-shriek, followed (like lightning) by a shower of wild emotional pain, a downpouring that lasted half an hour.

I never saw the dead patient or his family. My room-mate across the aisle arched his eyebrows at me, compre-hending the shriek and aftermath, and buried his head in a black hole that he burrowed in his pillow. And did not emerge until they came to take his blood pressure.

The roommate, Stuart, lay in the bed facing mine. When they wheeled him in, my second day there, he looked as if he were about half an hour away from dying: black half-moons under his eyes, that sidewalk-grayness of complexion, an angry, hunted, wild look in his eyes.

I hated him on sight. I thought he had a notably corrupt face, that he looked like a Mafia assassin—now at bay—and, I thought almost subliminally, was not much worth saving anyway, if his face was an indication of the life he had given himself to.

Not worth saving. In order to be just, to distribute my contempt equally, I then rendered the same verdict about myself: I was hard-hearted that day, unforgiving even of myself.

In the evening, Stuart still was bleak and obviously frightened. Something in me melted toward him. I went across the room and gave him a quiet speech, full of hospital-fervor (the love and disinterested fellow-feeling of the fox-holes): "You know, this passes. Stay with it, and don't be discouraged about it. You will be all right. You'll live. This happened to me once before, years ago. It passes, and in a year or less you will barely remember this. Stay with it and don't give in to it." He smiled wanly at me—not convinced, but grateful.

His family came en masse. I think that Stuart had a good deal of money. He was in real estate, he told me later, and seemed to have a large house in the Hamptons (where he said he would rather be). His brother came, wearing an expensive sports shirt and slacks so perfectly fitted to him that he needed to carry a small leather purse, a handbag for his wallet and Certs, I thought. He kissed his brother on the cheek, it was that kind of family. A daughter, much pregnant, and the son-in-law. The other son, who was a medico of some kind working in the hospital. A daughter-in-law, assorted friends. They could not cheer Stuart up for several days, for in the middle of the night his heart performed tantrums of arrhythmia that the doctors tried to control with drugs. The bouts of anxiety and arrhythmia left him exhausted in the morning, the half-moons under his eyes bigger than ever. I began to feel sorry that I had thought so harshly of him. He never asked me a question about myself, but he would look at me gratefully sometimes when our eyes met.

He got better. The dangerous improvised dancing on the monitor stopped. His heart settled down to a medicated steady regulation march.

The thought I had had about Stuart (the idle malice of wondering whether his was a life worth saving) kept coming back to me in regard to myself. A mood of futility and exhaustion. I cheered myself by thinking of an afternoon I had spent a few weeks before interviewing John Silber, the president of Boston University. Silber was holding forth, at my invitation, on his view of the world, and came to the question of extraordinary medical measures to keep older people alive. He said, in his forceful, fast-mouth Texas accent, "Hell! You think there is any question whether that money ought to be spent on care for my granddaughters or on care for me? Lance, I have *seen* the picture show. I have seen it four or five times. I didn't *need* to see the picture show again!"

In my hospital bed, I began wondering whether I had seen the picture show, and if so, how many times. And whether, on the whole, I deeply cared about seeing it again.

5

I transferred from St. Monica's Hospital sometime in the early morning, while the party in the coronary care unit was still going strong. The doctor who signed me out was an Iranian who spoke vigorous but barely intelligible English and seemed resentful that I was leaving, as if I insulted the medical honor of his floor by doing it. My pain and retching by this time had stopped. An ambulance took me to New York Hospital across town, through streets that were quieter than the CCU at St. Monica's.

* * *

At St. Monica's on the first afternoon, I was cared for by a nurse from England who was flamingly angry and could barely contain her rage. She hated America, she hated American medicine, which she regarded as inadequate and ridiculous. In my presence, she questioned doctors' orders, almost all orders. When one intern ordered a medicine, she rolled her eyes to the ceiling and muttered, "As if *you* knew anything about medicine." As a tactic I tried to win her sympathy by questioning her, between chest pains, about her life; and she told me only that she was trapped in America, obliged to work here at St. Monica's, as if she were an indentured servant, and wanted nothing so much as to go home. Toward dinnertime, she and a woman doctor had a screaming fight at the foot of my bed. The doctor shouted, "What is your problem?" It was a good question.

I was in the New York Hospital CCU for several days, supine and punctured. The nurses were a vast improvement. I had an Irish nurse named Mary who dropped an oxygen tank on her foot and sprained it, but hobbled around brightly enough nonetheless. I settled into the new bed, in a tiny room by myself, and felt considerable relief.

Yet I had entered into the highly provisional mode of those who are passively in danger: I expected little, I withdrew myself a considerable distance, even from my own body. Pain was easier in that mode. I said to myself calmly, "This will hurt," and saying so, I neutralized the pain, objectified it, and doing so, even felt a certain minute rueful pride at organizing the experience in advance and not coming upon surprises. Fear could be managed in the same way, I found—or minimized.

I feared the angiogram—or "cath" as the doctors called it. My cardiologist, Robert Ascheim, wanted one done as soon as I was stable, so that he might see how badly blocked my coronary arteries were.

The danger of the procedure, he said, was minimal, but I feared it nonetheless, mainly because I could so vividly visualize what could go wrong. And because it would be the first body invasion since my bypass operation seventeen years earlier.

But I negotiated with myself to institute a policy of

managed fear, which amounted to a policy of acceptance. And of self-admonition. I was, after all, I told myself in the shut-up-you-idiot mood, among the most privileged of the world's ill. I was ministered to in remarkable extravagance by nurses and doctors surely among the best anywhere.

Further, I had lived much longer than I had a right to expect (given the heart attack at thirty-six) and had not lived very wisely at that. For a man with a heart problem, I had eaten and drunk heedlessly. For a few years after my first bypass in 1976, I had been austere. Then gradually, as the sense of invulnerability returned, I behaved as foolishly as anyone. The night before my heart attack this time, I ate the dinner that is catered at the office on a late working night: shrimp and rice and, for dessert, two scoops of vanilla ice cream with caramel sauce. I ate the ice cream with a sort of suicidal defiance.

* * *

I glance up from my computer screen here in Dutchess County, and see turkey vultures circling in the air beyond our barn, above the far field. The vultures live in a huge maple out there in the woods in the fold where the ridge begins its ascent from the field—it is their condominium, their headquarters. They cluster in the maple like enormous bats. The tree is heavy with the ripe black fruit of bats.

* * *

The angiogram showed that the two old bypass grafts from years ago had closed down, finally. And new blockages had formed.

A new bypass was needed. Would it be do-able?

Ascheim dispatched to me one afternoon a surgeon

named Karl Krieger, who had not yet seen the movies from the angiogram. He entered my room wearing full operating-room regalia, all baby blue, the mask pulled down below his chin, the cap still in place on his head. His icy eyes were bluer than the uniform's blues. He had a perfectly planed and chiseled Aryan face and, it seemed clear, the heart surgeon's famous conviction of omnipotence. He discussed my chances of surviving a second bypass operation in such an angel-of-death way that when he left, I felt like a condemned man. My death was certain, the surgeon's manner said—unless a miracle intervened.

And of course he was right. I had not parsed it then: He would be the miracle. *Ex machina. Deus ipse.*

I fell out of the flimsy refuge of negotiated, managed fear and went into frictionless black free fall. The level of the game had changed. I had been sustained before not only by acceptance but also, I think, by an inner conviction that things were not that bad. Death seemed close enough, but somewhere in me I was still the matador to dance away from it. Now the flawless Aryan at the foot of the bed made me think I had been callow up to now. He had come to me from the real arena. The surgical blues were his suit of lights: He was the matador. What was I?

At four in the morning, I telephoned a friend in Paris, who was in St. Louis Hospital being treated for leukemia, awaiting a marrow transplant, and his gallantry cheered me.

* * *

The doctors moved me out of the CCU now and into what they call a "step-down unit"—one step down in the level of necessary vigilance. Blood thinner (heparin) dripped into my forearm from the IV, to keep the blood flow smooth through the narrows of the heart. Isordil slicked the way as well, and aspirin.

And so I trundled to the step-down. The first thing I saw on wheeling supine into the room was an old man, a wiry indignant bird wearing boxer shorts and trailing a hospital gown by one arm, intently ripping the IV needle out of his right arm.

The orderly wheeling my bed summoned a nurse, who flew into the room flapping: "Mr. Ajanian! Stop that! Mr. Ajanian!" and shoved the old man's sharp outraged fuddle toward his bed, confused but insistent and still gripping the needle and tearing it loose as he descended toward his sheets again under the nurse's weight.

Mr. Ajanian was ninety-two years old, I learned. He looked about seventy. He was a bundle of fiery peasant energy, his arms and legs taut with stringy muscle.

For the next twenty-four hours, I watched him try to escape. He had had angina pains at home and had been brought here. He wanted to go home. This was an outrageous captivity. He spoke almost no English. His son, who had brought him to the hospital, was nowhere to be found.

Whenever the nurse left the room, Mr. Ajanian began another escape. He rose out of his bed. Removed the IV needle. Pushed the IV pole aside. Stalked to his clothes locker and began to pack the shopping bag with his few belongings. Tried to get into his trousers, but failing that, decided to make good his escape wearing the boxer shorts and a shirt and his socks and brown leather street shoes.

The nurse would come (not summoned by me—I was rooting for Ajanian). He tried to strike her once, and this time she summoned the security guard, a monstrously large black man, six feet five or so, mountainous. He appeared and stood by the door, menacing, and Ajanian subsided into his bed again.

Now more interns and nurses gathered around the tiny wild man. An intern in horn-rimmed glasses, in his early twenties, it seemed, and looking younger, remonstrated in pidgin.

"Look what you do, Mr. Ajanian," he cried. "You attack woman! That's bad."

Mr. Ajanian looked chastened and ashamed.

"I want go home," he said sullenly.

The yuppie intern countered, "But Mr. Ajanian, you have a bad heart."

Ajanian stabbed his forefinger at the air. "I no have bad heart! *You* have bad heart!"

The answer was so unconsciously brilliant that it stopped the assembled yuppies for an instant. But then they closed in again. The intern took a needle from a nurse, and while two orderlies and two nurses (one stationed at each arm and leg) held down the indignant little man, the intern injected the tranquilizer into his arm.

Ajanian subsided for a little while, slowly, but erupted again in forty minutes, so quickly had his system disposed of the drug. And this time the SWAT team, accompanied again by the mountainous security man, tied Ajanian to the bed and injected him a second time, and he lay quiet.

Later, I said to Susan, who had witnessed the scene, "I wonder if there is a civil liberties issue involved in this. If he wants to leave, can they legally stop him?"

A nurse who had been checking Ajanian's bindings turned sharply to me, as if I were a bleeding-heart fool, and said, "There is no legal issue if he is crazy."

Ah. Catch-22, or a variation thereon: You do not have the right to leave if you are crazy. But you would be crazy

(Ajanian's point of view) if you did not want to leave. Immediately.

The fierce Armenian slept through most of the night. About three in the morning, he roused himself to strain against his bindings and the nurse materialized with a needle, after which he subsided, struggling but losing to the potion.

In the morning, the son appeared, a beefier younger dark-haired version of the father's focused indignation, and this time there was no argument about anything. No SWAT team, no tranquilizer. A nurse yanked the IV and left. The son packed the shopping bag, the father dressed with a wiry angry economy of motion, father and son all the while exchanging low mutters in Armenian. And then they both stalked out, the father rigid and tense with purpose.

I cheered. I clasped my hands over my head and shook them. Winner and still champion.

* * *

Each morning, the neighborhood dogs came frisking round: the doctors on their rounds, inconceivably young, tails wagging—and on their faces, expressions of a distant youthful bemusement as if the fleshly trouble they beheld in the bed before them belonged to such an alien order of experience, unconnected to them, that it was almost a form of entertainment. The gulf was enormous and for some reason angered me—perhaps with my memory of being that young and jauntily unconnected myself.

I thought of a day or two I had spent at West Point the year before, talking to cadets, having lunch with them in the cavernous dining hall where Douglas MacArthur had stood to say good-bye and said his last thoughts on earth would be of "the corps, and the corps, and the corps." Those cadets, unblooded, at least knew that they were, if all went well in their careers, headed for blood, for combat maybe, and that their death was part of the soldier's contract. The neighborhood dogs had no such contractual understanding with disease and death. They were yet outside its loop. What angered me was their unconsciousness, like an animal's ignorance of its own mortality.

They woofed and were gone.

6

Prayer was offered to Musisi, the god of earthquake, when he exhibited his power. . . . The Fijian addressed a prayer to his totem when he was in danger; e.g., a man who capsized at sea called on the shark-god, and a shark appeared and towed him ashore.

—*Encyclopedia of Religion and Ethics*

Capsized in open water, I prayed now in a way I never had—though I had surely prayed before. A glimpse of death opens the dimension of prayer and bathes it with unprecedented light and clarity. Now the matter of faith left the mainland of the rational: Sheer sightless faith itself, adrift, no land in sight, perhaps became true, functioning faith for the first time, and, doing so, acquired a power I had not felt before. Prayer was uncontaminated by reason, defied reason.

In fact, it amounted to a rejection of the entire reasonable world, on the sensible grounds that the reasonable world is a healthy and predictable one, not this night full of monsters and dangers. I was in the dark.

Elie Wiesel came to the hospital to see me one day and spoke of the dislocation that an event like this makes in a life, and he seemed to suggest what I say above—that prayer in such circumstances becomes different.

But I did not discuss it with Elie then. Visiting hours were almost over. Elie has a way of communicating a lot without speaking much. His voice is allusive and low, his face itself so expressive that his words become a kind of background music. He has his way of leading you to finish thoughts, to project ideas, to struggle with the problem yourself and thereby be stronger for having been brought to it by Elie and then left, on some higher but indefinite plane, to work it out.

Some months before my heart attack, Susan and I were having dinner with Elie and his wife, Marion, after a conference on hatred that Elie had organized at New York University.

I asked Elie, "What are you doing next?"

He said, "I am going to Yugoslavia next week."

He thought for a moment and then said, "Why don't you come?"

He spoke the sentence with just a ghost of that Transylvanian tone he sometimes has (he comes from a village in Romania), so that the question half-sounded like Bela Lugosi's bouncing iambs: "Vy *don't* you *come?*" But in Elie's version, the question was quizzical, a sudden inspiration, with arched eyebrows.

I did not look at Susan, who was talking to someone on her right.

I said, "Is that possible?"

"But of course."

"I will come."

Marion Wiesel rolled her eyes.

* * *

Elie's life (having risen from the ashes) is one of the miracles, of course. His presence beside my hospital bed was a sweet, wordless question: What is life worth? But also an answer. He came to see me because he knew that I was inclined to doubt, that I had a tendency to sink. No one had felt more cataclysmic sinking or more radical doubt than he. He wanted to tell me, by coming there, that my life was worth keeping. He wanted to tell me to live. And that I *would* live.

His visit to my bed and his visit to Bosnia—when I came along with him—were related somehow. He wanted to tell them to live as well.

But Elie's candle went into a high black wind over there. His fine illumination went against the big tribal rages that suck the oxygen from the room, that blacken the countryside.

* * *

Curious. Yugoslavia was one of my mother's passionate interests when she was a young woman in Washington, during the war and after. She fell in with broody, melodramatic Yugoslavs in exile there: Serbs, partisans, factionalists. She stayed up drinking with them half the night, she loved their dramatic, lugubrious, half-crazy and virile Slavic way. She liked the music and misted wolf-ridden mountainslopes of their minds, for she had not seen the other side of the slopes, not seen the amazing capacity for brutal killing. She had not seen the rapist at work in the Balkan scheme of things.

In my hospital bed in the middle of the night after Elie had gone, next to the forms of the men on the other beds in shadow, I saw the Serbian prison camp up in the mountains at Manjaca the night that Elie and I and the others came: the Bosnian Muslim prisoners lying in the dark in the vast dairy farm that was their prison, the dark dimly lit here and there by tiny smudged oil lamps.

It took a moment for our eyes to get used to the dark. And then the television crew that was with us turned on its glaring light, and in eerie silence we advanced—Elie in the lead, accompanied by the camp commandant—in the narrow aisle between the ranks of recumbent prisoners on their straw pallets, their few belongings hanging in cardboard boxes from the cow-milking rails that ran above their heads, and their shoes neatly arranged at their feet. They wore two-day whiskers. They did not look thin or starved, but had still a strong roundness of face and muscle. They mostly looked like country boys, and their clothes were mixed and tattered, worn in layers (sweatshirts, sweaters) against the rapidly descending mountain temperatures. It was late November, just after American Thanksgiving.

Now the camp commandant began to bark in Serbo-Croatian, explaining the camp to Elie at the top of his lungs. The commandant was a bristling, strutty man, about five feet six, with a military mustache, and the glazed, middle-distance gaze and motormouth of a by-the-book martinet.

I walked behind Elie with Sigmund Strochlitz, Elie's close friend who was in Auschwitz with him. Sigmund, I had learned in the course of several long conversations, is a man of shrewd judgment and humor. But Auschwitz, I suspected, was never far away from him. Now, listening to the camp commandant's loud, flat, hard barking, Siggie gave me a look. "I know this voice," he said. "I heard this voice before, at Auschwitz."

The commandant's words were being translated by a harried woman sent along by the Belgrade Ministry of Information. The commandant was explaining the humanity of the camp, the number of blankets the men received (two or three, he said), their sufficient diet, as good as his own men's ("But we are at war here, and we ourselves go wanting").

The barking echoed through the immense dairy. The prisoners were silent. Elie spoke to the commandant, asking questions, in such low tones, his wisping baritone, that I could not make out what he said.

Now he asked the prisoners questions. The television shoulder-held mobile light would swing from Elie's face down to the face of the prisoner he was addressing, and the boy's eyes would suddenly freeze like those of a night creature—a flashed deer, a rabbit in the road. Then, with the commandant glaring at him, the boy would noncommittally, mumblingly answer—half answers extracted from the prisoner as from a child answering a stranger's questions in front of his fuming father.

Siggie Strochlitz had told me, flying over the mountains from Switzerland to Belgrade a couple nights before, that at the end of the war, as the American planes flew overhead, the SS told the prisoners in Auschwitz that they would kill all the Jews regardless, so that no one would ever know. "Never, at any time," said Siggie, "did I have any hope, or any doubt that I would be killed."

I heard the Serbian commandant barking again, and the translator rendered his words: "I am a humanist!"

Over Manjaca camp there was a sliver moon when we came out of the dairy barn, and the air had a bracing late November chill. They said that the temperature in the mountains in a couple of weeks would be well below freezing—a deep, deep freeze, and that then the prisoners would begin to die in earnest. Elie pleaded that the prisoners should get more blankets.

Cold is always memorable: Trying to sleep in cold carves a memory on the bone like scrimshaw, since it is done in the half-light between sleeping and waking, a chilled child's rolling and turning to try to get warm like the Christmas Eve in Baltimore just after the war, when the temperature went below zero, and there was no coal for the furnace at grandmother's house on Garrison Street, so that Hughie and I slept in the same single bed under one thin blanket, pulling it this way and that to steal it from one another to warm the self, and Hughie's arms when I struggled with him half-asleep for the blanket were like iced bone and nothing else—no flesh, but ice-cold bone. Semiconscious and semidreaming, we dueled with each other all night with small boys' arms like ice-bones, fighting each other for a temporary warmth. We made no noise all night, and no protest, just as the Muslim boys in the cold were silent.

I think of dusk as the distinctive Balkan time, a sinister smudging and down-shadowing, giving off the menace that belongs to forests and wolves and superstitions and the—to Westerners—incomprehensible blood-hates of the place. Slobodan Milosevic received us in his presidential residence just after dusk one evening.

Milosevic sat on a sofa with Elie on his right. Milosevic had one leg cocked up on the seat cushion, toward Elie, and showed an expanse of hairless, pale calf above his black sock. Milosevic had a roundish, piggy face with tiny shrewd red eyes, a fresh pink complexion, and the sort of brush-cut that looks like static electricity.

"Truth is the first casualty of war," Milosevic told Elie with a flourish (and a subliminal wink as if to say, "Ah, you are surprised that I speak in your clichés?"). And then Milosevic proceeded to compose a self-pitying tapestry of lies: "There is no Serb aggression . . . merely protecting ourselves. . . . Everyone in Serbia is against ethnic cleansing," and so on. Besides: The Croatians "cleansed" the Serbs in years gone by—50 years ago, 700,000 Serbs died. The victim's arias: We're not doing it, and even if we are doing it, you should see what they did to us.

Memory justifies everything, and makes it all inevitable, every bit of it.

Siggie Strochlitz looked at the ceiling. As Elie sat on the sofa beside Milosevic, his face wore a pinched expression of painfully withheld judgment, as if he were politely trying to ignore a terrible smell.

* * *

And what of Karadzic? He is a published poet, and with a flourish he gave Elie his latest volume as they parted. He is a psychiatrist as well, a gleaming little narrative touch. Karadzic has theatrical wavy hair, thick expressive eyebrows, and a thousand-dollar double-breasted suit that looks Italian.

I had a good psychiatrist for years, a Freudian from Minsk, an elderly man, a kind of saint whose only fault, if he had one, was a curious sweet naïveté, which he maintained over many years even in the face of a billion fetid secrets poured into his ears. He died one afternoon in his late seventies, after leaving a message on my telephone answering machine, asking in suppressed and weary irritation why I had missed our session that morning. I thought, listening to the message, that I could hear the shadow of the heart attack that was coming up behind him and would knock him to his office floor and kill him sometime in the next hour or two. I played the message several times again, and felt the shadow rising more distinctly every time until it was a monster just over his shoulder.

I mourned the man. Radovan Karadzic is his evil twin. Karadzic sits in his command post in the mountains outside Sarajevo. The building looks like a suburban American high school built in the fifties on a small budget: low to the ground, cheap prefab materials. Our party has arrived here the hard way, in UN armored personnel carriers, with French soldiers holding automatic weapons peering out the peepholes, adolescents whose faces flicker from bravado to wonder to fear. Two days ago, a French UN soldier riding along this road between the Muslim and Serbian lines was killed by a sniper. He made the mistake of riding with his head sticking out of the manhole. Now the soldiers ride down below with us, all buttoned up in the windowless steel.

We wear blue UN helmets and flak jackets zipped over our topcoats. The helmets make our faces look faintly ridiculous. Elie's face is lined with worry and distress, clouded by what he has seen here; and framed now by his helmet, he looks like a Bill Mauldin cartoon GI from World War II—dyspeptic and underfed. Abe Rosenthal of the *New York Times* is riding beside me; his helmet looks like an absurd party hat. We hear a muffled explosion on the road ahead—a mine, we are told, but we can see nothing, and the soldiers will not open their hatches for a better look. They say this is precisely the spot where the French boy died the other day.

We wait ten minutes, then whatever was clogging the road ahead clears off and our armored procession starts again.

Karadzic greets us at his compound with a sort of Eastern European impresario's urbanity, eyebrows wagging over dark liquid eyes. On either side of him stand giant bodyguards in their early twenties. They wear twelve-inch-long black daggers in their belts, wear pistols and grenades in loops. They bristle with death and have, I think, the most violent faces I have ever seen—killers' faces, eyes hungry for mutilation.

So there is a dissonance buzzing around Dr. Karadzic, the poet-psychiatrist.

Karadzic styles himself the president of the Serbian Republic of Bosnia. He is the commander of the Bosnian Serbian military forces.

He leads us to his office—like a principal's office, with fluorescent lights, a rectangular conference table we sit around, and military maps on the walls. Quite spare and matter-of-fact, no personal details.

Elie's face is fixed in a metaphysically quizzical expression; his eyebrows have ascended to new altitudes of disbelief.

He asks Karadzic, "Why are you besieging Sarajevo?"

Karadzic: "We are not besieging Sarajevo."

Ah.

* * *

As I lay in New York Hospital, the news stories from Sarajevo grew worse. I had my son's Sony Walkman with me, and put on the earphones in the morning, after the Jamaican had drawn the day's first blood, and listened to National Public Radio's reports. The boundaries were broken down and all had become porous and interchanging, interpenetrating—public and private, one generation and another, even life and death.

Between my remembered Sarajevo and this one six months later, I thought of Gerard Manley Hopkins's shrewd anguish: "No worst, there is none. Pitched past pitch of grief, More pangs will, schooled at forepangs, Wilder wring. . . ."

Or was the slow death of Sarajevo now in truth only a diversion for me, a news hobby? It had the glamour of a doomed place the journalist had parachuted into and tootled around, being shot at, and then left in time to be back for drinks and a good dinner in Belgrade.

My chest, with its diseased arteries and the dangers flowing through those valves and narrowed passages, was my true Balkan dusk. Memory has its narrowed passages, its seizures, its violent inheritances. These things were all converging in my mind, tangling in the dark. Rages and occlusions. Balkan genetics. My family's rages, the black-red blind lashing that to a child is like apocalypse to the village.

It was blind rage, I was sure, that had gotten me into this fix with my heart, as well as genetics. In fact, the rage itself was genetic, as in the Balkans. The transmission lines trill and trill down the generations, ringing in the ears of children.

When I was in Sarajevo, a middle-aged Bosnian poet-diplomat approached me in the presidential palace where Elie was talking to Alija Izetbegovic, the Muslim leader. The poet-diplomat showed me his shirt—stuck two fingers down inside the space between the collar and his neck. His head came out of the collar like a dry stiff flower from a vase, and he said, "This shirt used to fit me."

The national library was gone, a blacked-out shell of itself. The Serbs denied that they had shelled it. They said that the Muslims had set fire to it to make the Serbs look bad—uncivilized. Bibliocide.

Mother, with your love of books, you would have wept and wept, or screamed the way you did when Roosevelt died.

Every building had lost almost all its windows. The

morning mist poofed through the bullet holes, and all walls bore the measle-marks of gunfire.

The people made their way through the streets in a hurried, dodgy, skittish way, their body English taut, over-stretched, the vectors pointing down. They had little water or electricity then, and as I listened in New York Hospital, bunkered in my own way, besieged, I heard that things in Sarajevo had grown immeasurably worse. I wondered how it could be that the city had not stopped, capitulated, or else turned itself outward in some lasting transforming gesture, all the people simply marching out of the place that had become a concentration camp at the edge of Europe.

But if they did that, I knew, the gunners in the hills would have gone to work on them, with that matter-of-factness of the land and its kill-culture, and would have finished off the remnants, pretty much, in one last effusion of violence. And little blue helmets would have rolled down the slopes like Easter eggs.

* * *

The last leaves were clinging to the trees in Belgrade. But the city, under months of sanctions, had a dismal, anxious look, like a woman with a stomach cancer gnawing her in the dark. An oil shortage cut down the traffic.

The Inter-Continental Hotel where we were staying—vast and glass-modern and new—was virtually empty: A ghastly hostess, the assistant manager, swept across the lobby to greet us every time we entered. She wore much livid lipstick, her mouth suggesting both sex and violence. She had a boxer's broken nose and heavy jaw, and came at us as if to say, in Dracula's iambs: "I *vant* to *suck* your *blood*."

7

The Hiroshima bomb fell on a hot and blinding August day when I was five years old and walking up Benning Road toward the Maryland border, at Coral Hills where the shopping center was.

The Kellogg's cornflakes box had a button in the bottom, buried in the cereal, that said V-E DAY. Hughie and I fished it out, spilling cereal, as we walked back down the hill from Maryland.

The hill was the farthest distance from here to there that my eye could take in—a wide, deep vista from the high Maryland side, looking down into the city, along the sweep of a boulevard, Benning Road.

Today, the entire neighborhood where we lived in Washington at the end of the war has become a miniature of its childhood self. Benning Road is a narrow lane. It runs through a black housing development that has the worst murder rate in the country—drug wars. Our tiny house, semiattached, has barred windows and a threadbare postage-stamp yard. The black family crouches inside. There is a black boy there who is the age I was when the bomb fell all those years ago. He repeats me, *mon semblable, mon frère*, but the violence in the neighborhood is now manifest, overt.

The bomb-bright August sky in 1945 was all flat light. Hughie got the button from the cornflakes box. The house was empty and oddly cool and dark when we returned. It felt as if the air had been sucked out of it.

It was not many days after that that Hughie, who got a Gilbert chemistry set the Christmas before, in 1944, made a bomb in the basement that, when he touched it off, exploded in a flash and then finished in a perfect—flawless—mushroom cloud. The sight of the smoke pillar and the ascending rings around it, now so familiar an image and so sinister, the new world, sent us flying up the basement steps. In our clearest primal memory, we had printed the icon of the perfect little bomb.

Roosevelt was four months dead. I still heard my mother's scream down the corridor of Children's Hospital. She heard the news of his death from a nurse while I was having my tonsils taken out. In my memory, I hear her scream as I go under ether, counting backward—the evil-tasting/-smelling vapor rising in my head, unforgettable and toxic as death; conked before I got to ninety, dead out, mother screaming for Franklin Roosevelt.

And now I wake, forty-eight years later, with a chain-sawed chest, after the long sleep, Hiroshima like yesterday.

* * *

At the museum in Hiroshima, when I went there forty years after the bomb, the halls were filled with Japanese schoolchildren, brought every day in hundreds of buses to see the black skeleton of the domed prefecture, to see the memorial park, and the gruesome photographs of burns and radiation, and the displays of drawings and watercolors that the children of 1945 made to show the horrors they had seen.

Japanese schoolchildren like to practice their English, especially on Americans. As I stood outside the museum, some children came out, having seen the displays. The children had that minted brightness of the Japanese young, and when one of them saw me, he approached me and smiled broadly and said, "Murderer! Hello!"

In Hiroshima, a survivor told me her story.

She had been six years old, and had been roused early on that morning so that she and her schoolmates could go around the city collecting roof tiles from the rubble of buildings that had been hit by American bombs. The tiles could be used in rebuilding. It was a bright day, and the girls went about their task as if it were a kind of play.

Then, in midbreath: The air was shredded by a thousand magnitudes of fire and light, the whitest white, blank-out, the eyeballs boiled, the world cindered.

The little girl found herself wandering now through a thousand lesser fires, the universe on fire. Fire-blackened forms of what had been people staggered out of what had been buildings, through what had been streets.

The little girl came to the river and saw it choked with people who had plunged in to escape the fire— seething people, screaming, drowning, yet still tumbling in from the scalding air, until the river boiled, as if with hideous irridiated black salmon spawning.

The girl cried for her mother. And there occurred a little miracle.

On a bridge over the river, a man who was a neighbor of the family recognized the girl and began to lead her back to what had been their neighborhood and her house. Which were no more. Where they had been were now mere grids, a blackened abstract of the neighborhood.

As the forty-six-year-old woman described to me the moment of the atomic blast, she showed me how she had raised her right hand and forearm to protect her face—and here in the middle of the 1980s I saw on her face exactly the swath of unburned flesh that had been protected by her arm. The rest of her face had been burned, and in later years patched over with grafts that restored her face somewhat but left the flesh with that ultrasmooth scar-shine of skin. But where she had covered the face with her arm the flesh was soft and untouched, like a child's.

The woman's voice was high and singsong, like a child's, and her eyes were wide and full of stricken amazement.

It occurred to me as she talked that the girl's clock had been stopped on that morning in August of 1945, at the end of the war. She had a history after that, of course—her life went on. (She never married, for all of those young people stricken at Hiroshima came to be regarded as genetically unclean, and they were avoided in marriage: And that was another sorrow.)

But her clock stopped, and the person I was talking to in 1985, in the library beside the memorial park near 1945's ground zero, was in most important ways still the same child the bomb fell on that morning: She was preserved in a sort of radiant amber, of the nuclear kind.

She knew not marriage, or sex, or much of the world's subsequent history, I suspected. In any case, the time that flowed on after August 1945 could not overcome the event at that instant, that morning. It was so powerful that it blew apart the universe and lodged her (a fragment of the city, a speck in the fireball) outside time.

With the time difference of twelve hours between Washington, D.C., and Hiroshima, between Benning Road and the bridge over the body-choked river, it was just after eight at night, starting to get summer-dusky, but I would not have been anywhere near sleep.

The German prisoners of war who rolled out Pennsylvania Avenue Southeast that afternoon in high-railed cattle trucks, with guards, had been settled down somewhere outside the city. I remembered their young Hunnish unrepentant faces and close-cropped spiky haircuts, and I demonized them talking to Hughie and Bruce in the threadbare grassless yard outside our house as the evening advanced. We had never seen such prisoners of war before, and never would again. They wore shirts with enormous letters POW stenciled across the back.

I tried to talk up some excitement around them, to say how dangerous they were. But in fact I saw even at my age that their faces were lost and confused beneath what looked like unrepentance. Mostly their faces were closed up, like tanks with eye slits, and watchful, and their body English tense. They looked healthy but unslept, road roughened. They looked like the young Muslims I saw with Elie that night in the mountains, at Manjaca.

There were no more air-raid warnings now in Washington. A year or so before, my parents had nailed blankets over the windows to blot out our light lest German bombers flying overhead might take a sighting on our house, and, heading to the northwest on a straight line along dimmed Pennsylvania Avenue Southeast, arrive over—*jah, jah*—the Capitol (*boom!*) and White House (*boom!*).

* * *

I was fascinated by the stopped-clock quality of the Japanese girl-woman's face. I have seen it once or twice on the faces of women who had been sexually abused as little girls, a look of something like permanent wonder and confusion, as if the normal processes of life had been interrupted, short-circuited, by a shock, an electrical/emotional overload. So maturing and aging simply ceased as of the moment. And among other things, childhood continued to go round and round the turntable, repeating and repeating the same notes and phrases, the same motifs of flash-frozen innocence. The eerily intact Atlantis of childhood, the whole universe and civilization of it.

This is the motif of the *nakba*. It is surely what I heard when talking day after day to Palestinians in Gaza and Nablus and Deir Dibwan and Amman. The *nakba* was "the disaster," the war in 1948, the great dispossession of the people from all that had been before: the Village, the Well, the Fig, the Olive. The paradise of the tribe was (in the Palestinians' origin myth of diaspora) shattered, in a flash, by the terrible alien Jews who descended, as if from the sky, after which descent all else changed, forever.

I would sit in the Palestinians' endlessly courteous rooms, one wall of which would be adorned by a large Kodachrome-vivid photograph of the golden Dome of the Rock in Jerusalem, backed by a deep blue sky, a vision of heaven. The picture was always hung high up on the wall, so that the eyes must be inclined to look at it. Elsewhere on the wall might be sinuous and filigreed Arabic quotations from the Koran: sayings, abjurations.

The Palestinian men (almost always men, not women, who remained deeper in the house, out of sight, in their own society) would line the room in rectilinear arrangement. The sofa and chairs were invariably squared off, everything at right angles. The air would be dense with

cigarette smoke, always Marlboros. As soon as a man finished a cigarette he would stub it out and another man
would reach into his shirt pocket and with thumb and forefinger withdraw a fresh cigarette and offer it, and take one
himself, and then light them with quick ceremony, and
after the little pause, the conversation would resume amid
the fresh exhalations.

The memory of the *nakba* had been polished to exquisite smoothness with endless retellings. The memory shone
with a mystical refulgence, an inner light. It had a life of its
own after a time, and in this way memory became a fact and
factor of ongoing history. The memory of the trauma of
nakba became an infinitely volatile explosive and therefore
an instrument of politics.

Each man, each family, wove the thread of its own
story into the larger tapestry of the tribal saga. The stories
differed in specifics (just as stories of the Hiroshima survivors varied) but were all fused beneath the surface, melt-
ingly flowing into one another in the tribal subconscious
until they formed the one powerful narrative of a primal
paradise that was stricken by apocalypse, after which the
people went into captivity or exile, and, drenched by the
Jews' injustice, began the long, long waiting.

The Palestinian men arrayed around the room and
telling me their stories in clouds of smoke seemed under
such compressions of rage and outrage and confinement and
frustrated manhood that I imagined them going down one
after another before me, slumping to the floor, clutching
their chests, their heart muscles dying. Or I thought their
eyes would shatter into tiny pie-shaped brown-black fragments and fly like shrapnel through the blue cigarette
smoke and stick in the walls.

The coming of the Jews was (the Palestinian men said)
an uncomprehended affront to the centuries-long order of

their world, an intrusion of aliens. The men always told the story of going back to the home they had been displaced from. One of them found a cruel Jewish family living in the house. The Jews, he said, drove him and his family away with cold insults. Another Palestinian man, in a refugee camp outside Amman, said the Jewish family living in his old house had the good grace to be not only polite but embarrassed. So what? The Arab still had to leave, his heart shredded.

And one man in a dim, cold upstairs room in Gaza told me that when he went back to see his old house near the coast, he found it had become Lod Airport.

Intrusion, interpenetration, rape: always the motif of some power tearing into the integrity of another's life—violating. The theme of anger is remembered violation. The rage backs up in the heart like a mob at the Dome of the Rock until all the dark streets and alleyways leading into the holy place are blocked and raging, horripilating with shaking fists and faces like fists, screaming.

When the heart dies, the poor thing is screaming for blood.

The curfews were hard on the Palestinians' hearts. They sat in their houses for days and days and days, sealed up with themselves, marinating in anger and frustration and ruined autonomy, the men smoking and smoking their Marlboros until they ran out. After which, deprived of nicotine, they felt even worse.

One afternoon I was in Nablus, talking to Palestinian leaders, when the Israelis' Shin Bet closed in on a fugitive eighteen-year-old in the streets of casbah (they had been looking for him for weeks; he was an important leader of the Intifada) and killed him.

We had seen the fugitive on the streets two hours before. I was walking with Jamil Hamad, the Palestinian journalist who worked for *Time*, when suddenly Jamil called out to a disheveled young man hurrying along outside a shop that, I remember, sold wedding dresses, its female window mannequin arrayed in full white plumage.

The kid looked unslept and wild, and startled when Jamil hailed him, but paused to talk to us a moment, politely but distractedly, the bride-mannequin smiling in the window over his left shoulder, and then he vanished up the way, into the casbah crowds.

Now we sat in an office not far away and talked to two PLO men who described how Shin Bet would induce Palestinians to become informers—using the bait of money and small privileges, luxurious minor exemptions from the misery and bureaucracy of occupation, leading them little by little, from a tiny betrayal (supplying a mere name or two) to a larger one and a larger, until they were hooked inescapably, and being now traitors, could not, under pain of death, rescind the betrayal and recover their innocence.

As we talked, word came in from the street that the young man we had stopped by the wedding shop had just been killed by Shin Bet agents, and that the curfew was clamping down now.

Jamil and I said good-bye and rushed for our car, to get out of the city. If we did not, we would be trapped by the curfew. I could talk my way out through the Israeli checkpoints, but for Jamil, a Palestinian, it might be more dangerous and problematic to try to leave.

We got into the car and joined a dense, honking stream of others fleeing the city, the Arab drivers' faces tight with anxiety and anger, leaning on their horns, right foot hopping from accelerator to brake, the car leaping a foot or two, then jerking stopped.

Here again was the occlusion, the heart's home stopped up, and raging.

* * *

In the Museum of Applied Art in Belgrade, Elie and I and the rest of the party went one morning to see a display of artifacts and photos that showed what had happened to the Serbs of Vukovar in November of 1991. The reciprocities of hate.

A Balkan morning: "Murderer, hello!"

Americans do not understand profound blood hatreds, I think; such blood-rages are essentially outside American experience, which (except for the black-white race hate) had always depended on mobility and shallow draft—no deep, deep Balkan laminations of tribe and place, no terrible, centuries-long suppression, no unforgettable wrongs (except, again—a big exception—for black and white). And always, usually, new money, to take the mind off blood-grievance.

The Serb says, "Croats are a genocide people." A beautiful middle-aged woman with soft brown eyes, Bosana Isakovic, led me through the displays at the Museum of Applied Art. She was a cousin of one of the victims at Vukovar—even showed me her cousin's body in a picture on the wall among many other bodies: charred flesh, corpses burned with gasoline in a pit. Her eyes brimmed with tears. Bodies thrown in the river. Mutilations both crude and ingenious. In one glass case, an instrument they say the Croatian *Ustashe* use—still—to gouge out Serbs' eyes. That eye-gouging is a trademark of the Croatian killers, the calling card. The instrument is crude steel, and shaped like a *U* with a handle at the bottom, or like a simple spur: The points of the *U* allow the brisk *Ustashe* to take out two eyes at once.

And there were *Ustashe* knives, which looked long and black, Satanic and yet shaped like a lethally radiant cross, like the knives in the belts of Karadzic's bodyguards in the Serb headquarters compound above Sarajevo.

In the town of Gospic, my hostess said, the Croatians gathered together all of the Serbian intellectuals—then murdered and burned them: the local judge, the professor of chemistry, the schoolteacher.

What distinguishes the new atrocity pictures from those of World War II vintage is not the crimes or ingenuities, but simply that the new pictures are in color and the old ones in black and white.

Now all the Serbian women—urban women, well dressed, educated, somehow French looking—are weeping around the photos of Vukovar, like a chorus formed around me: my eyes fixed on the bashed, burned corpses, and my ears taking in a surrounding stereo of grief.

When they drove us to the military airport later to find the UN plane for Sarajevo, I stood for half an hour among trees away from the runway, waiting, and gradually became aware that the branches all around me were heavy with silent crows.

* * *

Is death evil then? In itself?

If evil is detected by sensation, by feeling, intuition, then I was in the presence of evil in Bosnia. I think the mind could not account for the deaths there—in Sarajevo, and in the villages where the death is more intimate and blacker somehow, a glare, a vicious stab, flesh-to-flesh—without invoking evil and its theological atmospheres.

When my heart muscle started dying, it was nature going about its business—nothing metaphysically fancier than trouble in a clogged heart. But it certainly felt evil, rising in my chest—evil to me. Evil to me since I was the interested party. I labored under the most intimate of pathetic fallacies, that an infinitesimal individual fate proclaims a universal. We go up gasping and gesticulating like heretics in a dramatic smoke of subjectivism. *Nu?*

My brother Mike was only seventeen when he died. Mike's cancer felt evil, too. I watched it grow in his chest, on the outside of his lung, and conquer him over many months, appropriate his body and consume it: shrivel and immolate—slow, from the inside, dying. Mike's innocence and youth were the outrage there. He was gratuitously destroyed, like a child on an altar. But to propitiate whom? What monster?

Best assign death to chaos theory, I suppose, which will accommodate and override the petty human thirst for explanation: for fairness, justice even, for aesthetic satisfaction, for theological neatness. But chaos theory may be only a humbler though neoscientific approach—through new forests of the unknowable and unpredictable, new philosophical ordeals—to the same mystery, God and evil: theodicy.

Anyway, it is not wise to think too much about death. It makes one stupid, as obsession can. It shadows perception, like a smudge of kohl. It bends the mind to a habit of darkness. It also makes a man inward and boring.

Still, when death comes close, when your body brings the subject up, you are thrown into dark waters despite yourself, and have to swim in them, and never know if you will fight out of the turbulence, the black tumbling, and find shore.

I have just clawed up on shore again, coughing up salt water from my lungs. Is it the same shore that I left?

I hope not. There must be plenty of other shores. Let it not be the simple binary option of landing on this side or

else on the River of Death's doomy Other Side, but let there
be a different island, let there be another continent entirely.

* * *

I am ahead of myself. I look up now, shooting paral-
laxes, scurrying from Sarajevo to Hiroshima, from death
scene to death scene, widely separated though only by time,
which is negligible, trying to sight the shrouded star.

* * *

We left the crows and flapped up into the dismal
mountain mist, rising in a white two-engine UN plane carrying us and cases of Cokes and Palmer Export Beer into
besieged Sarajevo. The beer and sodas (for the UN people)
were strapped down by cargo nets. I sat cramped on either
side of the windowless gloom, dim cabin lights showing us
our own profiles.

The siege of Sarajevo began on April 5, 1992, at
Bayram, the end of Ramadan, when someone (each side
blames the other) started firing into a crowd of demonstra-
tors from a house near the Holiday Inn.

In the plane when I primed the Serbian photographer
beside me with questions, he talked and talked a narrative
line above the drone of the engines.

The photographer had shot most of the pictures I had
seen in the Museum of Applied Arts, the atrocity scenes
from Vukovar. The photographer, who told me his name
was Dusko Zavisic, said he had seen some 500 dead in
Vukovar that day. Some 50 or 60 were buried together in
the yard of a kindergarten.

"After I saw that, I was afraid to close my eyes because
I would see the bodies again—the smashed heads. . . . I

don't drink, but that night I had two huge glasses of slivovitz to try to sleep. I couldn't close my eyes for a couple of days."

It was the worst thing he had seen, he said, since he was fourteen years old and had been taken to the museum of the camp at Jacenev, the infamous concentration camp where the Croatians during World War II had killed (according to their victims) some 700,000 Serbs.

"The Croats," said Zavisic, who was twenty-eight years old, "seem to enjoy killing. They are competitive about killing. How can they hate so much, to do this?"

Competition. Of course, the world now said precisely the same things about the Serbs, about their massacres and rapes: that the Serbs are an atrocity people, that they enjoy it.

Dusko Zavisic's mother was a doctor working in the hospital in Sarajevo. He was flying into town on assignment for *Newsday*, and would perhaps get to see his mother, and then lift out again on the UN flight just before dusk.

Now our plane (thinking of groundfire) jittered and zagged in the air and shot steeply down, going fast, no gliding—down, down, and bang on the runway.

The UN troops were sandbagged into the airport. They did their best to be symbols of innocence: Their armored personnel carriers were painted white, and their helmets of course were UN blue, sky-baby blue. They were French and Egyptian and Portuguese, and had, I saw, a certain rueful esprit. As their mission was innocent and vulnerable, they did not pump themselves up to the manly combat aggressions, did not nerve themselves ("What's the mission of the bayonet? Kill! Kill!") to a fight to the death. Rather, being sent to interpose, to calm, they kept their air of slightly confused and fragile youth. Kids who would rather be at the beach, at the movies. If blood came their way, it would not be blood they spilled as warriors, but a mistake and a horror, an evil they were not fast enough to dodge. I was touched by the boys, for they were sacrificial lambs.

The United Nations signed us in and issued flak jackets and blue helmets to us, and packed us into armored personnel carriers that formed in convoy and then rumbled out of the airport toward town, down "Sniper's Alley." We sat in the APC in our helmets—Elie, Abe Rosenthal, I, and the others, looking like a row of Michael-Dukakis-the-Tankman dolls. Someone said the Muslims were doing a lot of the shooting at the UN, being angry, thinking that the UN supports the Serbs.

Grind to a halt. A UN face, frightened: "Hurry, hurry, they shoot at any time!" We crouch and launch ourselves into the late morning half-sunlight, mist cleared, seeing ourselves whooshed and shooed out of the APC and into an ornate nineteenth-century building that we are told is the presidential palace. Distant artillery crumps as we step inside into incongruous splendor, then mount a ceremonial staircase, rush-rush, to a ceremonial room that has been plushed to a hideous green.

More distant shells, to which no one pays attention. There on a brocaded couch sits Alija Itzetbegovic, the Muslim president of Bosnia, looking stolidly blockish and Western-tailored, vaguely like François Mitterrand. No aura of Islam about him. The room is filled with anguished local notables in chairs arrayed before the sofa where Itzetbegovic and Elie sit now, and in disorderly surges around the margins of the scene, the press, with TV cameras and sound booms.

An eighty-two-year-old poet speaks up, his indignant hair like spiky wild frost: He reminds me, now that I think of him, of Mr. Ajanian, the Armenian who wanted to escape from the heart ward at New York Hospital. The Bosnian is just as passionately focused. The poet speaks to Elie. He says he is Jewish. "I have seen three wars in the Balkans," he says through the president's woman translator. "And none has been as bloodthirsty and savage as this one."

When we leave the palace, the meager sun has vanished.

Our hosts—the local government—have arranged a strange, fast-forward tour of the city. Abe Rosenthal and Dave Maresh of ABC News and I crowd into the back of a battered white Renault sedan, I sitting in the middle and making jokes about having Rosenthal and Maresh as sandbags. Which is what they feel like. The car is not bulletproof.

The driver is a Russian—how he got here, we are not sure. He hurtles the car through the streets at a wheel-spinning, clutch-popping pace, swerving abruptly here and there for no evident reason, except the most important reason, which is to evade sniper fire.

There are clouds and mist again over the city, for which I make a note to be grateful, since presumably it defeats the snipers. I have a fantasy nonetheless of one man in the hills above the city, glowing with plum-brandy moonshine that he drinks from a canteen, watching me through his telescopic sight, my blue-shelled head bouncing in his crosshairs, like a robin's egg he wants to crack for fun.

* * *

We jolt across the tiny bridge where, I suddenly realize, the Archduke Ferdinand was killed in June 1914. The bridge is here and just as abruptly gone. I feel that quick strange deflation I felt on seeing the Jordan River for the first time—"Jordan's River is mighty and wide"—a miserable trickle barely visible beyond layers of Israeli barbed wire. The Sarajevo bridge produces the same effect: a sense of historical disorientation, of bizarre disproportion between the immense power of the myth and history and the banal, insignificant thing itself.

Abe Rosenthal questions the Russian driver closely about the situation in the city—food, electricity, water. Very little of any of those, the Russian says in thick English.

Abe says, "Well, does your wife go and draw water somewhere or how does she collect it?"

Driver, his face wearing a look of gravid woe that we notice now and understand for the first time: "My wife was killed by a sniper sixty-three days ago."

We are shocked. Abe says quickly, "Sorry," not knowing what else to say for the moment.

I am moved by the precision of the "sixty-three days"—the Russian has counted every one of them. We do not pursue him with questions further, though I wish that I could—could know why he stays in Sarajevo, whether he has children, how he came to be here in the first place.

The shops are closed and shuttered. The hospital is heavily sandbagged everywhere, with warning signs in English for the UN people, telling them (more or less) to be ready to die any second.

Something is inside-out at the hospital: Death is outside trying to get in, not inside as usual, with the patients. The UN general, a beefy Egyptian professional soldier, is sandbagged into the hospital.

My notes record this exchange between Elie and the general when we arrive.

Elie: "Is the danger increasing?"

General Ramiz: "It is always dancing."

I love the line, but cannot be sure he said it. He was speaking English.

General: "The infrastructure of the city has been completely destroyed."

Elie: "At night, what do your people do to pass the time?"

General: "We are telling stories."

At that, I thought of a correspondent from *Time*, Bill Stewart, who was assigned to Beirut during the Israeli invasion of Lebanon and siege of the city. When Bill and I were riding on a press plane going to Ohio to cover a Ronald Reagan campaign rally at Bowling Green State University in 1984, I asked Bill, "What did you do during that tremendous shelling? You couldn't have gone outside. . . ."

"I stayed inside my apartment," Bill said, "and watched videotapes of *Brideshead Revisited*."

The Chetniks wear full black beards, the tribal mark of their ferocity and some Slavic brutal holiness, a mystic pledge, manhood and monkishness and unkempt mountain wildness: a reek, a nest for the burning eyes. Guerrillas avenging.

The place is filled with these black priesthoods. The Croatians have their *Ustashe Hos* and *Hov*, elite units. The Serbs tell me that the *Ustashe* burned a synagogue in Zagreb last spring. And that in Zagreb you can buy Nazi souvenirs and blackshirt *Ustashe* items, so thick is the Croats' nostalgia.

When leaving Karadzic, Elie had the perfect, quiet line. "Well," he said, "I hope that God is a psychiatrist."

Karadzic—psychiatrist, man of letters, patriot, nationalist, liar, thug—is a Renaissance man. A patient who would want a murderer for a psychiatrist must have interesting problems.

And what is the superego in such a land, in such tribes? This is morality inside-out, discipline, patriotism, blood-loyalty turned to the blackest uses. In Freud's terms: The id writes the rules for the superego.

You begin hallucinating almost the moment you go into Yugoslavia. The terrible moral landscape is infectious; it draws you in with its cracked perspectives, its unthinkable cruelties: the Balkan faultlines.

Elie and the rest of us came to the prison in Sarajevo where the Muslim authorities held men charged with this and that.

The day was cold, and the inside of the prison colder than the air outside. The military men in Sarajevo have a look in common: unshaved faces, uncombed hair, complexions red and raw with cold and wind, their bodies much bulked by the layers and layers they wear—undershirts, sweatshirts, sweaters, tunics—and their hands, hard, raw, dirty, with a casual hold on a rifle or machine gun.

The soldiers guarding the prison looked like that. Their eyes hardened when they saw us. The prison director went into a fluster of panic when told that the president had ordered that we should speak to the prisoners. This seemed absurd to the warden and guards, like bringing chocolates to rattlesnakes.

The prison had the derelict look of bombed-out buildings. It had been a factory, improvised for its present use. The guards, with darting eyes and misgivings, led us now along a corridor lined on the left with tall, blank, locked steel doors with barred peepholes.

Elie pointed to one of the doors and directed that it be opened. The guards complied, looked in, stood back. We looked inside and saw four men blinking in the unaccustomed light. Two were standing, one sat, one lay on a thin dirty mattress on the concrete floor. All blinked at us in curiosity and fear.

Elie, through his interpreter, asked Red Cross–type

questions about what they were getting to eat and whether they were warm enough, but the men, almost too frightened to speak, could barely answer, and at length David Pincus, one of our party, a friend of Elie's, gave the men candy bars, and we withdrew. The guards, like zookeepers, buttoned up the cage again.

Elie pointed to the next door. The guards opened it. This time in the suddenly light-flooded dark we saw two men: one old, one young. The old man wore a look of crafty abjectness and ingratiation. The young man was very tall and thin, with a triangular-shaped head that was too small for his body: a high, high rhombus of forehead, a long nose, and the worst eyes that I have ever seen in a man's head—not dead, exactly, but deathly. He was twenty or twenty-one years old.

Seeing the young man, I thought at first that he was a gangly, inarticulate country boy, and I felt sorry for him, for the instant before I caught and held his eyes. Then he looked away, from me to Elie, and then to the floor, where his gaze remained.

Elie questioned the old man first. The man, sixty-two years old, said he was being unjustly held, and then, lest he offend his jailors, he softened that—it was all merely a mistake, a mixup.

Elie sighed. He turned to the tall country boy.

"What is the charge against you?"

"Murder . . . rape."

Elie's eyebrows rose and his head swiveled in a half-recoil, a glance aside, and then his eyes returned to the young man. The young man did not look up.

"Did you do it?"

Shrug. No denial.

"Why did you do it?"

"I was ordered to."

"Ordered by whom?"

"By my captain."

It dawned on me: This was Herak.

Herak, a Serb fighter, was charged with raping and murdering some seventeen Muslim women. He had talked to a reporter from the *New York Times* and was in the midst of a day or two of modest international fame.

Elie said, "There are serious charges against you. Do you understand them?"

It had occurred to Elie, and to me, that the boy might be an idiot. Or too mentally disturbed to know what he had done. But when the boy raised his eyes again, there was comprehension, all right.

Herak was a monster, the real thing—the dead-deathly eyes, the triangular reptile's head. And a certain low, buzzing energy in him. I wondered if the old man, his cellmate, was not terrified to be there in the dark with him.

But there were many monsters loose. And when Herak said "My captain!" had ordered the rapes and murders, I was inclined to believe him, as rape and murder had become a systematic policy against the Muslims, a way to drive them out and demoralize them so thoroughly, to lay waste their lives and salt the earth with such defilements that they could not come back, ever.

The door closed on Herak, and we walked on through the gray, shattered prison, which made me think of Berlin in 1945. Behind me, an Italian journalist described how under bombardment the Sarajevo children sometimes lose their voices. "They are getting more and more cases every day."

Franjo Tudjman, the Croat leader, in one of his books quoted Toynbee: "All peoples must decide whether they choose to be the carcass or the vulture."

8

I have been my father's delok. He has been mine. Each has hovered over the other's recumbent self when one or the other has had a heart attack and been cracked open to repair it. We have brought each other messages from the middle distance.

The last time my father went out of body, he did not return.

It was not so long ago. In retirement, my father and his wife, my stepmother, moved out of their enormous house in Bronxville, the one with the ill-smelling ghosts and mildew of the past, and moved across the Hudson River to a small, neat, one-story house built on a Japanese model—a house and garden all enclosed by a high wooden fence and shut off from the surrounding world, which was suburban enough. As the Bronxville house had been as grand and decayed as Miss Havesham's, the Japanese house across the river had air and light: glass walls on two sides, birds (finches, doves, robins, cardinals, invading blue jays), and trees. In spring and summer, the house was a sort of rectangular solid of green light. And the swimming pool that my father loved was a rectangular solid of blue light that pleased him and gave off sparkles in sunshine. He would walk abstractedly around the pool, carrying a flat square net at the end of a long aluminum pole, and with it would skim fallen leaves from the water, or bits of twig, and be happy when he had completed two or three rounds of the pool and found that the rectangular solid was as pure as a gem again, a shining, bluish, geometric dream of illumination.

We cleaned the pool's bottom with some ceremony, using a vacuum at the end of another long pole and pushing and pulling it back and forth, back and forth, in slow motion. The bottom debris and scum would disappear in stripes as we proceeded, and the vacuum would leave an ever-expanding undersea plain of clean clarity. The process drew my father into a state of peace and satisfaction. The swimming pool was his Zen garden: clarity, blankness, illumination.

We stared into its clarity when we talked about things: about my brothers and sisters, about politics, about my divorce. And saw that cleaning the pool was a mental and spiritual exercise somehow, a sort of outward parallel enactment, and that when the twigs and leaves and bug and bee corpses and film of bottom scum were gone, our minds would be clear as well.

None of this was premeditated, but rather a kind of companionship. My father kept a large whirlpool hot tub in a patio just outside his bedroom, and before his heart grew worse and could not tolerate the heat, he took a lolling, oriental pleasure in the tub, its bubbling, jostling, amniotic warmth. He invited children and grandchildren into the tub, and there presided with a pasha's satisfaction.

These liquids played their light across his mind. They seemed to satisfy a state of some sensual innocence within him, some bright pool of childhood.

So he was happy. My stepmother tended to him. The high wooden fences kept out the world.

* * *

I am sitting in the country now, just after dawn, a fire in the kitchen fireplace hissing, and rain beating pleasantly on the roof. It is late October, and the flaming leaves are two-thirds down from the trees and wetly plastering the ground.

It crosses my mind that I am, here, rehearsing for the retirement that he went into. He left his old life with a sense of relief that was almost audible—an air-lock's whoosh—and he passed through the intermediate stage, the gate, the birth canal, and emerged with a look of stunned happiness into his Japanese garden.

Wherein would be no politics, none of the large male public mendacities that go with it, the swagger and wink, the deals, the balls, the postures, the swellings of the Big Bogus, the television cameras, the burned-out reporters, the caffeine and Chrysler Imperials, the bombast, the Nelson Rockefeller of it.

* * *

My father worked for Rockefeller for twenty years, as a speechwriter and political adviser and press secretary, and had been the man who announced Rockefeller's death to the press the night the former vice president had a heart attack while with his mistress in a townhouse on West Fifty-fourth Street. My father, shocked and thinking fast behind his handsome and impassive exterior, told the reporters at Lenox Hill Hospital that Nelson, statesman and art lover, had expired in his Rockefeller Center office while working late on one of his art books. An edifying death.

Then a day or two later, the newspapers found the ambulance drivers who took the ex-governor and ex–vice president of the United States from the townhouse, with his hysterical girlfriend along, and my poor father (not poor Nelson, surely, who had gone out grinning, a man presumes) was left to represent private infidelity and public untruth placed in one bundle and tied up with his tongue.

After that, my father's natural good-natured ruefulness sank to a sidelong introspective rue, self-second-guessing and fruitlessly incensed at a dead man who inflicted one last casual, outrageous humiliation (not only on my father, of course) as he skipped out the door: catting around, then leaving in the air the ghost of a Cheshire's grin, while underneath, my father lied into the television lights.

My father walled himself into his rue until it was time to leave the feudal employ of the Rockefellers, that thin Protestant court of earnest public ideals and a grim exuberance of private sexual itches. (My father had told me of an apartment house on West Fifty-fourth Street, just down the way from the townhouse where Nelson died: The apartment house was occupied by many of the pensioned-off mistresses of the Rockefeller boys over the years. There were older women from the era of World War II, somewhat younger mistresses from the postwar era, on down the line. All most genteel, and no one ever talked. The family had a lawyer whose business it was to minister to these women, to see that they got mortgages on the most favorable terms in the apartment house. The women, as far as I know, never talked in public about the Rockefeller family.)

So my father went off to his Japanese garden and now

enjoyed the kind of peace that King Lear dreamed about but never got. My stepmother conspired with him at creating a private world and an inner peace.

When my marriage broke up, I would take my two sons on weekends up to the Japanese house. They gave it a raucous noise that my father liked. We had water-pistol fights in the bushes around the pool.

Thinking now of those days, I feel a sudden inexplicable drenching of shame, a quick downpour I cannot account for—except that I think of the pool, unused for two or three years now, the leaves and branches fouling what little remains of the water in it, a sad stagnation: the bright blue water gone to the muck that we used to clean so carefully and dreamily.

* * *

My father made ceremonies of small routines. He voyaged forth on expeditions—to bank, to hardware store, to supermarket—as if setting out for other worlds. He carried an attaché case on those missions, filled with extra glasses, reading glasses, sunglasses, antacids, checkbooks, portable electric razor, mints, flashlight, all the grappling hooks and duelling pistols of encroaching old age in the suburbs. He installed the briefcase beside him on the passenger side of his beloved old blue Mercedes, and set out.

He had a navigator's pride in knowing the way, not only the main routes but the back ways, the secrets, the hidden surprises, the alley shunt that would miraculously debouch upon a big familiar spot from some wholly unexpected angle. This knowledge made his driving seem oddly inventive and adventurous. He was the Lewis and Clark of suburban exploration.

Sometimes I would set off with him, and often bring

along the boys. If the destination was, say, the pool-supply store on Route 59—say that he needed more chlorine pellets to clarify the waters—we would leave the driveway of the Japanese house and at the corner turn right instead of left (surprise), then slide by elegant zigs and zags through unfamiliar (to me) neighborhoods, through residential eddies and backwaters that could not have been used by any but those who lived there, and then, in shorter time than the usual trip would have taken, we would glide into the pool store's parking lot. And my father would give a small triumphant high beam–low beam of his eyebrows, followed by a subliminal wink.

The navigation was like crossword puzzles, which he also spent his hours solving every day, to my bewilderment. The day did not proceed without his getting through at least 50 percent of the New York Times' daily puzzle. My busy Puritan's soul regarded this as an enormous waste of time and intellectual energy, but I was missing the point of the play, the sly clicking-into-place of patterns (which was the satisfaction that he got, I think, from the working out of roads).

My father asked for directions with great reluctance, and only if driving in territory totally unknown to him. And he would allow the instructions to be given only once: He would never repeat them, and would politely interrupt anyone attempting to reiterate the route: "I've got it, thanks." With that method he found his way through any puzzle. Like a hunter who allowed himself only one bullet with which to kill his prey. A point of pride.

Hunter-gatherer of the mall tribes.

It was thus, in small routines and wanderings, hunting the small game of an immediate life, that he regained some of the peace of mind and personal sense of scale that he had given up in the years of playing Polonius and Duke of Kent in the courts of powerful American neurotics and lover boys.

He talked about them sometimes while we sat in the kitchen of the Japanese house, my father in his imitation-leather BarcaLounger that tilted back to set him at the angle of an astronaut taking off. This was the unencumbered recumbency of retirement: He had his channel-changing clicker at hand and surfed through the electronic flashes, looking for a good wave.

He talked about the dukes and princes and kings and their procurers that he had known—about Reagan and Nixon and several Kennedys and many Rockefellers. He had spent many years in American politics and yet oddly— or perhaps for that very reason—he had no politics that I could discern, no ideology whatever. He was the most thoroughgoing American I have ever known: his memories and instincts and contexts all American, small-town Pennsylvanian, bred up in him at a time before America had truly entered the larger world (he was born toward the end of World War I in a town that had little business with Washington, let alone with the capitals of Europe). His boyhood was thoroughly local, and installed a kind of lifelong localism in his mind, a small-town boy's sense of proportion and scale and human drama. When he left that smaller realm, and like the country itself, went off into the bigger world, into huge complexity and power, he carried the instinct of the local with him, and it made him a decent human being. He found ideology ridiculous, a flimflam, a species of con. When he met political True Believers, he would classify them and judge them in the same way that he would identify wild animals or breeds of dogs, which is to say, impartially and expertly. And a mongrel would be a challenge: "I think he's got a little boxer in him, don't you? Boxer and maybe a little Lab in his coloring." The same with candidates, senators, presidents, ranters, ravers, dreamers, sword-swallowers, and those who practiced politics with three walnut shells and one pea. He judged their skills of argument, of dudgeon and cajoling, their mannerisms, the range of their unamplified voices in a hall, their capacity for drink, their weakness for women. And the spectacle amused him in an affectionate way. His face would cloud and sometimes even harden into a snarl when he remembered some act of cruelty or meanness. But I think he instinctively sensed that in his version of democracy, the worst and biggest harms were evanescent. As a man assembled out of the materials of the twenties, the Depression and World War II—and as his mother's favorite child—he believed that everything, no matter how bad, comes out well in the end.

My father had undoubtedly been marked by the Depression, shadowed by it, chilled by it. He was one of eight children born to a Pennsylvania country doctor and his wife. Dr. Morrow had been late in going to medical school (in his thirties), late in marrying (in his forties), and late in having children—and having to support them. He set up a series of small-town Pennsylvania country practices but often seemed to live somewhere in the vicinity of the threadbare, since there were so many children, and the patients were mostly farmers from roundabout who could not pay much for their treatment and sometimes left apples, corn, chickens instead of money. Still, it was small-town America in a Booth Tarkington version, and its harshnesses were not traumatic. They had even a little of the lingering American romance of frontiering, of conquering nature. My father from the age of thirteen drove Dr. Morrow on his rural rounds, and remembered years later the snowstorms that obliterated the roads and obliged him to back-and-

butt the Model T Ford to clear a path through the blizzard,
like an icebreaker through the whiteout countryside.

My father ran traplines for raccoons and foxes, and
sometimes came back from his early rounds stinking of
skunk. Only a sponge bath of tomato juice would clean off
skunk smell. He said that sometimes two or three boys
would be sent home from school because their clothing
stank of skunk and the teacher could not teach under such
conditions.

* * *

Here in Dutchess County, as I write this now, I find
that if I raise my nose and sniff, I can still catch the lingering smell of the skunk that came several nights ago. It
seems to have found its way into the basement, probably
through the cats' door, and tangled with the cats, and
sprayed, and trundled off in the dark.

My father had skunks on the grounds of the Japanese
house. A family of them lived under the shed in one corner
of the yard, and they would come out late at night. They
became so tame that they would waddle into the pool of
kitchen light that poured through the glass doors. The
light made them look half blinded and incompetent,
though they seemed to do well in the dark. My stepmother
put out the dinner leftovers for them.

I knew that the Great Depression was always somewhere at the edge of my father's mind, and that, consciously
or unconsciously, he consulted its lessons. His instincts
made their decisions on the basis of what he had seen and
absorbed of a world that had taken a hard fall and broken
many of its bones. Whatever successes may have come afterward, for himself or for the country, he had the caution of
the catastrophe. He was conservative in the nonpolitical,

personal, career-man's sense: He advised me against taking chances, against jumping from one safe job to a riskier proposition, since he had felt himself the wild black panic of free fall, with no net and no bottom. He had a sort of memory in his fingernails; he knew what it was to hang on. And be afraid.

So even under the seignorial protection of Nelson Rockefeller, my father had his sense of hanging on, to some extent, at least—the memory of chipped paint and impermanence. Of actual hunger.

So he liked to eat well, eat often, and eat quickly. He wolfed down food, ate elegantly but rapidly, with a sort of alarming, animal's voracious intake, inhaling, vacuuming. He drank in that way as well; no sip and leisurely savor for him, but a clugging urgency. Strange. In the act of eating or drinking, he would lose himself for an instant in an almost savage concentration, as a cat or dog will, as if the hunger-and-intake had become all there was, a little like the all-else-obliterating focus of sex.

But all that animal hunger was partially hidden—and satirized—by the delicacy that he brought to the table, by the air of amused fastidiousness that accompanied and commented upon his voraciousness. He absorbed food and drink by an interesting legerdemain, not by gross shoveling but by sleight of hand and mouth: Now you see it, now you don't. And after it was gone, why, then would come the elegant beast's beaming smile of well-being and satisfaction, a well-upholstered nineteenth-century afterdream of indulgence.

* * *

The rheostat of my father's life—his light—turned down so gradually over the period of those years that we almost did not notice the dimming. Or did not admit it. But when I returned to the Japanese house after not seeing him for weeks or even months, I would find him sometimes in his BarcaLounger staring off at nothing, blankly. And I noticed that as time passed, it became harder to recall him from those moments, which had a chill and iron gray about them. But I did not associate them at the time with fading light and a gradual approach of death; rather I thought to myself, with some irritation, that he was depressed again—a contagious depression—and I could see that my sons began to avoid his company a little, as if they found him strange, and not quite all there.

That was precisely it: He was not quite there. He had begun to be elsewhere. A kind of vacuum of dusk made its way inside him.

Or perhaps what he was doing at those moments was trying his wings, for his out-of-body flight capacities. But I never thought that at the time. I thought he was more and more becoming Emerson's moping dog.

He could be cheered out of the moments, but I could watch his mind, which I always associated with a pure light blue, begin now to turn to a vague muzz of brown. He was browning out.

The doctors found heart problems—irregularity of beat, some blockage of the arteries, they thought. His heart was not getting enough oxygen.

One evening toward late March, the winter lingering, I went out to the Japanese house and found my father full of anxiety, premonitions. He was scheduled to go into a hospital nearby in a day or so to have an angiogram, which would determine whether a bypass or angioplasty might be possible.

My father had almost never been sick in his life, never took pills, or medicine of any kind, until his diabetes began to encroach upon his system seriously as he reached old age. Now he took insulin by needle every day, and other pills my stepmother kept track of and administered. But still he never had a sick man's frame of mind, or any of the emergency parcels of fatalism that most of us carry with us and break open to calm ourselves when in medical danger. He was still, somewhere in his mind, I think, a robust child, his mother's favorite, and therefore invulnerable. It was a very American quality he had, that sense of invulnerability, of never having lost a war.

So now the idea of wheeling around on white gantries and having his body invaded by surgeons playing a serious game disturbed him, shook him, I think, to his core. I could see in his eyes a question that had never been there before.

My sister Cathy, a doctor, came down from Maine to interpret for him, for the rest of us. The angiogram found bad blockage in three arteries. He would need a triple bypass, they said.

The weather warmed toward spring, the temperature in the fifties, the trees getting their first buds, the first hints of blossoms—featherings. My father lay in Valley Hospital in New Jersey, just across the border from his Japanese house. His complexion had now grown blotched and liverish, and he lay among his plastic tubes and monitors, his face wearing an expression of somewhat dreamy and incommoded woe. I thought for an instant he looked like a very sweet dog that had been brought to the vet with an illness he could not, of course, understand, the dog making big eyes of confusion as if to say, "What's going on? Why have you done this to me?"

Then all his children gathered in the room, and his wife, and gradually they simmered up a mood of warming rue that began to pop bubbles of hilarity, until my father himself was laughing in his bed, but scared still, as the nurses bustled in and out to draw blood and squirt creams here and there on his body for the EKG, fastening the awkward little squeeze-bulbs that detect the blood's rush and bump through the piping. He laughed and remembered that the Muzak when he was getting an angiogram played *All That Jazz*, the Bob Fosse movie about having heart surgery and dying. My father whooped and barked and shot out a high screeching drawn-out soprano word of outrage and amusement: "Jeeeeeeeeeesus!"

* * *

The bypass operation went well. And then just as he was coming out of the anesthesia, he had a stroke. And so he stayed down under the ice, in deep water, trying to break back into the upper air.

This began a long misery. For days we debated whether he had been suffering in the struggle, or was just drifting, floating up and down. He never fully regained consciousness after the operation. The stroke paralyzed the left side of the body. For days he lay in Valley Hospital, Room 226.

Sally, who comes from Mississippi and has in her that valiant southern woman's blood, a high competence and endurance and dogged, persistent responsibility, never left the room, except when she went downstairs every few hours to smoke a cigarette. She slept in a chair that was never meant for sleeping in. My father slept, then quarter-woke, never opening his eyes, except when his eyelids rose and revealed two unfocused brown moons, the left one wandering, because of the stroke, in business for itself.

All week it rained, cold rain, the weather unnaturally

cold for March, in the thirties. And at night in the twenties.

*   *   *

At first we were certain he would die. I learned the word *apnia*, meaning that his breathing would stop for long, long seconds, as if the body had forgotten to breathe . . . and then would resume, as if nothing had happened.

And the breathing came out in arias—of lung and throat noises, and hiccups that emerged as small whoops, as if a small stupid panicked bird were trying to escape the cage in his chest, the bars of the ribs.

And then he began to seem better. He had periods in which he could understand the voices around him, could make conversation, or acknowledge it, with squeezes of the hand. He could talk only in incoherent (mostly) mumbling, a sad business to watch, for his mind knew what it wanted to say. He gave the command to his tongue, and out came nonsense, or the crudest, remotest approximations of sounds.

My brother Patrick brought a tape player and some jazz recordings (Louis Armstrong, Duke Ellington) and played them for hours, hoping that the music would stir something in his memory, would mingle with the voices of his children and his wife and stir up the surrounding colors and associations of his life, and bring it back like a Polaroid photograph slowly developing and finding its clarity. He seemed to respond for a time, to know what was being said around him. He opened his eyes and looked around the room at the people there, and seemed to recognize us. But his eyes were filled with a look of despair, and he remained in a remote country.

Days passed. He seemed more deeply exhausted than anyone I had ever seen before. He slept for long, long periods, making walrus noises, as Sally called them. He dined through a feeding tube down his nose. When he woke, he was sometimes lucid, his eyes full of their old intelligence. But comprehending the imprisonment.

The brain was still swollen on the right side, where the stroke occurred. A stroke is a fascinating and appalling transaction in which reality itself goes haywire: The brain explodes. The image made me think of Céline's Europe in 1945, all the bricks of the continent flying apart, a centrifugal world. Stroke was like that, I thought—the mind's big bang of violent disorder.

My father would lie sometimes on the bed like a fish struggling to breathe, but his mind still there, so I thought of his clear mind imprisoned in a gasping fish, like some terrible mythological reduction, a downward metamorphosis.

I went back to the Japanese house, and at two in the morning, as I sat in the kitchen, the yellow cat came yowling at the glass door, importunate through the pane. And I thought of my father struggling on the other side of the glass.

He came in and out of consciousness. I read to him from Russell Baker's book called *Good Times*, and he recognized the names of some of the newspapermen Baker was writing about, his generation of the thirties and forties.

As I was leaving that afternoon, I said, in Yiddish, "*In drayim mit de goyim*"—to hell with the Gentiles, the tag line of an old joke from years before that had become a kind of private salute. And he repeated the line to me, in a slurred, tongue-muddled way.

And the next day, as part of a little joke about his doctors, he gave the finger, flourishing it in the air. The gesture was satirical and almost merry, not angry, and had a small extra charge of subtle meaning because on a couple of famous public occasions, Nelson Rockefeller had been photographed satirically, defiantly, gaily giving the finger to various hecklers and would-be tormenters. So my father's gesture was a reference to that as well.

His temperature spiked alarmingly. His eyes were wandering moons. He aspirated some of his vomit and the fear then was he would die of pneumonia. I found myself wishing he would die of something, for he had endured the torture long enough, and should not have been forced to go on. The doctors wrote a DNR (Do Not Resuscitate) order on his chart, thank God.

They brought a new bed for him, ingenious in design, to prevent bed sores. Envelopes of air stacked tightly upright beside one another, each adjustable, inflatable individually. He lay on air, or the closest thing to it. His heavy body (though getting lighter and lighter as the days went on, living on IV fluids) would levitate almost. His soul already was hovering, out of body.

Once, when Patrick spoke to him in the Patrick style, blustering and profane and filled with a mock outrage about something or other, my father raised his right hand as if to conduct an orchestra—a perfect gesture for him, rather elegant, ethereal almost, or anyway a satire of elegance: He held one forefinger in the air and wagged it back and forth in a tempo withheld to the rest of us, and he even tried to say something, though no sound came, his mouth trying to round itself around phantom words.

I thought that his mind was going deeper into the dungeon, and was becoming windowless.

At length there was no improvement, or little. There was talk of his going home. It was almost time to open the swimming pool, but it would not be opened that year.

I wondered whether he would choose to live as he now lived, or to die. Then it occurred to me that he had chosen

to live already, his body being so resilient despite everything. It, any rate, had not given up.

* * *

It is good to think about the dead. It helps them.

I have heard that is true, but helps them how? Warms
them somehow? The heat of human love projected in the
blank chill? Speeds their flight through cold space to next
life? Cheers them that we loved them so, and hold them
still alive in our minds—the holograms of them, the virtual
reality of memories by which we reconstitute them, put
them so splendidly back together that they are even slightly
better than themselves, more refulgent in the retelling?

What else do we have?

This is what I wrote down:

SEPTEMBER 25—*Pop died this morning at 9:50. He
stopped breathing, a quiet death.*

He had been breathing in shallow, laboring breaths, and
it seemed that his lungs were filling with fluid, so Sally said,
and his kidneys were failing. The urine bag had a small
quantity in it, and it was dark pink, that ominous color. I
came out late last night after Sally called and said that he had
had another stroke, a bad one, and it seemed that his right
side was knocked out. I had not been here for a long time and
felt ashamed about coming now, but also was grateful. I was
in the room when he died, Sally as well. She listened to the
breathing, then the way it stopped, and she knew.

I thought for the longest time that I could see him
still breathing. I imagined the imperceptible rise and fall of
the hospital gown, and thought that his face moved
slightly. But it didn't, of course. Last night he was very very
cold, sweating and very cold. His hands were shockingly

cold to the touch and wet: refrigerated. Kidneys failed, and the fluids came out through the pores.

Then the funeral-home guys came. They were two fat, Irish-looking characters with stubby legs and leprechaun faces, tiny little noses. They looked somehow perfect for their mission. They had brought a body bag and a narrow stretcher. Sally said good-bye, I said good-bye, and they zipped him up and wheeled him out of the atrium and into an old station wagon, and went off.

Before that a cop named Coogan came to check it for the police, nice guy, self-effacing and efficient. Paramedics came but were not needed. One of them went to the body and grabbed the lower jaw and wiggled it to test whether Pop was dead—interesting test—and seemed satisfied.

The body retained its heat. We waited for a long time, almost an hour, after he died, because we did not want paramedics coming and trying to resuscitate him, banging on the chest, all of that. So we waited, and the body kept its heat, and only gradually cooled.

Just at the end, I held his hand, and he had by morning regained some of the strength in it. His right hand was quite strong; he moved his right arm a little, as if the strength were returning.

His color had been extraordinarily good, perversely good for a man in his condition. Then after half an hour, I saw his complexion begin to darken, and mottle, until I grew alarmed and thought he might eventually, soon, turn black in death. But after another half hour, his complexion went a clear, pale color, and he looked quite serene, rather handsome. I watched his face for a time in death. Quite a noble face, the high brow, the nose, the well-set eyes. Still intelligent as he lay there, and I reminded myself that his intelligence had now left the room. Sally had told him during the night that she wanted him to walk toward the

light, because his son Mike was waiting there, and she repeated it again this morning just as he was dying.

*October 21 on plane heading east to New York from Los Angeles—
I dreamed last night that Pop came back from the dead. We could
not explain it, he was there among us again, looking rather overweight and not very steady and a little flushed, but then, he had
been dead. I helped him walking, and then after a time, he fell,
onto his back, as if he had fallen into a campfire and couldn't get
up, and caught fire, and burned and burned, and then was dead,
and we had to mourn all over again.*

*November 1—Seneca Lake: I made many calls this morning to
arrange Pop's memorial service. I left a message on Russell Baker's
answering machine at the* New York Times. *An hour ago, my editor at* Time, *Dick Duncan, called Susan here in consternation and
said that the* New York Times *had called him and wanted to
write an obituary on me, because they had heard that I was dead.*

* * *

At the moment Duncan called, I was on the lake, fishing in a canoe, casting on motionless water with a bushhog
and a Mepps, trying for bass. But it was too early in the
day, or too late. The weather hazy, fall-ish, but warm
enough, in the fifties and sixties. The lake flat, and then the
wind coming up from the north and northeast and blowing
me out toward deep water. I fished over the weed bed, letting the lure sink down just to the top of the weeds and
then pulling it in, rapidly flashing in the water, which now
is colder and has killed the algae, and so is clear enough to
see bottom for hundreds of yards out. No nibbles, nothing,
though a pleasant drift.

And then Susan hailed me from the dock and told me

Time had called to ask if I was all right, because the *New York Times* had just called for an obit.

October 12, San Francisco—I dreamed that the earth beside my father's house was dug up by bulldozers, and then the hole remained in the ground, and the bulldozer was left there to rust on the ground beside the house, so that the house was in danger of falling into the hole, was impermanent and falling apart. In the dream, my father's wife died, and he was left alone bereft in the ruins, trying to figure out what to do with the house, with the damage. I asked him what he was going to do and he gestured vaguely, a typical gesture for him, as if to say, I've got to get organized about this sometime. . . .

I think of the morning of his death: the strange metaphysic of his visible absence, lying there on his inflated deathbed. For so many months, all the medical equipment was like furniture alive and electrified and animated and only his brain gone dead, emptying out, his eyes like dead bulbs, dead planets, old moons, rolling in space, lost and useless, but still nonetheless hooked up to something, I could not say what, connected to something beyond, and only intermittently seeing into the world where we still were. We could see him swoop in for a moment or two into our earth orbit and seem to recognize us, and understand, and then he would fly out into space and death again and be lost to us, receding, receding, the husk only left to lie here on the bed and make his death-breath noises. He breathed through his mouth snarfling and snarfling, pig noises, regular, punctuated.

He waved at his face, his hands restless always, arms making spirals irregular, as if trying to get free, as if he were trying to fly, but the wings were injured, so he beat the wings in some unconscious memory of flight but went nowhere, and we watched him as if he were some crashed bird with its systems ruined. Watched him sometimes with the detachment of the living, the curiosity almost, of the well who see a self-contained nightmare from the outside, and wonder that the creature cannot fly, that such a tragedy should have occurred, but the eye of the healthy is (in secret) triumphantly dispassionate as it looks on death. But then one crashes too, and internalizes the dying of the loved one, mimicks it, and the heart breaks. It cannot fly either.

When he died I felt around his carotid artery and around his wrist for a pulse but there was none. The pulse sometimes seems a hallucination anyway—now you feel it, now you don't—and so I thought, Ah, it is hiding in there somewhere: Pop's pulse is running somewhere in the inside corridors, but I could not catch it. After some minutes, I realized that it was truly gone, vanished. I think of the day when James was five years old and hid from me in a large crowded playground in Central Park, hid from me so well that I could not find him for ten minutes, fifteen minutes, twenty minutes, calling for him, calling his name louder and louder, more and more panic in my voice. My imagination went more and more specific and more and more alarmed: the fear that he would be gone, gone, irretrievably gone, like Etan Patz, vanished, so vivid and then just a sort of afterimage on the retina. At last, James grew tired of the game and emerged from his hiding place. He rematerialized and I rushed to him in anger and relief.

* * *

At the wake for Pop, in a funeral home, they had a closed casket, but a picture of Pop holding his grandson Arlen when Arlen was a baby. A cheerful and happy picture. The casket. The relatives, the Morrows from Baltimore.

All the old prominent Morrow Roman noses. Very funny. Dr. Seuss died the same day as Pop. So did Klaus Barbie. The Morrows looked like a tree limb full of Dr. Seuss creatures, sort of hook-nosed and birdlike, vulturelike almost, though sweet.

May 31—Sunday morning. 7 A.M. Cold rain. Heavy skies over the East River, the slosh of tires up the avenue.

I was thinking of the universe when I was a child. It was unstable. It consisted of dark vacuums and strange tensions and then, of red wild eruptions, when the house (which was the world) shook, and the sky screamed. Doors exploded and black-red rage leaped out, then door slammed shut and monster made its noises inside there, muffled, banging distantly, thrashing, thrashing.

I therefore hid. Became invisible. And have, so to speak, remained invisible. I learned, of course, how to put on proper clothes, and good language, and complex ideas—a manner, an armoring, a semblance. But I remained, inside of that fortress, invisible: vacuum myself. And inside my mind the doors still exploded and imploded, still erupted (silently, internally), and thrashed and thrashed: the prisoner-patient, straitjacketed, eyes bulging. All life a self-containment, for I was warder to myself, doctor, turnkey, and child attending this violent internal rite of gods erupting. The gold-red engulfing lava flowed down the slopes of the house, down the walls and stairs; the island would be engulfed in fire, the house in a hell's *poof* fired, and gone. Appease, appease: make self small and harmless. Things will settle down, storm pass, monster fall asleep and slumber stirring now and then in the middle of the dark, if stay awake pop-eyed and listen-listen-listen-listen to housequiet and afterrumble, aftergroan, afteranguish, then dark again. . . . Until first gradual creeping

light on windowshades and room takes shape again, bed-
posts familiar, countryside of covers, hillocky, close mountains drawn up to the eyes. And listen: no sound at all.

They would sleep late after such midnight storms. As
they sleep, Hughie and I in pajamas walk downstairs, find
kitchen knives, and then begin to dig at the walls of the
dining room, gouging holes until the holes form white
craters whiter than the surrounding wallpaint. They look
like bullet holes that we make. And keep at it all Sunday
morning. The wall becomes St. Valentine's Day massacre:
murdering mob-children having vengeance. And tell them
when they come downstairs, "We heard mice. We were
looking for the mice where they were hiding." Then they,
sheepish, hung, exchange the guilty-shamy glance. Do not
at all punish, but breakfast, Sunday papers, funnies.

* * *

Wartime: I dimly have begun to read, or rather to decode. Headline: A-BOMB. Huge. Much solemn talk, all
earnest now. The bomb has stilled their own violence and
made them . . . what? Not as anxious as children surely, but
triumphant and anxious too. Such power.

V-J Day comes. The Washington *Times Herald*. Up
across the Maryland line on Benning Road, the store sells
cereals with a V-J Day button packed among the cornflakes.
Walk down the long hill into the district again: asphalt and
roadside dust, the telephone poles all creosote-smelling
where dug with jackknife, the cheap wood splintering if
dug with the blade. But throwing, must hit the pole in the
center directly, blade's point dead-forward. Otherwise, knife
bounces off, deflected, dangerous, the blade flying sharp,
half-closed again by the blow into the rough-dimpled black
handle: I see the knife exactly in midair, as if it had stopped

there forever. Then the blade is in the dust, and I see Hughie's face, scared. He picks up the knife and pushes the blade all the way back into the handle and slides it into his pocket: quick heavy metal drop.

Find Bruce and the others, coming toward us with cigarettes. They have gone into Bruce's father's car again, to the carton in the glove compartment: Pall Malls. Matches. In the woods in a circle out of sight from the road, Bruce unzips the red pack and hammers out a butt the way he'd seen his father do it, *whap-whap-whap* the pack against the left hand's first knuckle 'til the white tubes with brown centers leap out. All eyes on the pack, we pass it round and each one takes a butt, then Bruce (in his father's motions again) strikes the fire: Eight-year-old Bruce, eldest of the bunch, becomes his old man eerily, becomes the fleshy big presence that smells of grown-up. He passes around the fire; the boys, we, hold the tubes in thumb and forefinger, intent-intent, and suck once, twice—the younger unprepared for what comes now: The dense evil poison in the white cloud hits inside just beyond the mouth. We gag, explode it out again, then try to cover up the gagging, choking, puff again, cough, puff again: And the evil goes all through the body now, green evil through the brains and eyes, and the entire body becomes a gag reflex.

Looked in the bathroom mirror, as if to see how the self, what there was of it, could have turned so sick. I felt a sense of betrayal. And many years later, when I was having a heart attack in Kansas City—a heart attack after thousands of packs of cigarettes, four of them that same day—I went to the men's-room mirror and looked at myself a long long time to try to see inside at what was happening: felt sick the same way, betrayed the same way, although of course in each case I had done it to myself.

My mother saw me sick when I came out of the bathroom and she gave me her ironical look.

9

In the hospital I woke up thinking of Mengele and the Gypsy boy.

Siggie Strochlitz told me the story as we stood in the presidential palace in Sarajevo and listened to the distant, almost conversational pop-pop-pop-pop-pop-pop of sniper fire coming from the surrounding hills.

"You know," said Siggie, "we knew that the Nazis were getting rid of the Gypsies. And we wondered, because Mengele had a Gypsy boy as a kind of pet—the most beautiful child I have ever seen, about five or six or so. Mengele brought the boy everywhere with him, and seemed to dote on him. We wondered, naturally, what he would do with the boy when he had killed all the other Gypsies. Would he spare the boy? Or what?

"And you know," said Siggie, with a look of amazement and disgust and resignation and outrage all mingled, "when the time came, and the last truck, Mengele took the boy and threw him in and slammed the door!" And as he said it, Siggie made a gesture, as of Mengele holding the boy by one hand and swinging him into the meat wagon— the last Gypsy being the most beautiful and innocent.

Siggie stared at me intently as if he had asked me a question and was waiting for an answer. Then I saw that he was simply speechless again, before the facts of the case.

* * *

The diseased Balkans went on dying, like a bad heart. I put on earphones and listened to the news for an hour in the morning as the floor began stirring, the nurses and aides formally bustling in the transition from night to day routine by taking blood pressures and pulses, temperatures and blood and weights and collecting the night's urine in the white plastic urinals hooked to the guardrails of the beds.

Later, about the time the frisking neighborhood dogs came around, a Pakistani news vendor would call, "Newspapers!" in the hall, and I would call back, *"New York Times."*

Sarajevo was dying by inches, still—instant by instant, cell by cell. I thought of the Russian driver, and the poet with the collar that used to fit him, and wondered if they were still alive. Sarajevo was staying alive the way my father stayed alive: with an almost perverse will to live and animal strength to endure that would outlast all else, including the civilization that the strength once supported. My father had been such a civilized man, full of nuance and information and wit and feeling. A civilized city of a man. And then when the stroke befell him, he had to live in the ruins of himself and boil grass from the public parks. He was besieged by monsters. The library of his mind burned down.

I thought of Sarajevo in this way because of Elie, mostly. He had brought me there: I went to the city, so to speak, under his protection, to the city of the dying. He had a license to guide in such places, an authority that derived in part from his Nobel Prize and his media celebrity, in larger part from his character and its shrewd, steady focus, but of course from his having survived Auschwitz.

If Elie could, as a child, emerge from the factory of death, then he must ever after be immune, untouchable in lesser holocausts. He is an ur-victim of the twentieth century, suffering emeritus—a fact that embarrasses him as a human being, I sometimes sense (enough of the Suffering, enough of the Mr. Holocaust!), and might make him a monster in any case, if he did not have a pure heart and a sense of humor.

When I met Elie in the lobby of the Inter-Continental Hotel in Geneva, he embraced me, the first time he had done so, and I walked him to the newsstand, where he (a thin man with austere face and unpolluted complexion) bought an enormous stash of chocolate candy—not the good Swiss stuff, but Mounds and Almond Joys and Baby Ruths and M&M's. He paid and stuffed them into his flight bag. "I have a sweet tooth," he said, sighing.

I asked him, in the journalist's way, "What do you hope to get out of Yugoslavia?" He flashed a smile and opened his palms toward me in a Yiddish gesture and answered, "I hope to get out!"

The Yugoslavian government was cooperating with the trip because, I think, it believed that Elie would be able to see its point of view—not entirely the Bosnian Serbs' point of view, but the more complex perspectives supposedly available at a remove from the fighting, available if the past were brought into the picture, all the Serb sufferings of decades and centuries gone by. The brutal moral ecology of the Balkans.

Perhaps the Serbs thought that Elie would at least sympathize with them as fellow survivors of the Nazis. Perhaps they thought that Elie, as a Jew and supporter of Israel, might harbor an anti-Muslim streak: To think so would have been to think in the Balkan mode, of course, where sympathies of tribe are overriding, where any dynamic outside the imperatives of blood is inexplicable. The Serbs, so accustomed to thinking in this way, building their politics on tribal expectations, must have believed that Elie would see their side of things, and more—and would vindicate them. I doubt they ever said it, though. Elie must have known, suspected, that some such thought was concealed in their gloomy hearts.

The imbecile Italian said it directly. He was a photographer from a journal in, I think, Milan. I rode with him in a car one day from the hotel in Belgrade to a meeting in a synagogue. The photographer, as tall and muscular as one of Karadzic's bodyguards, festooned with Nikons that he wore like necklaces, in broken English retailed the conspiracy:

"Whole trip is paid by Israel, you know. They want to stop the Muslims. The Serbs want to stop the Muslims. Suuuure. Big plot."

The Italians were not well represented on this trip. One of the Italian journalists covering it was a short, fat character with tiny, piggy spectacles, who fell in with the photographer's theory, bobbing his head up and down: "Cor-*rect*! Cor-*rect*!"

The candor and ripeness of European anti-Semitism is always a shock to an American. How matter-of-fact: part of the compactness of Europe, perhaps, and its tribalisms. And its rotten historical habits. Americans, even if harboring anti-Semitic opinions, would not advance them thus: before strangers, in a professional context, with coats and ties on. No, the ground would have to be prepared, possibly by alcohol. Anti-Semitism in America is not respectable, and in fact goes a long way to destroy respectability except in circles disreputable to begin with, or among the old WASP-insular and dying.

But Europeans . . . The Italians riding with me in the car saw that I was a Gentile, and assumed that, as such, I must be receptive to an anti-Semitic conspiratorial interpretation of our venture. What gave relish to the game was the thought of that paragon, Wiesel, so moral, with his Nobel Prize and his moral pretensions and posturing, that, that, Jew! And all the while he was on an unclean secret Jew-mission.

I told one of Elie's friends what the Italians had said. I said, "These guys are anti-Semites, you should throw them off the bus." But they stayed. I think Elie did not want to start a loud, messy controversy that would distract attention and give publicity to an anti-Semitic conspiracy theory that would play well with certain predisposed constituencies anyway.

So the Italians stayed.

* * *

In trying to describe—or even to think about—what goes on in the body, the politics of the body, we exhaust the simple vocabularies almost immediately (*hurts here . . . numb . . . sharp . . . dull ache . . . sore*) and must invent images and metaphors. These images take on a life of their own, a reality, because they describe an internal world of sensation that is real enough but hidden and subjective in the sense that all nerves and pains and bodily moods are subjective even though the Needle People can control those subjectivities most minutely.

So I thought of the heart-attack sensation as a glowing toxin of some kind at the core of the chest. And the toxin becomes, despite myself, real to me, and toxic.

My mind works in that way when I think of anger. Ever since the second heart attack, I have felt that I brought it on by harboring, inside myself, an accumulation of palpable rage that finally, after years, arose against the saner regime and tried to stop the heart, and killed the muscle, taking it as a kind of tribute, a sacrifice of myself to the rage god.

Anger recollected in tranquillity, or in the place that it has led to—the coronary care unit, not distant psychically from the war zones. The dynamics feel eerily the same, the eyes of the anger are the same: the violent, incoming irrational weather, the wild ride of anger, the murderous adrenal rush, a kind of black ecstasy that is at the same time aura-ed in its righteousness and self-pity, that exquisite tenderness that brutes feel for themselves when they are committing a crime.

The body's *lex talionis* is the clutch inside the chest and the killed heart muscle. I do not believe that anger clears the coronary tubing, or is cathartic in any way. Not my anger. And not the hates and angers I know about. Instead, I think they eat the heart out. Or else they fill it up with dark silts that choke the flow.

My father was not an angry man. Nor is Elie, who has cause for anger; he is not angry on any level I can detect. The molten base metal of his anger, it may be, has over the years been transformed into something else. So I think.

My father was possessed of a serenity that made me think often of a clear blue air. I thought that it derived, far back, from his mother's love for him, which was absolute and unseeingly worshipful. He was not her firstborn, but the first of her nine children to survive. Her first baby, Leslie, died an infant. My father was the miracle that arrived not long thereafter. He became, in some sense, an only child. He kept, all of his life, a mother's boy's sense of serenity and entitlement. That was maddening, I suspect, in a hidden way, to his younger brothers and sisters, but there it was: the favorite, the prince in splendor—like Sara Roosevelt's Franklin in the Hyde Park mansion on the Hudson.

* * *

Even when he lay dying, my stepmother ever in attendance, merely dozing in her recliner through the nights lest he wake and need her, even then in such medical misery, my father had, to the end, his mother's attendance, the soft, caring, maternal, dreamlike dimension that rocked him between waking and sleeping.

When he lost his temper, it was an event of benign meteorology—noisy maybe, but harmless and brief. My father could not have nursed a grudge if he had focused his entire conscious being on it. His little tantrums were those of a child. The dull enduring rage was not in him. He was not that breed of dog.

My mother, on the other hand, had a genius for big storms, few of them harmless. She had a sightless rage in her sometimes, for understandable reasons that went a long way back, as they usually do. I got that rage—among other, better things—from her.

It is the inheritance a long way back that you think about, after a heart attack has landed you in a meditative position: on your back in a hospital bed with needles dripping glucose and calm-down potions.

The sobering landscape before long raises the question of whether these inherited things—like rage—can be overcome, changed, put to rest. Whether you can struggle to a negotiated bargain: If given another chance, will you stop all this, the anger, the fatal predisposition to repeat and repeat? Is it possible to change, in other words? The American fox-hole convert/self-improver thinks so, for a little while.

But then thinks of the Balkans, and wonders if he is not, in miniature, something of the same gene-drenched, history-ridden fanatic of the tribe.

Some of the principles involved are the same—the important ones. A memory of being wounded, for example (in the Serbs' case, try 800 years of Ottoman Muslim rule), an inherited grievance, or else one so embedded in the early self (a memory of the 800 years) as to seem the prior dimension of fate. Electrons and selves and families and tribes have their distinctive trajectories. All memory is powerful folklore. By what trick or metaphysic can the biographies be kicked into different flight paths, into higher states of energy?

Other principles and dynamics in common: habits, customs, certain addictions. I know no tribe that is not ceremonially addicted to itself. It would not be a tribe if it were not self-intoxicated in some sustaining way. So, too, the family selves, which have their own ceremonies, sometimes terrible and destructive. I have seen them at work all my life, in rich elaboration.

The fierceness of the custom and addiction is what brought me—in the embarrassment of middle age, when one should, we think, be past such things but we never are—to the medical meditation room, my enforced retreat. Death, said the old joke, is nature's way of telling you to slow down. Or not to be so angry all the time. I am, at this pass, seriously considering the advice.

When Susan was in the desert once, an Egyptian friend admonished her, in Arabic, "You know, my people

have a saying: If you run around too much, you wear yourself out." Ah, the ancient wisdom.

* * *

Dr. Krieger has seen the movies of the angiogram now.
I get the word that, having scared me to death a few days
before with his angel-of-death house call, Krieger has now
decided that my heart is, after all, operable. The statistical
odds on survival may remain the same, but the drift now is
toward confidence. Routine, says the Aryan god.

The surgery has become so commonplace it seems
banal, and it seems silly to make a big deal of it. I know a
doctor in Geneva, New York, who had nine bypasses inserted
not so long ago, and now he writes me encouraging letters.

There is this disjunction, this odd *either/or* of perception.
Either this is a thoroughly routine procedure, done a thousand times a day, no problem, in and out. Or else it is a hairy
business performed in dangerous territory, wherein the chest
is cracked open, the beating heart exposed in a certain Aztec
way and then repiped by the beneficent priests attending.

It may be routine, in other words, but the enterprise is
spooky, as well—being so bloody and intimate, the rubber
fingers working inside the metaphysical center, the heart,
after all. *Mi corazon.*

* * *

It would be done. But first we must wait two weeks
for the heart to recover a bit, to get over its irritability.

And the blood will be thinned, so small are the passages it must get through without incident. I will be
weaned from the thinner heparin, which is only given
through the veins, and put on Coumadin, a thinner they use

in rat poisons to induce internal hemorrhages. I will leave the hospital for a little while, but stay quiet as a mouse.

* * *

We have sublet my apartment in New York, and Dutchess County is too far away (two hours' drive) from the hospital. Susan and I check into the Stanhope Hotel, where a friend has arranged a suite for a ridiculously low price. The Stanhope, now owned by Japanese, is a hotel of the Laura-Ashley-hunt-prints-on-the-walls genteel school, cousin to Ralph Lauren's Brooklyn-born idea of English aristocracy.

I move slowly now, carrying in my mind a vivid picture of straitened arteries through which the flow of blood must remain thin and unexcited and smooth. The rat poison, I imagine, has my blood down to the texture of pink water sliding through a cloggy, mossy weir.

A heart attack leaves an afterimage, a ghost of its pain, that is a long time fading. You have been spooked, and respond with that inward, hunted expression. I had been through all of this seventeen years earlier: the evil surprise in the chest, the panic-and-scramble, the diagnosis, surgery, recovery, and gradual back-to-normal.

I felt this time, curiously, as if I were getting a little too old for heart attacks, that I should not be reverting to this earlier stage of my feckless and self-punishing evolution. Surely I should be more serene now, a budding Buddhist.

The truth is that the restless, unsatisfied scuffling goes on and on: It never smooths itself into happiness.

At the Stanhope, waking in the middle of the night, I take up Edmund Wilson's journals of *The Sixties*, when he is bumping and rattling into serious old age—still drinking too much, to my amazement, still learning languages (Hungarian, for God's sake), still having money trouble, dodging the IRS; a life filled with a strange blend of grandeur and humiliation. The triumph is there in the books he has written, his accomplishments, his dinner at the Kennedy White House and lunch with André Malraux. The humiliation is partly the crumbling defenses against old age: his angina, his ruined teeth, his gout gone to rheumatoid arthritis, his old-man's blubber, his "mailbox mouth." He reads old reviews of his work, in the middle of the night, to reassure himself.

Wilson has always been one of those whose work I read to steady myself (the vigor and certainty and strength of his sentences would give me courage). But now, for the first time, in the sixties journals, I found him disturbing. I felt a waver in his prose, the tackiness of age, a kind of piddle-staining in the ideas.

I was unsettled, and put Wilson aside. The tackiness felt a little like my own, as if age and bad health were a failure of nerve, and I was being prematurely dragged into Edmund Wilson's senescence.

Wilson's senescence, of course, had more fire and energy in it, some days, than most men's youths. Still, he is making sounds of resignation: "When you realize that it won't be so long before you fade out of life, the activities of so short-lived human beings begin to seem rather futile and the beings themselves flimsy. Does it really matter that much? And all that energy and worry expended on merely getting themselves reproduced."

I got up for a glass of water and drank it in the dark, looking out the bathroom window at the Upper East Side of New York, at the roofs and back windows of the city's sleeping gentry; then heard a siren that started far down Madison Avenue, out of my view, and came up quickly in a screaming Doppler, like a sharp, blood-red incision of sound, moving south to north, until it hit peak scream and passed, going up to Mount Sinai in Harlem.

I went back to Edmund Wilson, reading him by an Itty Bitty Book Light while Susan slept. He was writing about the early sixties, when I was at Harvard. He regarded himself, as he said, as a "man of the twenties." The man in the nineties, reading him, bursts out laughing now and then, as when James Baldwin comes to dinner one night and starts using bad language:

> When Elena left the table, to go into the kitchen, he turned on his adjectival "fucking"—like the people in his novel—and the Brandeis man answered him in kind. I had been wondering whether ordinary people really talked to one another that way now. I reflected, after seeing *Who's Afraid of Virginia Woolf?*, whether most of the dirty language in fiction and on stage didn't occur in the work of homosexuals. . . . It is, I suppose, true that though these writers do often deal intensely with women, they have no awareness of the presence of ladies they want to please—and if I say "ladies," it is because most women one wants to please have to be treated as ladies.

How long ago and far away. I comprehend, at the earlier end of my life, the lost world in which such statements could be made, and comprehend the different world at this end, too. It was quaint and somehow endearing of Wilson to write as he did, to feel as he did.

Quaint and endearing as well that he wrote this entry, which I read just before I went to sleep: "Echoes from the past: Edna Millay's saying, when I had made love to her for the first time in my life to anyone: 'I know just what you feel: it was there, and it was beautiful, and now it's gone!' "

10

I enjoyed an interval away from the hospital, a sort of false peace. James and Justin and Susan and I went to restaurants for dinner.

One night at Brasserie Pascal on the West Side, Luciano Pavarotti encamped at a table nearby with his party, the man a festive bonfire of mountainous Italian well-being, I thought, and then thought again that he ought to start worrying seriously about his coronary arteries. I walked slowly from the restaurant, almost slow motion, into the late spring heat.

I moved like the Bomb Squad, my heart being the unexploded bomb. I listened to its tickings. Having a heart attack and waiting for another at any moment results in an especially wearing and unlikeable introspection. It is a physical introspection entirely, an in-peering anxiety, my focused self standing like a peasant outside the castle walls, awaiting the caprice of a lord who is given to drunken rages.

Families are filled with concealed bombs. Even what are now the quietest landscapes have been so fought over and savaged that just beneath the surface of normality lie unexploded mines and shells. This territory, ingested and internalized, is bad for the heart.

What were the causes of all this anger and bad family blood? Alcohol was certainly a motif—generations of alcohol. The Serbian fighters above Sarajevo have the same traditions. Slivovitz warms and loosens the trigger finger, if it does not improve the aim. All sides of the family have a taste for the poisonous inner glow, for the way alcohol behaves in the system and heats the mind while numbing it in that interesting, addicting way. My great-grandfather Morrow, colonel of the Ninth U.S. Cavalry at San Angelo, Texas, and other godforsaken posts in the years after the Civil War, was court-martialed for being drunk on duty and temporarily relieved of command. Like most other members of the family, he quietly took the hint and did not drink again. I liked the touch of rueful manliness in that.

Yet over against that chastened, sobered streak there ran a deeper irrational vein—a weakling atavistic love of booze and fights, revenge, recrimination, blind rage, apocalyptic follies. My mother's father seemed to be a wellspring of that tradition. He was an elderly Pittsburgh steel broker who had a lot of money and a mansion in Sewickley during the twenties but fell, as people did, on hard times during the thirties. His hardest times were marital, however.

Old Tom had married a younger woman, a delicate Alsatian named Hildegard who had a musical gift. Tom Vickers's sensibilities belonged to the nineteenth century: He was born in the 1880s and married late. Her parents were against it. Tom Vickers dressed expensively and carried a gold-headed cane, and rode to work in downtown Pittsburgh in a Pierce-Arrow with enormous headlamps, driven by his chauffeur. He was a small man—about my size, five eight, or a little smaller—but walked with a strutty, brittle dignity. He surrounded himself, as they did sometimes in the nineteenth century, with an aura of drama, a vaguely Shakespearean something, a grandiloquent self-importance that was then thickened by the Byronic.

Tom Vickers wrote atrocious poetry, my father told me once: heroic, overblown, bombastic in the fashion of the time. He had a sense of drama about himself, and perhaps something of the drinker's sense of grievance and affliction. There were murky stories, years later, of the old man physically abusing his wife and daughter, my mother.

His wife, oppressed and musically inclined, seems to have gone softly mad. Something like Ophelia. Among other things, she had some involvement with a clarinetist of the Pittsburgh Symphony. Tom learned of it. He launched into a King Lear display of histrionic self-pity and moralism and vindictiveness. The Bard's great moments in Pittsburgh: Lear threw Ophelia and daughter, my mother, out of the mansion, and after their life of privilege, they landed in a boardinghouse downtown, living on a dribble of crumbs the old man allowed to fall from his table.

My father did an imitation of old Tom Vickers meeting a friend on the streets of Pittsburgh or in his club, and grasping the man by the lapel, piteously, and saying, "Have you heard of my tragedy?" And then he would tell the story of Hildegard's betrayal.

My mother hated the old man all her life, and she refused to go to his funeral when he died in Pittsburgh in the sixties. I never met Tom Vickers. I became acquainted with him only through my mother's blood-red rages, when she would curse the man and as she did so, throw glasses or plates at the wall. I associated Tom Vickers with vivid splashes of alcohol against walls at the end of Georgetown dinner parties, after the public figures had left, and with dangerous flying glass, and with that rage that came out of Tom's daughter like a wall of fire.

I have always been curious about Old Tom, have entertained a kind of perverse liking for the idea of the man, though I knew little about him. I liked, somewhat, the nineteenth-century buffoonery about him, or rather the W. C. Fields version of it—or I did until I heard in later years that he physically abused women, at which point he became to me only another vicious drunk, self-righteous, self-pitying, charmless.

The generations are boxes within boxes: Inside my mother's violence you find another box, which contains my grandfather's violence, and inside that box (I suspect but do not know), you would find another box with some such black secret energy—stories within stories, receding in time. Like a Balkan oral history. In the Balkans, the motif is revenge. In my family, the revenge came to be exacted internally.

Edmund Wilson drank like a fish for years. I have always been impressed that he could do so and still retain his capacity for hard work and clear thought. He drank and ranted, often enough, and sometimes abused people. But he kept an eerie matter-of-factness and objectivity about it, and the morning after, when he came to his journal, he wrote about his drinking as if it were any other phenomenon he happened to observe. He placed little moral onus on himself about it, or so it seemed.

I found this an interesting kind of emotional double-jointedness. It is difficult to believe that Wilson, so intelligent and observant, with such long experience of alcohol, would fall into the most primitive kind of obliviousness and denial on the subject. But of course, he belonged to a different period; his talk about the "ladies" and about Bald-

win's cursing might suggest something about his attitude
toward drinking and its effects. My parents' generation,
only somewhat younger than Edmund Wilson's, grew up in
the twenties and thirties. When I watch one of "their"
movies—especially their favorite, *Casablanca*—I am
amazed at the amount of drinking and smoking that occur
in the movie. None of the major characters is without either
an alcoholic drink or a cigarette for more than a minute or
two. I have meant for some time to count each character's
drinks in an uncut version.

There is a gallantry in the drinking—people under severe self-control, under great external pressure (Nazis closing in, a war to be won, love thwarted by circumstance).
The only time anyone gets drunk and stupid and self-
pitying, it is Bogart late at night in his café, when he takes
out a bottle of bourbon (which he calls "boorbon" in the
Main Line Philadelphia way) and remembers Paris and Ilsa.
The next day, he has the good grace to be embarrassed and
remorseful about it. Otherwise, the astonishing world-
historical downpour of alcohol in the movie, attended by
clouds of cigarette smoke, is quite matter-of-fact. It is in
fact part of the aura of heroism. Brandy, Cointreau, cham-
pagne cocktails, bourbon, these potions are attributes of the
good guys. No one asks for ice water (but in Casablanca
that might have been dangerous too). The only nonalco-
holic drink in the movie is the ceremonial thimbleful of
Arab coffee that Ferrari (Sidney Greenstreet) serves to Vic-
tor Lazslo and Ilsa Lund the morning they come to the Blue
Parrot.

Edmund Wilson persistently drew connections between his drinking, often excessive, and his behavior, including scenes he made at parties the night before, or
cranky unpleasant behavior, or worse, toward, say, his wife
when he had had too much. But it never seems to have

occurred to him to quit drinking. Perhaps he was not an alcoholic. He was able to perform remarkable—heroic—intellectual work for many years while drinking heavily. If I look at his picture from 1963 or so—the year I graduated from Harvard, when Wilson was living in Cambridge and would be seen by friends of mine around the Loeb Drama Center, taking in the experimental productions—his skin looks clear enough, without that bloat and reddened crapulence that booze gives to most marathon drinkers.

It still seems astonishing to me that a man could for so many years sail back and forth between sobriety and drunkenness without eventually being shattered against the rocks. Our family motifs of rage and pain were almost always enacted within some context of alcohol, whether it was the cause of the trouble or just an attendant circumstance.

Edmund Wilson mentioned *Who's Afraid of Virginia Woolf?* He spoke of it not in the context of alcohol but of its (Edward Albee's, and homosexuals') bad language. My own long dislike of the play (which opened on Broadway that same spring of 1963) was based not on its language (that never would have occurred to me) but on its central conceit of alcohol as a truth potion that, as the night goes on and on, will bring forth deeper and deeper cathartic truths. I thought that as playwriting the conceit was slovenly and childish. But more important, I knew that alcohol is far more a destroyer than a truth-teller, that it is a distorter and flame-thrower.

I had listened to alcohol declaiming on too many nights, had watched it make too many eyes go damp and unhooked and glazed-wild-dull, to think it was a truth serum. I had seen it call forth too many slurred stupidities to buy the sophomoric line, *In vino veritas*.

On the other hand, alcohol's very distortions, once

lodged in a family, eventually establish their own new truth, their own unhappy and dangerous secret. They become the hidden unexploded shells, the casings of rage around black shames. They breed entire systems of bad truth: pseudotruths and booze humiliations, errors, abuses, incests, debts, illnesses, and so on. And the deeper into the systems you go, the more a prison alcohol becomes, and yet the more it seems all there is—real life itself.

11

Booze is first a smell—conspicuous and offensive if you are not drinking and it hits you from someone else; or else a pervading unnoticeable fact, if you are drinking hard—eventually becoming like an amniotic gas. There are many smells of booze. They correspond to the mood and even to the socioeconomics of the boozing. I learned to distinguish many of them as a child.

Beyond the hill at the edge of Maryland where I first felt the atomic bomb as a boy lay a foreign country. I knew Washington well enough as a southern town. I knew the black housekeepers (maids, we called them) lived in another part of the city that looked very different. But I was mostly innocent of that difference until later.

My father would take me along when he drove the maids home, over across Florida Avenue or down the river into Southwest. My schools were all white. The swimming pools were white. I never thought of that. I did not sense violence in Washington, racial violence.

But I knew that it existed somewhere very close, across the borders, in Virginia and Maryland—especially in Maryland, which gave off an energy of meanness, a border-state squint of the vicious, that somehow I did not detect in Virginia. I had more experience with Maryland, it may be; I recognized its faces and accents. I had a surer sense of that hard little white man's murder in the washed blue eyes, of Maryland white poverty and relish in nigger-hating.

That violence smelled like stale beer in empty long-necked bottles, bad local beer: National Bohemian in the roadhouse trash. Thin and squinty white men sat in bars hunched over, smoking Luckies and Chesterfields, kind of humping the stool a little, realigning the pelvis, grinding, talking about the nigger gals: a shotgun rack in the back of the brain. They were cowards, and niggers were great to bully, and kill now and then, maybe, or talk about killing, if they could get away with it. I never saw any such thing. I sensed it, feared it.

I heard the bragging once or twice in a roadhouse somewhere on the way down to Charles Creek, Maryland, late at night when Hughie and I were older, nine or ten. My father would stop for a drink, a scotch and soda (which had a different and acceptable smell, the admirable Press Club smell). My father would look over the boys, and they looked him over, the locals, my father with that little dare in his eyes that he got when he was drinking, a truculence (lightly, the arched eyebrows, the faraway eyes: *You gonna do something about it, fellas?*), and then he would bang his drink down on the bar for emphasis (*No takers, the shoe clerks folded, time to go, boys,* was the thought in his look) and lead us out the door.

Or else he would have a second drink, and the boys at the bar would relax a little, might say something. Or else go back to their own talk, but talking now for his, the city boy's benefit, and say something about *niggers*, just to see what the city boy would do. The city boy would turn away and look over the rest of the room, slowly, as if he wasn't going to be drawn into their cracker games, and they would *nigger-nigger-nigger* a little more, turning up the heat.

And then it really would be time to go, because the temperature in the room would have changed, the racial pressure: The boys at the bar would feel goaded a little, would feel the city boy's superiority and be irritated, and in their beer, be looking to do something about it themselves, maybe say something that would require a direct response, a challenge, something a man could not ignore. Things would ratchet up toward that, amid the punctuations of the gulps and sips and glasses banging and cigarettes drawn out and lighted, the Zippo snapping hard closed, the smoke exhaled in just the way my father did it—the first smoke of ignition not inhaled but exploded from the side of the mouth in a quick burst like a lily of the valley, and then to the serious business of inhaling and smoking. The first burst was somehow ceremonial—or so it seemed to me. Perhaps he only meant to get rid of the smoke from the lighter fluid that he had taken in, the first impure smoke of lighting up.

The gesticulations of smoking, the prop of the cigarette, waving, held this way, that way, the helix and ripple of blue-gray smoke in the air, now serene, now disturbed, agitated, the glow of the cigarette's firehead, expanding ash, the bellows of the body taking in the clouds and concealing/transmuting them and then giving them forth again. The mouth when not talking was doing this kind of talking, these other kinds of articulation, and all of this had content, meaning.

My father's smokes would mingle in the air above the

bar with the smokes of the other drinkers, who would squint through it—study and ignore, or comment aside.

The black men would come to the window behind the bar, a black face appearing suddenly, and ask for a drink, the window like the opening to a cage; the black makes application for a drink and is served a long-neck bottle, not a glass, his money shoved forward first to pay for it, *thank ya captain*, and the black face disappears. The eyes of the face would remain there in midair hanging, rheumy, red eyes, drinkers' eyes, then they too would vanish. The jukebox all the while with its multicolored bubbles, the little bright cathedral of platters and light, gives forth "Your Cheatin' Heart," and other country maybe, but the juke, I think, was a special occasion and mostly silent: save the money for the National Bo.

Alcohol always got the boys started. A bully gets inflamed at the black face near, a certain energy of viciousness brought up by the booze needs its release and the energy goes to the boot to kick the nigger—these drunks as a rule being sly enough not to fight with other whites when blacks are available. The redneck grievance rises in the drinker's brain—the opportunistic rage, maybe nothing more complicated than old tribal antipathy, the black face pissing off the white, all very basic and mean, no subtleties required.

* * *

Drink had a sort of ritual importance, I thought, in my parents' lives. I had early learned to make their drinks for them and for their guests because the knowledge—how to make a martini, for example—seemed to admit me to their world somewhat, to one of its mysteries. Their world excluded me, and so the sacrament of the alcohol—with its transformational powers, magic not always of a happy kind, but magic nonetheless—would, I thought, admit me to their secret, a kid's pretend, like trying on the old man's hat. I started smoking for the same reason. I experimented at five or six and got sick. I endured some weeks of sickness from Camel cigarettes when I was sixteen, but at last my body came to tolerate the poison, and when I smoked, I did so with the same explosive first burst of white cloud (the uninhaled cloud was white, the smoke that had been inhaled came out bluish) that was my father's style.

When I started to learn to drink, at sixteen or seventeen, I began with beer, never my father's drink. My father's drink was scotch and soda. It seemed to me an urbane drink: My father always wore a suit, it seemed, when drinking one.

I heard him once order a stinger. He had driven me and Hughie from Washington to New York City, to Grand Central Station, so that we could catch a train to take us north to a summer camp in the Adirondacks, and as we waited in the station for the train to arrive, he ordered a stinger, a drink that mystified me. I did not know for years what went into it; it seemed thick and lethal, a concentrate of the sacrament.

The bar in Grand Central was almost empty, darkish with the New York polish that I hated and mistrusted— still hate and mistrust. Perhaps my father obscurely felt the same unease in the city and wanted a stinger to brace himself for . . . what? I am imagining this now: brace for some cruelty and exclusion in New York, the old American story, an echo of it, the boys coming in from the country and being humiliated in the city (the social class) they were not quite good enough, smart enough, rich enough, to handle. New York seemed to promise some shame, threatened always to send us back where we came from, humiliated, and so here I sit, New York City clubman, twenty-five years there, and imagine his wariness.

The barman in Grand Central wore a uniform white jacket but had an upholstered New York middle-aged ease, an odd distinction—he might have been, in a different uniform, a banker, a stockbroker—and made the drink and set it down on the rich brown bar. In a stemmed glass like a flower with nitroglycerine in it. It was early in the day. My father took up the drink from the bar in the spirit of gingerly concentration, the surface tension shining darkly, and sipped it with an air of speculation. Hughie and I drank Cokes.

We made the train, and as we rode north I read *Life* magazine's piece about King Farouk being overthrown by young colonels, led by Neguib. Another named Nasser was mentioned, I think, but maybe that is mere retrospective knowledge, maybe Nasser was still concealed offstage.

12

Drinking was one of the central ceremonies of my father's profession. You worked and, when finished working, drank with people you worked with; the routine was almost that binary, that rigid.

I wonder now why, when I came back to Washington as a young man to work as a reporter for the *Washington Star*, I never joined the Press Club. I never went there at all. I never had a drink at the Press Club bar in all the time I worked in Washington.

When I was a child, the gargoyle drinkers would come swimming through the Press Club bar to grasp my father's hand and buy him drinks, or have him buy them. Sometimes my mother would be there at the Press Club, either in the small lounge off the front lobby that was known as the Tampax Room (because it admitted women) or in the (women-allowed) rear dining room, which I always hated, far in the back of the club, a sort of steerage, the equivalent of the back of the Maryland roadhouse where the blacks would do their drinking, begging drinks from the white bartender through the hole in the wall.

The men's bar had about it the twilight muzz of an alcoholic brain, a certain slow-motion depressive air. The gargoyles were men who had, I vaguely understood, lost their jobs as Washington correspondents for papers like the New Orleans *Picayune* but somehow managed to hold on to their Press Club memberships and to pay their bar bills. I suppose there was a much larger tribe of those who had lost their jobs and did not keep the bar privileges but faded and died as drunks do or else perhaps sobered up and were seen no more in the Press Club bar in any case.

It was harder to sober up in those days, I suspect. There were none of the rehabs that today are a mass industry. Or rather, there were drying-out tanks and private clinics. I doubt there was anything like the medical insurance to cover the treatment. And so little of the lore of recovery, the technique of it. There was Alcoholics Anonymous, of course. My father joined it for a time in the midfifties. He never talked to me about it at all, but sometimes went out on missions in the middle of the night to help drunk friends and get them into detox.

The Washington press corps was filled with alcoholics; drinking was pretty much what a man did. It had its lore and style, its gallantries, its angers and codes. In that world, borrowing money was an art form and a way of life. My father borrowed and was borrowed from with regularity—not huge sums, but $30 here or there, up to $100, I suppose, which in those days was quite a lot of money and would buy the groceries for many days: would drive whole packs of wolves from the door.

I remember an elfin alcoholic named Philip who worked as a Washington correspondent for the *Denver Post* and was forever deeply in financial trouble, a tiny Irishman with great charm, a Celt of the redhaired kind, wiry body, wiry hair, reddening face once handsome and hands that shook and shook. When I was ten or so he walked me around downtown Washington on some errand or other.

And here, forty years later, comes my perfectly clear memory of bright sun, the corner of Pennsylvania Avenue and Fifteenth Street, at the U.S. Treasury near the bend of the avenue—Philip and me waiting for the traffic light. He reaches to take my hand, and his hand shakes with such a frank, unconcealed steady trembling that I watch it for an instant in pure curiosity before (reluctantly) taking it and crossing the street, Philip all the while maintaining his gay, nervous patter of conversation, which as I remember it was full of delightful Hibernian swoops of fancy and deadly perfect imitations of all the Washington characters of the day. His Robert Taft was a perfect rendering, I knew even then; his Truman with the wigwagging head for the flat midwestern emphasis, his dark dark Joe McCarthy like a paranoid stormfront—these all poured forth.

Philip, being a drunk and slightly childish himself, never condescended to children. He assumed I knew everyone in the cast of characters he was parading, and in retrospect I appreciate the gallantry of the performance (although maybe he was mostly performing for himself) because he was taking me to the Press Club to meet my mother for lunch and there is no doubt that the destination promised what he badly badly needed: a drink.

When we arrived at the rear dining room of the press club, Philip ordered a double scotch on the rocks, held his rib cage 'til it arrived, and then drew it off in two draughts.

13

A gray cold this morning after days of thick bright heat. The air suddenly feels like fall. But it is still the end of July. My chest hair is beginning to grow over the Frankenstein cuts.

I have been reading Elie's lecture on Ezekiel, man of extremes, visionary and psychotic. Elie says the psychoanalysts have been through the Book of Ezekiel many times, and concluded variously that Ezekiel was paranoid, or catatonic, that he suffered from "narcissistic masochistic conflicts . . . fantasies of castration . . . unconscious sexual regression . . . schizophrenia . . . delusions of persecution, delusions of grandeur."

It strikes me now, looking across the hayfields toward the coyotes' tree line, that Ezekiel might have been rabid, in some metaphysical way.

Elie described him as a genius of extremes, a visionary alternately of horror and of beauty:

When he is harsh, he seems pitiless; when he is kind, his generosity spills over. In his worst outbursts, he declares his own nation ugly and repugnant; but suddenly he recovers his compassion and everything and everyone radiates sunshine and serenity. He oscillates between the shame of sin and the grandeur of salvation—for him, there is nothing in between.

Ezekiel is the prophet of imagination, Elie thinks. If he does not have the prestige of God's voice behind his messages, then he is another hallucinating crank, a street crazy. When he warned the people of Gilgal of the coming exile, says Elie, he paraded through the streets carrying a knapsack, to tell them that they too would become wanderers. Often in the seventies, I saw a man parading up and down Fifth Avenue, wearing, even in the hottest weather, a Burberry trenchcoat and a muffler, and carrying a full knapsack on his back. Front and back he wore signs warning of cosmic conspiracies (which he conflated with his ex-wife's plots against him) and entreating people not to kill him, since he had already suffered enough.

I am drawn to Ezekiel's mood swings, his cosmic trapeze—not a question so much of unstable temperament, given to exaggerations both up and down, as of an effort to expand the vision, to comprehend a universe that is not moderate but given to such extremes of temperature as heaven and hell, good and evil, life and death.

I felt the temperatures of extremes during that suspension between my heart attack and my surgery. I thought that sex would be unwise, but I was repeatedly unwise nonetheless. A strange sensation in the middle of the night, the warmth of love and energy of passion, working so close to the cold, to a fear of immediate death.

Why was I incautious? Stupidity, perhaps. A calcula-

tion that the medicines I was taking—blood-thinner and
some others—made another heart attack unlikely. It was
not erotic to think I was making love on the edge of a dark
precipice. No gambler's thrill. On the contrary. It was an
anxious risk, like driving at night along a cliff road beside
the sea. Nerve-wracking sex.

Edmund Wilson writes about that in his journals of
the sixties, when he made love to his wife despite angina
pains. He felt as I did, I think. A certain baked-Alaska effect, no doubt—having sex and death so busily present,
with only a thin wall between them.

*   *   *

Reading Elie's lectures on the Hasidic masters and
biblical prophets, I have started to dream about them. I fall
asleep very easily, usually just after noon. I read Elie for a
few minutes, then put the book aside and almost instantly
drop off. The stories come back to me with that distorted
clarity of afternoon dreams.

Yesterday, I was repeating the name of Ba'al Shem Tov,
the Hasids' Besht, over and over, and trying to get the syl-
lables in the right procession, but it kept coming out Sha'al
Bem Tov or some such. The dreams were full of argument
that reflected the terrible, obscure conflicts among Hasidic
factions, my brothers and sisters sometimes falling into the
parts of Hasidim and Mitnagdim, old enemies. I conjured
in one of these dreams the fight in which (Elie wrote) Rabbi
Itzak Meir Rutenberg—later known as the Rabbi of Ger—
left his master, the Maggid of Kozhenitz, to join up with
Rabbi Bunam. The Maggid commented, "'Poor, poor Itze-
Meir, he has disturbed my Sabbath. I am afraid the same, if
not worse, will happen to him.' And indeed the Rabbi of

Ger had thirteen children and lost them all. Every one died on *Shabbat*."

I would wake from these dreams with refracted clear-water afterimages lingering for a moment or two: Hasidim and Morrow siblings intermingling, fighting. One day, there were Hasidim I did not recognize walking slowly through my father's ruined, tumbledown house—my recurring dream image of a place (family) gone to ruin, the windows broken, the floorboards rotted, the lathes showing through broken plaster walls and the stairs without banisters. The Hasidim, dressed of course in black, creep slowly into the house as if investigating a place they have never been before. My father, still alive but barely, lies as if in state upon a sort of kingly bed, a Viking's hero-altar; yet the rest of the house all around him is ruin, dust, neglect.

Just waking and trying to remember the dream, I sit on the edge of the bed and think to myself, suddenly laughing, *In drayim mit de goyim!*

The ultimate messages, visions, arrive by the vehicle of dreams. Or at least they do in the minds of Elie's prophets and masters. My favorite variation on dream revelation (very modern somehow) was Nebuchadnezzar's trick (in the Book of Daniel). He would summon his magicians, his astrologers, his charmers, says Elie, and say, "I have had a dream. Tell me what it was." He said that if they could not tell him the dream, he would have them executed, a perfect perversion of power in the face of mystery and spirit. And Daniel came forth and told Nebuchadnezzar his dream: "You saw a huge statue of extraordinary splendor. . . . The head was of pure gold, its chest and arms were of silver; its belly and thighs were of bronze, its legs of iron, its feet part iron, part clay. As you looked on, a stone came loose, hit the feet of the statue, and broke them to pieces. Then the whole statue broke and the wind took it away without leaving a trace."

My father and his house were past their splendor in my dream that afternoon when the black Hasidic figures worked the margins of the scene and my father lay upon his hero's pallet. I see my father now being consumed in flames, dying again. But the house does not burn down. It is ruined already. My father's noble profile is like a death mask, eyes closed; and then the flames and smoke obscure it, but he remains as white and chaste as marble, but vanishing now in the rising fire.

Or the story of Daniel and Darius the Persian, successor to Cyrus the Great. Daniel is one of the prime ministers of the kingdom, but is caught praying to his God, through the open window toward Jerusalem, and the saddened king must, therefore, give him the usual punishment, which is the night in the lions' den.

Here Elie breaks off his account of Daniel for a moment for this gag: "In Africa, two men stand at a river, which they are about to cross, when they notice crocodiles looking at them. 'Are you afraid?' says one to the other. 'Don't you know that God is merciful and good?' 'Yes, I do,' says the frightened man. 'But what if God suddenly chooses right now to be good to the crocodiles?'" The shrug, the Jewish rue.

Then Elie asks, "How could Daniel be sure that tonight was not going to be the lions' night?"

* * *

So in a state of suspension, with a clogged heart and blood thinned down to a sort of salty rosé, I have distorted afternoon dreams in which Ezekiel and Daniel mix with Morrows, and Elie is an offstage impresario.

I think about death from the inside and death from the outside. What I fear now—and am fixed on—is death from the inside: the danger of my own body, at its core, annulling itself, its life. And there is death from the outside—Bosnia, say—where the shells rain down through the air onto Sarajevo and tear apart people waiting in line for water and bread. My Russian driver's wife had death-from-the-outside.

Death from inside is somehow more difficult. It is a drama enacted in the dark, inside the intimate alien of the self, and conjures up all kinds of fetid recriminations.

Death from outside may possess more honesty and poignance—if less justice. It has more narrative clarity; not slow disease working in the dark, but blast, fire, steel, death. (Perhaps that is why Hemingway chose the shotgun—narrative clarity.)

Why the latter should be preferable to the former I cannot say. I find myself wishing I were in Sarajevo now: some boyish impulse to show off, be brave, court danger—be outdoors and death-defying, not lying here invalid (awful word—no validity left), taking pills, afraid to move too fast and set loose a dread black iceberg in an artery, twirling slow-motion toward the fatal impasse just north of the Left Anterior Descending.

Better to be dodging bullets and shells among the defenders of the city. To be sending out dispatches as the end comes: articulate before the horrified, admiring world.

I should know better. Piggy Milosevic and Wolfie Karadzic have torn almost all of the meat off the bone by now. They sit already, like Masai warriors, at the Balkan meat-feast: drying ribs and organs strewn about, the inedible tidbits empurpling in the dirt, blood blotting up pine needles, and human hair in matted clumps at the edge of the campfire.

A big tin bucket filled with filthy water and human hearts steams and boils on the hot coals. The Balkan dusk comes on. Slivovitz all around.

* * *

Am I superstitious? Do I fear the Maggid's *Shabbat*, like the one on which he lost all his children?

I was superstitious about my father's bypass operation: It was followed immediately by the stroke that left him so wrecked, unable to speak or walk or move his left side or rise from bed for the last eighteen months of his life. I kept imagining myself entering the same operating room and coming out shattered.

The day before my bypass operation was Father's Day. I took my sons and wife to a brunch on the East Side. As we entered the restaurant at Ninety-second Street and Madison Avenue, it occurred to me that it was just on the sidewalk outside, when Justin was two, that I had said to him, "Hey, Justin, what's new?" And he had grinned and replied, with, for him, complete accuracy, "Everything."

I had been moved by the moment. Now Justin was twelve. His brother James was nineteen, home for the summer from Georgetown University. James was now a thin, handsome young man with a distinctive public manner and self-possession, an elaborate set of political opinions that he had researched thoroughly and could defend with a Jesuit-trained mind, and a bluish beard like Richard Nixon's. Unlike Nixon, James was extremely funny.

Justin was in the summer between his sixth and seventh grades at a private school nearby. He and his friends were deeply involved in moviemaking just then. I had bought him a video camera. The boys sat up late writing movie scripts, surreal stories that involved a certain amount of assassination and betrayal, and cosmic moneymaking scams. It was *film noir* speeded up for the nineties and then inexplicably performed by twelve- and fourteen-year-olds. The narrative logic belonged to the school of Deconstruction. I had seen the first of the movies—a rough cut, Justin insisted. It had a certain amount of snarling and many chase scenes down the corridors of Justin's mother's apartment building. The death scenes would require some ketchup later on. The best scene was a moodily lit "I've-got-you-now" confrontation in a stairwell.

We had a Father's Day brunch that I did not enjoy. I felt apprehensive and sorry for myself. Afterward, we walked a bit, then took Justin home, and James and Susan brought me to the hospital, to be there at four o'clock or so, get checked in, get restored to the hospital mind-set: the pajama'd passivity, the intravenous needles, the tubing that leads to the IV pole that must follow you around, even to the bathroom, the heart monitors, the bouncing, beeping cardiogram.

Ah: the coyote's leaps and springy gait, a wild animal's body English. These patterns of motion I had seen for weeks before on the electrocardiograms at the hospital: a certain animal bounce and fall, a jaunty, relentless persistence.

I had to talk myself into being back in the hospital, had to review consciously why I was there, the attitude necessary to sustain me (tough, clear, aware, but accepting, and always with the seriousness of this thing in the forefront of the mind). Otherwise, I would writhe and whine and think, Why me? That would be a foolish and ungrateful question, for of course I was lucky to be there, to have such surgeons, such technique, and an operation that could undo the slow natural damage to my heart of many years.

Still, I was superstitious. I thought of my father's horrible terminal fix, the nightmare of that captivity.

I was installed again in a four-man room, but since I would be there only overnight, I only nodded to my roommates—all heavy men in their fifties and sixties, grizzled and stolid, I thought at a quick glance, except for the one to my right, who spoke with a fast, loud Brooklyn accent to a man in the chair beside him (his brother or his business partner). I did not want to get to know them. I was thinking about myself.

I had the phone connected beside my bed, and the tiny television that hangs from a big flexible arm and swings down into your face when you want to watch it. My sister Cathy had driven down from Maine to stay with Susan during the operation and offer medical interpretation.

The word came down from the surgical team through the nurses that I would be the first case of the morning. Which pleased me—no waiting around in suspense in the morning.

A woman in green from the surgical crew came to interview me in intense detail and write down the answers on forms on a steel clipboard. The woman was thin and over-caffeinated, with taut, stringy biceps and black circles under her eyes, and a melodramatic air that was not entirely reassuring: Her tension bespoke life-and-death issues. Her hair was wild. She looked like a bloodthirsty Frenchwoman sitting at the foot of the guillotine. She had that light in her eye.

She completed the impression she had made when she listened to my heart, cuffed me for blood pressure, needled my arm for blood, and then, before leaving, gave me a jabbing rectal examination.

In the morning they changed the plan and said I

would be the second operation, not the first. So I would wait until 11:30 before being wheeled down.

I began to relax and readjust my clock. I had learned the trick of segmenting time, of dividing it into compartments and entering only one chamber at a time, not thinking about the next one until it was time to do so. The technique of sanity in tight spots.

So I settled into the morning waiting chamber, and just as I was getting relaxed in it, the nurse came and said I would go immediately down—I would be the first after all.

So the doors to the other time chambers were flung open, and for a few seconds a black anxiety rushed through them into the chamber where I was. Then the anxiety passed, and I settled into a prearranged fatalism, the attitude I had been putting in order the night before.

Otis comes with the gurney. He is a tall, amiable black man who works with the surgeons. He has a quality of Magic Johnson about him, an open friendliness that helps with his mission.

Otis rolls me out of my time chamber and out of the room, down the corridor, Cathy and Susan walking beside the gurney. The ceilings need painting, I see as I slide along—flaking and water damage. The hospital is undertaking a huge new building program—one billion dollars. These old floors will be gutted soon.

They have put Valium in the IV, I believe, to ease the ride. The hospital's touches of squalor, here and there, can remind me of my frequent dream, wherein my father's house is crumbling. We have the atmosphere of mere survival, of doing the best we can in the aftermath.

Aftermath of what?

I cannot say.

We come to a polished steel box and its doors slide open. Otis pushes me inside, Susan and Cathy stay in the corridor, reaching toward me. Each blows a kiss and I do the same, and then the steel doors slide shut. Otis smiles, and we descend.

We come to the Yenta at the Gates.

She is a woman in her forties who sits at a desk as we enter. This is the anteroom of surgery, she is the keeper of the gates.

"Did you shave him?"

Her voice is a raw complaining New York.

"No, they didn't tell me to shave him upstairs," says Otis.

The Yenta explodes now in grievance and indignation: "Didn't shave him? Nobody listens to me!" Like King Lear on the heath: *"Nobody listens to me!"*

Early in the process, just after I had had my heart attack, I had schooled myself not to get angry—not worth it, too dangerous, counterproductive. But if I had not had the Valium just now I would get angry now.

Otis fumbles with his electric razor. Yenta bullies Otis further. Otis with his razor begins a remarkably rapid harvesting of my ample chest hair, the high whine-buzz of the razor not quite overpowering the Yenta-cries.

Otis uncovers me and I lie naked on the table, getting barer and whiter by the second as the razor in Otis's black hand in sheep-shearing loops denudes the flesh down to stubble. He takes chest hair, stomach hair, pubic hair (*Careful there, Otis*), then marches south along the thighs (lifting the legs to take the backs as well), then calves.

What a gleaming specimen I am left, what a plucked Caucasian!

And all the while, the Yenta has not stopped her line of Otis-bullying, self-pitying outrage.

When I am totally naked at last, she turns full face to me and says:

"Nothing by mouth since midnight, right?"

Here we go.

"I had a peppermint two hours ago. . . ."

"You what? Woy? Woy did you have a peppermint? Woy?"

Am I, naked and hairless on a table on the Upper East Side of Manhattan on the first day of summer, to argue with the woman about a peppermint?

I cannot. I shrug. I can feel my penis, naked under the lights and rhetoric, withdraw a little in one of those motions of self-defense the autonomous organ makes sometimes. The testicles rearrange themselves before her gaze, and think about heading north a little, to ground that is less exposed.

But I am groggy now and starting to drift. I feel myself sliding into the operating room. The swimming faces of the anesthesia team—masks and goggle eyes—peer down and attend to their potions. The stadium lights beam down in blinding clusters.

Then I am gone.

14

Just now in the middle of the summer, there came death so quick and quiet and unexpected that it seemed an unobtrusive magic trick: bright sun, green water, black magic. We blinked, and Gary vanished.

No commotion. Now you see him, now you don't. The surface of the canal where he went under (the strongest swimmer, a bull of a man, crossing a mere canal on a summer day) was instantly smooth again.

The telephone rang in the study, two rooms away from the bedroom where I was dozing in the early afternoon. I heard the phone, and muffled talk. Then Susan came into the bedroom, sobbing, and said, "Gary's dead."

We packed the car and started upstate, driving west across the Catskills and then straight north to the Finger Lakes, and got to the cottage on Seneca Lake by nine o'clock.

Gary lived in a house on the same bay as Susan's parents' cottage. He was a hunter and trapper and fisherman, and his basement was filled with guns. I once counted nearly 100 deer rifles racked upright along the walls down there. The room bristled, a dark masculine armory that had something of the animal's cave about it. Gary collected guns, buying one, it seemed, almost every weekend at one of the gun shows in Rochester or Syracuse or Elmira or Corning, or privately from another of the gun brotherhood in the countryside. Gary favored lever-action .30-30s and .30-06s, I thought; there seemed a huge redundancy of them (all ages, all states of polish or disrepair) in the basement collection. He owned assault rifles—at least one Uzi, and at least one AK-47, and no doubt the American models as well. He had many pistols as well, I am told, and at least one of them he kept loaded against intruders.

Gary shot as many deer as he was able to take in a season. Until the fish-and-game people arrested him—on a bogus charge of using a snare—Gary ran traplines across wide territory, taking foxes and raccoons and coyotes. He sold the furs and sometimes used them to make coats for his friends. Susan has a coat made of eastern coyote, the fur rich and wolflike.

For a time, Gary kept a half dozen wild foxes in a metal-bottomed pen outside his house. The floor was slanted, and Gary collected the fox urine and bottled it and sold it to the fancier hunts, including, I suppose, those that tally-ho through my home territory in Dutchess County. Sometimes old hunter types would buy the urine, not the mounted foxhunters of the gentry but Fenimore-Cooper geezers of the forest. These men, Gary said, would stick their forefingers into the bottles of fox urine to sample it before buying: "No, no, too sweet . . ."

Gary had other home industries. For a time, he kept fish heads and carcasses in tanks in order to sell the oils of their decomposition. Once the same game warden (later sent to a mental institution as a paranoid) who arrested Gary on the snaring charge came round to inspect his decomposing fish tanks and, looking into the muck and bones, advanced the theory that Gary was a serial killer who disposed of his victims' bodies this way.

No one was busier than Gary. He was a big man, with strong muscles and an incipient pot. He wore glasses and had a ruddy face (Irish and Polish), sunburned in summer. He was forty-seven when he died, but with a boyishness about his face, an eagerness and gleam, a combination of relish and self-deprecation that seemed to me very American, like his competence and his air of being able to handle himself in a fight, should the need arise. I never doubted that he could switch, with that American suddenness, from the amiable man he was to the fully mobilized fighter and even killer. It was not an ugly or a menacing trait in him, but instead owed something to the James Stewart or Gary Cooper tradition of American males: "I'm not looking for trouble, but if trouble's looking for me, I won't be hard to find."

Gary rose before dawn and in all weather he would push out onto the lake in his cruiser.

Seneca Lake was one of the deep gashes left when the glacier fingers of the Ice Age clawed through the landscape. The lake is 1,000 feet deep in some places and has not frozen over in generations—mystical depths. I sometimes imagine monsters down there—coelacanths, sightless oddities.

Gary engaged in a kind of factory-fishing that I never found enjoyable, partly because I was simply along for the ride, or to hold the net now and then. Gary did the work, somewhat manically, watching the sonar for fish, calculating their depth, rigging dozens of lures (bright metal flashers with hooks, a temptation in the depths) on the endless factory lines that he unreeled and sank for hundreds of feet into the dark water. Lake trout swim deep. He would drive the boat and talk, and watch the lines outrigged on either side of the boat and trailing into his wake, and could tell by a little thumping disturbance on the line when a fish had hit somewhere deep below. I could not distinguish a real hit from the tug-and-thump the lines made dragging through the water in a wave-bucked boat. Every hour or so, I would take the wheel and Gary would laboriously haul in the lines (it was hard, grinding work) and harvest the lovely but exhausted lake trout he had enticed with his flashers.

He loved this fishing: The harvest meant a lot to him. We have three lake trout in our freezer that Gary caught two Sundays before he died. I think we are afraid to eat them, as if to do so would violate a taboo. Transgress death, partaking of the forbidden fish.

Gary had enemies. One was the game warden who pursued him like Javert. The warden's case against Gary (catching a rabbit with a snare, the warden said) made the newspapers. Animal-lovers' groups were roused. They certainly hated Gary. Gary for a time lost his licenses to trap and hunt and fish and, after his appeals were exhausted, he had to serve ten weekends in the county jail for his alleged unsporting rabbit assassination.

My own inclination, because I was always on Gary's side, was to dismiss the charge as absurd, and further, to think that even if it were true, so what? The moral difference between catching an animal with a shark-jawed leg-trap and taking him with a snare seemed to me, let us say, Thomistically fine.

And you heard stories sometimes suggesting potential violence against humans. The massive gun obsession seemed a little unhinged—or would have, had I not known Gary. He talked about his life only with a jocular guardedness, usually after he had been drinking a little with the judge. There was the night when he and the judge were having a drink in a bar somewhere and a man who was certainly drunk and probably psychotic pulled a knife and said he was going to kill the judge. Gary, as the judge told it, shot out of his chair in one deft, seamless motion and hit the man so hard in the jaw that he lifted half a foot in the air and was sound asleep when he hit the floor.

And there was the mystery of Vietnam. We always thought that Gary had served in Vietnam, had seen a great deal of killing, possibly done some of it himself—that he was captured by the North Vietnamese and that the experience had left him traumatized and mute on the entire subject. We never knew for certain, even after his death. Some said he had been a helicopter pilot and had been shot down once while evacuating American soldiers; or that when pulling out of a hot landing zone, a soldier who grabbed one of the skids at the last instant had held on for a moment or two and then fallen to his death from a height of several hundred feet.

There was the story that he had been captured and held in a Communist bamboo prison, where the Vietnamese tormented him with sharp sticks—and possibly harder forms of torture—and the spiders of Indochina left him with a screaming phobia. I had a notion (my own ex post facto fantasy based possibly on Gary's career as hunter and trapper) that he had been one of the Lurps, those who went on long-range patrol, lying motionless in grass for a day or two at a time and waiting for the enemy to come by and be ambushed. Or that he did some other stealthy, solitary, bloody work, and that it had possibly left him with a leaning in that direction.

But maybe none of those stories was true. Gary let

them hover around enigmatically, and may have enjoyed the bloody glamour of their influence.

The guns and stories make Gary sound like a dark, violent man—what D. H. Lawrence said about the American male: "hard, isolate, stoic, and a killer." But that impression (which the animal lovers took up when they heard about the snare) was all wrong.

He was a hunter, it is true, he shot and butchered wildlife, he was pretty rough with living things. But Gary loved the wild world with a love different from the Sierra Club version, and he was in it, tooth and claw and muzzle.

In the set of Edgar Rice Burroughs that Susan kept in her bookcase in the cottage at Seneca Lake, I first read the Tarzan stories: Before, I had only seen the American-sanitized movies. In one episode, Tarzan in the middle of the night hunts like a wild animal and sinks his teeth into the warm, raw, bloody flesh of a gazelle that, like a lion, he has run down in the moonlight.

Gary was a little like Burroughs's Tarzan. The hunting side of him was animal. He possessed an uncanny sense of smell: He could pick up game on the wind. He knew the animals' habits better than they knew themselves. He knew where they would come to eat and drink, and when. He knew all their tracks and scats and habits, how well they could see, and smell, and hear. He was, in other words, connected to them. And the connection was, on his side, quite passionate.

Gary had been born, oddly enough, in New York, on the Lower East Side. His parents were poor, apparently. The *New York Times*'s Fresh Air Fund sent him, when he was eleven or twelve, to spend a summer on a farm in the forests of central Pennsylvania. There he developed such a passion for the woods that before long, he was adopted by the farmer and moved into the country. That was when he learned to hunt and trap.

When he grew up, Gary went through a period when he raced cars and became, he told me once, a national champion in one category. He became a professional drag racer and had his own car, which he trailed around the country to competitions. He described (in loving, recondite detail) the necessity for the winner to have exquisitely perfect timing, to catch the starting lights to a nanosecond, the massive rear tires quivering and quivering against the brakes in ready animal energy tensing, the blast, the struggle to hold the car on the track as it shot out. You could be killed.

What made Gary a splendid man—what transformed a character that in some other man might have been a mere beer-guzzling, game-shooting loutishness; he had a sign on the back door that said IS THERE LIFE AFTER DEATH?/COME IN, AND FIND OUT.—was his energy and generosity, the direct and simple way he focused his love. He lived alone in the lake house with all his guns. He was divorced and had two daughters, whom he dearly loved and protected.

To Susan's family, he was a kind of guardian angel. He first made friends with Susan's brother David when they were fishing for bass near one another on Seneca Lake. David, then fourteen, had an authentic genius for fishing; he was a national junior champion bass fisherman and traveled the country winning bass tournaments. At first, David was outraged to discover that Gary had found all of the same spots that David knew—the same weed beds and holes—and was pulling in fish even faster. They began talking about fishing and became friends. Six years later, when David was killed in a car crash in Connecticut, Gary consoled the family and became, in time, its most reliable, enduring friend.

He was a presence: close, strong, competent in all

things. Earlier in the year of his death, after Seneca Lake
was lashed by days of winter storms and the family's long
dock (like many others around the lake) was destroyed,
Gary undertook to rebuild it. He pounded in the steel piling-
pipes by hand, with a sledge hammer, and had a friend float
over a pile-driver to pound in telephone poles to make a
double boat-hoist. (The project was half finished when he
died.)

The judge helped Gary with his legal business (including the game-warden trouble), and Gary helped with everything, and took the judge fishing on Sunday mornings, the
judge presiding in supervisory judicial capacity as Gary put
out the factory lines and then hauled them in with heavy silver trophies. And at the appointed hour (10 A.M.) they
would open a ceremonial beer, and drink, and savor the sight
of the fish, the blowing water, the sunny morning.

Gary earned his living as a telephone lineman, work
he did with an expert's avidity and, again, a love of the outdoors. He liked the challenge (and the overtime) when
storms tore up entire landscapes of telephone lines and he
had to go out in rough conditions and sort out the damage.
He was good at the work. He was a patriot of the phone
company, a knight of the labor.

The morning he died, Gary and his crew, three other
men, were dispatched to run new fiber optic cable along an
existing line that crossed the Erie Canal on the edge of a
town called Lyons.

The phone company's working manual ordains three
possible methods of stringing line or cable over water: (1)
use a rowboat to bring a towrope across, then attach the
rope to the cable and pull it across; (2) put a man in a small
cable cart, something like a bosun's chair, and have him
pull himself across the existing line: this requires an existing line strong enough to support his weight and not break

and a man strong enough to pull himself and the cart up
the slope of wire on the second half of the trip; (3) shoot an
arrow across the water with a light rope attached, then pull
the cable across with the rope.

Gary's crew had no rowboat with them. They had bow
and arrow, but the bow was broken. They had a cable cart,
but no one likes to use such things: They are time-
consuming and arduous to use.

It was a warm summer day. The water at that spot on
the canal was only 160 or 180 feet across from bank to
bank. As I looked at the water later, it seemed surprisingly
clean for a canal: tinted green, a sort of radiant emerald as
you followed the sunrays down. From the bank, I could
look into the water to a depth of five or six feet and see
mossy rocks and tendrils of weed, wavy but thick and ropy,
not gossamer like Ophelia's hair.

And so: Gary took off his work boots and socks and
stripped off his shirt and lineman's work belt and trousers.
He tied the towing rope lightly around his waist and, making jokes, jauntily stepped down to the water by the black
shale fill-rocks beside the canal and slipped into the water—
with a hoot of pleasure, I am sure, at its coolness on the hot
morning—and began to swim across.

He was swimming from the south side toward the
north. Two of his co-workers stayed on the south side, the
other was on the north. He got halfway across the canal by
Australian crawl and then switched to a breaststroke. The
men said he was joking as he went.

Two-thirds of the way across, something happened.
Gary called for help (the newspaper account said, "Hurry,
hurry!" which sounded unlikely to me). He seemed, some
said, to hunch his shoulders. He went under once, resur-
faced for a second, no more than that, and then he went
down below the surface again, and did not come up. He

disappeared. *Poof*. The water closed over him, greenish and still.

The rope that had been tied around his waist pulled loose. The linemen on either bank now frantically took off shoes and work belts and plunged into the canal. They dove and dove, repeatedly, but could not find him. Minutes passed. They found a telephone and called police and fire department.

The water at that spot is twelve feet deep. A lock-keeper nearby told me two days later that there should have been no current. But another man who knows the canal said he would not think of swimming there. He said that every year or two a kid drowns in the canal, because it looks innocent but has a vicious undertow produced when a lock opens and quantities of canal water get suddenly exchanged.

* * *

The rescue squad went in rowboats and grappled for nearly an hour before the hook caught Gary's undershorts and they could drag him to the surface.

I thought: If it had been dead winter, then maybe Gary, like a child fallen through the ice, would have been frozen into suspended animation and might have been revived. I have never understood that magic trick, though it happens once a year or so—the boy two hours under the ice brought back to life, Houdini-ed out of the cold blue coffin. In Russia during the Second World War, the combat surgeons would have severely wounded men tossed into snowbanks outside the field hospital, and there, frozen in some metastable state between life and death, they would await their turn on the table.

But of course it was summer, and Gary was gone in an instant.

It was an hour or so after they pulled up the body that the phone rang in Dutchess County and Susan came into our bedroom sobbing.

No one could understand how a man as strong and vital as Gary, a powerful swimmer, could drown in the Erie Canal on a morning's five-minute swim.

Some people thought he must have had a heart attack. The hunched shoulders would argue that. So would the lack of struggle. Gary was proof against any attack from the outside, we thought, but perhaps an unexpected attack from within could have taken him.

I subscribed to that theory at first, then I swung round to the canal's undertow.

The autopsy said he died by drowning. No evidence of heart attack. But suppose a heart attack had just begun— not enough to throw off the enzymes that proclaim the infarction, the dying heart muscle—and then he went under and drowned before a full heart attack could take place? We grew intricate in our speculations.

The guessing was pointless, of course. But it helped to deal with the shock of the death. The odds against Gary's dying this year, next year, anytime in the foreseeable future, seemed overwhelming. He was the strongest of us, the healthiest, the most accomplished survivor.

The funeral home in Seneca Falls was so new that it smelled still of fresh wood, fresh glues, fresh paints. Gary's might have been, for all we knew, the first body laid out there.

The casket was open. Gary lay there with a certain waxworks shine on his flesh and an expression of dull truculence about him. He wore his glasses (for our benefit, not his—nothing for him to see, after all). In death, people usually look smaller than in life. Gary looked somehow bigger, as if he had been shoehorned into the suit (he never wore one—except most recently to our wedding, almost five years before), as if he had been shoehorned into the casket itself, and it was a tight fit and he wanted to break out. His face had the unreality of a bad sidewalk caricature, the most important something being missing, the end result being a travesty of the person, a sight that makes you angry for a moment, and then (in the case of the corpse) obscurely relieved, comforted perhaps by the knowledge that the essential person has indeed gone elsewhere, so it is all right to dispose of this husk.

It was a Catholic service. There was a large crowd, many of them telephone men, and Susan and I and her parents and brother had to sit with the overflow of people on folding chairs in an adjoining room, so that we did not see the casket or the priest, who spoke with a thick accent that was difficult to place. Eastern European, evidently. Croatian, I think.

* * *

That night and the next, sleeping in the cottage at the lake, I had violent, murderous dreams.

The first night's dream took place in New York on the far West Side, among abandoned buildings with broken windows and floors covered with shattered glass. In one of these abandoned rooms, three men were attacking a fourth, savagely. One of the attackers had dwarfish legs. The three attacked the fourth for no discernible reason, but for the violent pleasure of it. They beat him until he was badly bloodied and then lifted his body savagely to a window and threw it down an air shaft many stories to the street. That done, two of the men, including the one with the dwarfish

legs, turned on the third and began to attack him just as violently. At last, the dwarfish one had the victim down on
his knees, and pounded his face and eyes with a kind of
wrench until the eyes were a bloody jelly, and then the two
threw the third down the air shaft. And the dwarfish man
turned on the last. . . .

At that, I woke up, my heart pounding.

On the second night, I woke again after a violent
dream, but could not remember it.

* * *

There were Perseid showers that week, and we stayed
up late at the lake to watch them. But the atmosphere was
hazy and we could not see through it. All that summer, the
air was like that—heavy, darkish sometimes, and promising
rain that rarely came. After midnight, the night of my second dream, the lightning and thunder finally arrived at the
cottage, and I watched the storm through the skylight just
over the bed.

Unable to go back to sleep, I looked for something to
read and found a text that Susan had used in college: *Nine
Short Modern Novels*. Her undergraduate signature, just the
last name, appeared inside the front paperback cover. I
started on *The Death of Ivan Ilych*—not escape reading. It
seemed to go with the summer.

I had last read *The Death of Ivan Ilych* when I was
twelve years old and plunged more or less indiscriminately
into the Russians, missing a lot but absorbing the atmosphere. I sat in the R Street branch of the Georgetown Public Library in Washington and conjured with Prince
Myshkin and Raskolnikov. I was bewildered by Ivan Ilych,
almost missing the revelation at the end, the light and
peace and transcendence.

I thought the Russian brew was too dark and rich and foreign, and I let it alone for some years after that, until I arrived in college.

Now I lay under the skylight, with the rain hammering heavily, pleasantly, on the clear plastic doming, and read Tolstoy by flashlight, not wanting to wake Susan. The steel flashlight was cold against my neck and shoulder, and then it gradually warmed. The beam made an astigmatic circle on the page, and I had to run my eyes along the lines of type as if I were hiking through rough country, with some clusters of words quite bright, like clearings, and other words murking off into shade.

I seemed to merge Ivan Ilych's terminal revelation with a thousand other moment-of-death descriptions, and with Sogyal Rinpoche's Buddhist sense of death and transition—the bardo of death.

I thought of my father's death that morning in Rockland County: Whatever happened to his soul at that moment was of course hidden, as always. He did not come back like a delok to report. I certainly had no sense of light, but only of a quiet extinction—the end of a long, long twilight and the almost imperceptible coming of night.

Gary's ending, on the other hand, came so suddenly and unexpectedly that I had wondered if he had, in the instant going under, experienced the flashing playback of his life. That of course is not the same as the Ivan Ilych moment of clarity—which amounts, I guess, to a kind of reunion with the larger truth.

I was still disturbed by the dreams, which had violently thrashed up the surface of my mind, as if a crocodile had come up for dinner.

I had not had such dreams for years, and never had a dream of violence contained this element of sadism—methodical, relentless, mutilating cruelty. No Tolstoyan mys-

ticism here in the jagged abandonments of the West Side.
But for an instant I thought the murder building in my
dream came from the jail in Sarajevo. Both buildings (real
and dreamed) had the same gray concrete, cold and broken
quality, the same visual cruelty.

* * *

I read for an hour. The sweet rain pounded on the
dome above me, and then gradually abated to a pitty-pat
and intermittent dripping. I turned off the flashlight. Susan
stirred.

I listened to the rain and then rolled and tried to
sleep. But the bone still hurt where the surgeons had cut
the sternum in order to get at the heart. When I lay on my
side, the rib cage on the down side pressed against the
upper cage, and my body's entire architecture of bones
would hurt, as if misaligned.

So I lay on my back again and appreciated the rain
until I drifted to sleep.

* * *

The priest in the fresh-minted funeral home in Seneca
Falls droned in a doleful Carpathian way for an hour: God's
ways are hidden from us, we could not know His intentions
in taking a man so young from us so unexpectedly, we must
have faith, drone, drone, all true but droning. The words
aroused at first an indignation at the banal formulas being
retailed here, over a waxworks corpse, and then came a resignation: *All right, all right, I suppose you are right, I'm sorry I
got angry, what do I expect you to say?*

The priest labored out some such thoughts about the
hiddenness of God's intentions. They struck me as touching

in their futility and in the dogged decorum of the form: dressing up and singing hymns as the ship fills with water and slides under the surface and vanishes.

* * *

They took Gary's body by truck back to the farm in Pennsylvania where he had been happy as a Fresh Air kid and first learned to hunt.

We stayed in Geneva for several days and then drove downstate again to the farm in Dutchess County.

We were haunted above all by the sheer suddenness of the death, and by the absurdity of it: Now you see him, now you don't.

Our farm nests in a valley that is bowl-shaped on three sides. The farmhouse sits half up one slope and looks across pastures and the pond (now drought-stricken and drying up) to the wooded ridges beyond. The fields are given over to hay now harvested. Once, they quarried marble from the hillside opposite, and from the house we see white rock outcroppings high up the ridge. At the foot of the ridge is a dynamite shack where they kept the explosives for quarrying.

When we returned from Geneva in late afternoon, we walked across the pasture and climbed up through the woods and sat almost to sunset on the high rocks. We looked out across the valley. Lush summer trees hid the road, and we could see only our farmhouse and barn. It might have been the nineteenth century. A hawk worked the currents above our valley.

We looked for the coyotes. Normally we could see them in the pasture opposite the house. Gary thought that the ones we saw were quite young, still under their parents' supervision, and that what we were watching was organized play. The pups would hunt field mice in the pasture while the parents watched from the concealment of the trees. The pups moved with the *boing-boing* gait of the light and wild. When one of them found a field mouse, he would make a hyperbolic leap, like an Olympic diver leaving the board, trying for altitude, and then come down on the vertical, paws first and nose, jaws immediately following. The method seemed to work. Through field glasses we could see a pup come up shaking something in triumph, something small and alive.

The farmhouse cat, Bruce, hunts lower to the ground, as cats do—with that quivering feline tension and alertness in the grass, the tail switching electrically behind, the eyes lasered in on prey. Bruce pounced on a chipmunk he had been stalking. Caught it, and brought it back in his teeth to the yard by the house to torment. Bruce released the chipmunk, which evidently had a broken leg, and watched it try to escape across an expanse of grass, the chipmunk leaping a little like the coyote pup, but in terrible pain, trying to make for the bushes. Bruce let the chipmunk get fifteen feet away, let him make a last desperate break for it, and then in a sure, efficient, terrible rush shot across the grass—blurred fur—and hit the chipmunk on the back of the neck, just behind the head, took him up again in his mouth and brought him back again with sinister satisfaction, like a Christian martyr fetched to the middle of his Roman lawn. Little playtime pageants of animal death.

That night, in memory of the chipmunk, we gave Bruce so many leftovers to eat—grilled swordfish—that he ate for a while in overwhelmed bliss, and then could eat no more and stood contemplating the remaining fish in a bloated stupor, in a glutton's dilemma. But he could eat no more, and we threw the rest away.

* * *

Up on the white cliff rocks just before dusk, we talked about Gary's death and how difficult it was to absorb it, to accept it, to understand it. Can death ever be understood? Certainly. I understood my father's death and accepted it perfectly. The death of an old man at the end of a long illness conforms to one's sense of fitness in the nature of things. Gary's death in the Erie Canal on a summer morning when he was apparently healthy and strong and prime offended the unconscious expectation of justice. The expectation of justice is unjustified, of course, by experience, but it lives on in the mind, like a residual tail.

Watching the hawk's dreamy drift over the valley, sitting on the marble outcroppings, I gave Susan a talk about death. I said that death probably did not mean much. That in any case, it was not the important thing, that life was the important thing, and death was something like a stupid mistake. (It was in Gary's case.) I said we should not expect to understand very much from death: that it did not have much to give us. But it must be accepted, patiently. That the meanings of lives and deaths can be absorbed only with time and patience, and at levels deeper than the conscious.

Was I not inspirational?

15

In Key West in the spring of 1948, my mother sat writing through the afternoon at a card table under two tattered palms in the backyard of the little conch house. The palm trees gave almost no shade.

My mother was still only in her midtwenties, and was not a cautious character. She veered from precocious brilliance to a heedlessness that was almost childish. On this afternoon she was being a fool (precocious and childish simultaneously) about gin and subtropical sunlight. She labored for hours at a portable typewriter. She kept beside her a bottle of gin from which she periodically poured a drink. The level in the bottle descended. So eventually did the sun. Amid the garish pinks and oranges of Key West sunset, my mother staggered into the house, stricken from her backyard labors, and passed out. The writing life.

My mother had chosen Key West to make her escape because Ernest Hemingway had lived there. Of course, Hemingway was at least marginally wiser in his working habits. He got up early and did his writing in the morning, before his drinking day began. I was impressed by the self-discipline and seriousness of his schedule. And he wrote standing up, at a sort of lectern, with the cats rubbing now and then against his legs in their languid electrostatic curl. At least, no matter how much he had drunk at Sloppy Joe's the night before, and no matter how much he would drink after, he worked every day in that window of sobriety in the morning.

Now, in 1948, Hemingway had long since departed to Cuba, where he lived with his fourth wife, Mary.

My mother loved Hemingway. She felt an identification with him. She loved the ostentatious masculinity—loved it not necessarily as a woman is attracted to a man, I think. Some part of her wished to be Hemingway, wished to be similarly, swaggeringly manly. This was a confusion of identity in some way, but not of sexuality. It was a sort of preference of attitude and style—and power. She wanted his freedom and invulnerability.

My mother was herself quite feminine and in many ways girlishly immature. She had leaping mimetic gifts of spirit, an artist's capacity to go into another's character and inhabit it, and at this time of her life, a powerful part of her wished to inhabit the Hemingway character. Quite a leap.

Maybe it was a matter of generation: Hers was filled with writers, male and female, who tried to ape Hemingway's prose style and living habits.

My mother had her own accomplished prose style, which was rich and supplely intelligent, and so I doubt she tried to imitate Hemingway's distinctive, increasingly irritating mannerisms. (Funny that the writer who began as the stylist of spare, hard, relentlessly simple truth ended by turning that style—that is, himself—into a swaggering fraud and a bully.)

I suspect that it was what my mother thought of as his freedom that she liked about Hemingway and wanted: his license to go where he pleased and drink what he pleased and live as he pleased, and be free.

Perhaps it was the size of his personality. She was a tiny woman, an inch over five feet tall. Yet possessed, when she wished, a character of considerable size.

How strange—or what a close appropriate fit between Hemingway and my mother—that Hemingway profoundly hated his mother all of his life, as my mother hated her father. And that (so I think, anyway—hardly an original insight) some part of Hemingway deeply hated women. Hated them, needed them. Maybe it was not so much that he hated them as that (neediness compounding rage) they made him very angry. A small perverse symmetry in all of that.

* * *

The slouching, unbidden thought of suicide, when it comes round, always stipulates the shotgun, the dark polished instrument in its white canvas sleeve, and, rummaging, proffers the shotgun shells that are concealed behind the bathing suits.

I have routed the thought, the temptation, and lately it has stayed far away.

One morning last week, a journalist I had known for years killed himself by diving out of the Upper East Side Manhattan high-rise apartment where he lived. My reaction on hearing of it was shock and anger at the man for having done that to his wife.

Then I felt ashamed. I learned the details of his months-long (even years-long) depression, and of other illnesses. He had been made almost immobile by the black, staring weight on his mind. My anger gave way to a confused sorrow. Inevitably, I tried to look into his mind that decisive instant, to imagine just how he might have—must have—felt, and what he might have thought, when he went to the window and decided.

Or was he overtaken by a fierce blindness washed of all thought, a sort of spasm of will brought from somewhere so deep as to be involuntary: death having the pull of a terrible black magnet?

When Hemingway killed himself that early July morning in Ketchum, Idaho, of course it was with a shotgun. I cannot imagine Ernest Hemingway killing himself in any other way. Not with pills (a woman's way). Not by going out the window (he rarely went into buildings tall enough for that, in any case). Not with carbon monoxide (too passive). Not by slashing his wrists (closer, but aggressive-passive, first you cut and then you wait). Which critic said, so nastily, that Hemingway's fatal shot was "the only one he ever fired that found its mark"?

Hemingway, of course, was sick in mind (*mens morbida in corpore sano,* another critic had said years earlier), and tried to walk into the propeller of a small plane a few days earlier at an airport on the way back from the Mayo Clinic. Or anyway, he was empty in mind, he could not write, the electroshock treatments annulled the crucial something in his spirit. Or the Mayo's shocks finished the work on his brain that alcohol had begun years before, a punishment given emphasis now and then by some tremendous blow to the head (a skylight falling on him in Madrid, Hem head-butting his way through the window of a crashed plane in Africa in the fifties).

What a callow youth I was that morning (the sort of twenty-year-old about whom the phrase *callow youth* was coined), coming out of the American Express office in Paris,

seeing the headline about Hemingway's death in the Paris
Herald Tribune, buying the paper, absorbing small waves of
shock and irony in the news, and then, with three equally
young and callow friends, driving south toward the Spanish
border, toward Pamplona, where San Fermin was in
progress, the bullfight fiesta of *The Sun Also Rises.* We three
undergraduates from Harvard, with one hitchhiking Co-
lumbia dropout, were having Hemingway dreams—light
from the dead star. We were in fact enacting them (an unconscious funeral homage) on the very day Hemingway
walked downstairs in Ketchum, while Miss Mary was still
asleep, and chambered the shells and swung the heavy gun
awkwardly around so that its muzzle would fit in his
mouth.

I have been more haunted by the story of Hemingway's father's suicide. I have an unclear idea of the man; his
wife, Ernest's mother, is more vivid and formidable. Dr.
Hemingway seems smaller, inward, self-baffled. He shot
himself with his father's Civil War pistol. Afterward,
Ernest's mother mailed a package to Ernest that contained
(1) a cake that she had baked for him; and (2) the pistol
that the doctor had used to kill himself.

Ernest took the pistol and dropped it into a very deep
lake in Wyoming: He watched it flashing down into the
darkness, out of sight.

Why did his mother send that package to her son?
Her doing it suggests mental illness of her own—or else a
malice toward her son so profound as to amount to illness.

Hard to fathom. The pistol is still there at the bottom
of the deep lake. Those are pearls that were his eyes.

Maybe Ernest Hemingway was overpowered by a
mother as my mother was overpowered by a father, and each
went into a kind of lifelong stylish rage about it. They had
in common that child's sense of absolute outrage and ab-

solute vulnerability. Children are absolutists, dogmatists, totalitarians.

* * *

What disturb me as I grow older are the seeming inevitabilities of lives—most of all, my own. The Buddhists' endlessly repetitious Sea of Samsara, I suppose: the dark tossing sea.

We struggle on, and at the end of a long passage, when we thought we had left behind the past, we find the past again: the same shapes forming before us as we fight toward them, shapes coalescing like a Polaroid picture to our eyes, gradually, magically, fatally. Until ourselves come clear, again—but to our disappointment.

We circle to it in the dark, to the past. The fossils that we find are our predecessor selves, and our present selves, eerily, exactly, repeated. We recognize them.

* * *

The Greyhound barreled south from Miami across the causeways in clear bright April sunlight, the magic-colored water just below us as we rode—blues, greens, turquoises, emeralds, aquamarines, the colors shimmering and quick-changing as light and shadow shot down through them. We looked for sharks; we had been told they were down there, the solid sliding shadows, flicking and sinuous.

I had never seen such colors. Or such trees—palms that I recognized from storybooks, shapes that therefore cause a primal stir of recognition.

Hughie and I rode in the Greyhound in a state of giddy surprise, struck dumb, daydreaming. My mother had taken us out of school in the middle of the spring term, before the Easter vacation, out of the patched ice and gray and cold of Washington, and propelled us south. We rode for a couple of days on the Southern Railroad from Washington to Miami, dozing and waking, eating astonishing southern fried chicken in the dining car (we had never tasted it before, or seen a dining car) or else buying sandwiches and orange drink in cardboard cones from black men who came aboard at southern towns and went hawking down the aisles with shiny brown polished cardboard vendors' boxes around their necks, crying out unintelligible offerings. The sandwich bread was thickly soft and white and held the indentations of the fingers that had made them. The orange drink was a liquid warm and wan. We watched the telephone wires falling and rising between the telephone poles, bouncing and bouncing and bouncing in endless hypnosis. Rolling beside us, the diorama of a country we had not seen before: the mule wagon at the crossroads, tobacco fields, black children staring at the train, and closer in, the black rain-ditches, flecked with a coal scum. The trackside backsides of towns, and then, again, the interminable stunted piney, piney South going by all afternoon until the light began dying off to the right of the southbound train and the lights of the car came on. We drank warm, metaltasting water from Dixie cups at the water dispenser at the end of the train car. Then walked back down the aisle to our seats on expert train-legs, our bodies having learned the motion, bracing laterally against the jolts and rocking in a kind of educated stagger. And sank back down onto the unplush plush of our seats, a sort of horsehair deluxe, which was grating to the cheek as we tried to sleep.

So we had come down in a dream, and now awakened to this most vivid dream of our lives: the unprecedented heat and light of the Florida Keys.

My mother was installed already in Key West. She had

rented the conch house, a modest, one-story, two-bedroom house with faded white paint and a front yard of verdantly tough grass that felt to the bare foot like sisel.

On either side of the property were lots of overgrown grasses that were, to me, chest-high. Exploring there on the first afternoon, running through jungle paths that someone else had made, I was about to put down my foot when I saw below me a coiled coral snake. I had a second's sight-flash of its bright rings and little head and black BB eyes, and with my back foot propelled myself in a jump beyond the snake and shot out of the jungle.

When Hughie and I returned there in the days afterward, we armed ourselves with sticks and probed through the grass, almost paralyzed by caution. It was a complicated thing to have a hiding place so perfect and find that it was infested with a danger worse than the one we were hiding from.

We discovered that even the sun was dangerous, the ultraviolet air. The first day, we went with my mother to the beach, and bathed and played in the sunshine, and waded in the beautiful water, looking for sharks, and watching the Portuguese men-of-war, those luminous blue floaters that looked like a clear bubblegum bubble crimped at one edge and trailed (we were told) long, long stingers that, if you touched them, would nearly kill you with pain.

Such dangers were attractive. But we did not know about the sun. And came home so sun-poisoned that my mother had to call a doctor. He was a youngish man. Hughie and I lay in agony in a darkened bedroom. The doctor shook his head in disgust (at my mother's stupidity, mostly) and prescribed nothing more serious than Unguentine and days of shaded rest.

We blistered. We peeled off our skin in long delicious

sheets. In four or five days, we began to get better. And we went out into the new world.

The spring in Key West was a shining gift to us, a gem of time shot through with colors and light, and freedom. We did not return to school when the Easter vacation ended. We stayed. My mother worked at her writing. We rarely saw her. We vanished from the house almost at first light, and did not return until after dark. We were as free as dogs on the loose, with entire days to roam in, and islands to be explored.

At a trailer camp a block from the conch house, we found a store that sold sodas and candy bars and rented bicycles for two dollars a week. We would leave the conch house, my mother still sleeping, and would pump off on the bikes, standing on the pedals and thrusting the frame from side to side by the handlebars to torque forward, down the hard gravel street and off for our explorations.

It took some days for us to see all of the island of Key West, and after that, we tried pedaling north across the causeway toward Indian Key, but we grew discouraged by the distances, which left us stranded on a causeway over mangroves as the sun went down. And so we specialized in Key West, and learned every inch of it.

In those days, Key West was a rough town with three or four principal ingredients, all of them distinctively masculine. One was the U.S. Naval Base (Harry Truman vacationed there), which spilled sailors into the downtown bars and streets on Friday and Saturday nights. The sailors would get drunk and fight sometimes. The first thing Hughie and I did on a Sunday morning bike run was to check the plateglass window in front of the big hotel on Duval Street. It was a favorite recreation for the sailors to throw something, or someone, through the window during a Saturday night fight. Hughie and I were disappointed if we did not see the glazier in the morning working to replace the window. The hotel must have been the glazier's chief source of income.

The sailors were transients. Key West was home to sponge and shrimp and conch fisherman who constituted the community and anchored the economy. But the layer of middle-class respectability in Key West was a little thin. The atmosphere of the town—which delighted Hughie and me—was one of laissez-faire and lawlessness at the margins. A long history of smuggling and shipwrecking and ship-looting had left over the keys a moral atmosphere that was 180 degrees and a thousand miles to the south of New England: a scruffiness and easiness and laziness and above all a sense of isolation from the rest of America, which was a heavy presence up to the north somewhere. The Keys half-belonged to a different principle, something lying to the south, brilliant and watery and hot, subject to weathers and dangers (hurricanes, piracies, sharks) that the North knew nothing of.

Key West was a man's town, which was no doubt the reason Hemingway had settled there, as Hemingway was the reason my mother had been drawn there. Its masculinity was raw and unsettled, as the sea is raw and unsettled and ungoverned and unpoliced and unconfined. Key West was out of the way, morally; it was out of the main American currents of power and constraint and culture. It allowed a freedom unavailable farther north. It had gotten Hughie and me out of school, had it not? Out of snow and cold and slogging bleakness. We had become invisible to authority, immune. We did not belong to the place; adults did not ask why we were not in school. My father had remained in Washington, but he was part of our conspiracy anyway: He'd helped set it up.

Hughie and I biked to the town docks in the morning to see the fishermen come in with monsters that they had taken out in the Gulf Stream: enormous stingrays, for example. One day—it was Easter Sunday morning—we saw one twice the size of the skiff that was towing it in, a Jules Verne creature, sleek as a nautilus or spaceship, and pale and tiny-eyed in death, ignominiously dragged along the side of an infinitely inferior craft, wooden and oar-driven and manned by hairy, ungainly, weaker creatures who possessed, nonetheless, enormous (for their bodies) heads and eyes. The men in the skiff were bare chested and bare footed, wore knives in their belts, and they struggled in to the dock against a wind, but with an air of triumph and conquering. The hair under their arms was so long that it blew in the breeze as they oared in, standing and kneeling in their skiff incautiously, like Washington's party crossing the Delaware.

It was a drinker's town. My mother had discovered the double whammy of gin and sun. The two went together in a natural if lethal way. She knew another writer who had come to Key West in Hemingway's footsteps to write great books. The man, a freelance journalist from Washington, installed himself and his wife in a tiny, one-room cabin under palms, and brought in cases of beer and sat down to work. He never wrote anything—a few pages, I heard, for the beer would slow him down as the morning progressed, and heat got worse, and beer got colder, until at last the composition of prose degenerated to a stare at the half-written page (now slightly off-focus), and the hands that had been typing (a little) now occupied themselves entirely with lighting cigarettes and smoking them and opening cans of cold beer and drinking them, until a case or so would be gone, and the American novelist, subtropical, would muzz his way to the unmade bed and a drinker's afternoon coma.

What his wife did I cannot say. I was obscurely shocked to hear about his drinking from my mother (sidelong tut-tutting and cluckings of regret) because I knew that the man was Jewish and the behavior seemed to me un-Jewish in a basic way. But he was a weak man, and I suppose he thought he must be thoroughgoing in his imitation of Hemingway if he wanted to partake of Hemingway's power. He seemed to think (as they did in that generation, and the one before and the one after) that alcohol was a sacrament with transformative powers. Magic: typing turned into literature. It didn't work.

Or the magic worked in the wrong direction; the only transformation was downward, a darkening of the brain, and finally the virtual disconnection—lurch and snore and awful smell. Night sweats. The stories to emerge from the process would be a few scraps of paranoid drinker's dreams.

My mother, curiously, never went around to see the couple, although they had been good friends in Washington. I wondered what had happened to their friendship. My mother did point out their house to me one day: It looked like a cabin in a low-rent roadside "motor court" of the day, one step up from a migrant worker's shack. In front of the cabin was a bare dirt yard, the dirt mingled with the fine-ground coral, hard on the feet, that is the foundation stone of the Keys—that is, in fact, almost all there is to the Keys except for a little soil and tenacious mangrove and stunty pine, the clinging, stringy-muscled survivor life-forms that can make it through a hurricane.

The writer and his wife had no such muscles. They were flaccid, aliens who had come down as if from another planet. As my mother and Hughie and I had done—escaping.

What was my mother escaping from? We did not know or care much. Adult business. It would have concerned us in Washington, and there we would have speculated about it, resented it—felt its encroachments, some sense of loss, the oxygen it would have deprived us of. In

Washington the adult business was always almost taking something away from us, leaving us. And leaving us angry.

But now, in Key West, we knew that whatever larger issues had propelled us here, we could not resent them, for they had given us something blazingly unexpected and bright: a rich concentrate of paradise-childhood. It seemed a wild compensation and overcompensation for former bleaknesses and chills.

That was the biggest change. In Key West, Hughie and I were not angry anymore. We were adventuring, autonomous, and happy.

The Keys had sunlight, mystery, enough danger to excite us, a foreignness. And we were outlaws, too, playing hooky and far, far beyond the reach of schools.

When I had been in school that winter, daydreaming through a class, my fantasy conjured a tiny fighter plane that I could fly in and out of the school windows—the wide, tall, many-paned institutional windows that had to be opened with a long varnished pole like a marlin spike whose hook far, far up in the air and, wavering, would fit into the latch-ring at the window top—the job performed by some assiduous brownnoser, never, certainly, by me. My fighter, like a fierce metal insect, powerful, would fly in and out of the windows, firing its little spitting wing guns relentlessly, I in the open cockpit, having my revenge of course, but not only that: being (necessarily) the center of attention.

I got the idea of the fighter (the noise of the engines, the pilot in goggles, the spitting wings) out of the endless World War II movies I watched. Curiously, I never saw myself simply getting into the plane and flying away, but was always, in these schoolroom dreams, entangled, flying in and out of the windows, boring in upon the others.

Now in the Keys I had truly fled.

A favorite sport was to buzz Sloppy Joe's bar on our

bikes in the morning when the drinkers were just getting going. One side of Sloppy Joe's was a series of wide, arched doorways open to the sidewalk, so that Hughie and I on bikes, going fast, could weave in and out of the bar (like me in my tiny fighter airplane going in and out of windows) and leave the drinkers (as we liked to imagine) virtually spinning on their stools, and before anyone could stop us, be gone down Duval Street. We could not try this every day, of course, because they would be waiting.

Hughie and I were Huck and Tom in the subtropics. Thank you, Mother.

* * *

She had left school, left her mother and the father who had evicted her, and married at the age of fifteen. By the time she was seventeen, she had two children: Hughie and then, eighteen months later, me. She was herself essentially a child, impersonating a grown woman; a beautiful and gifted young woman who seemed to fire headlong, full of ambition, into a world that belonged to other people who were utterly unlike her and yet whom she understood perfectly and in sly daughterly variations—that is, she launched herself into the world run by men like her father.

Except for Franklin Roosevelt. My mother worshiped Roosevelt, I think, precisely because he was a father with none of the characteristics of her father. Tom Vickers's Republicanism (strutting, bombastic, self-important) had taken the country off the cliff. It was a fraud and a ruination. FDR was the Good Father.

The Bad Father, Tom Vickers, was a brittle man in his early sixties, smoking with dudgeon. My mother was the elder of his two daughters, and in middle-aged disappointment that he did not have a son, he seems to have raised my mother as if she were a boy. He was a well-read man with an immense library that he opened to her at a precocious age. My mother was a brilliant pet, a theatrical little girl who could recite Shakespeare in quantity for the guests at dinner parties in Sewickley. He raised her in the late twenties in moneyed style. They traveled together. He showed her off.

And ultimately cast her out, along with her mother. The two women moved out of the mansion in Sewickley and into a boardinghouse in downtown Pittsburgh. The old man—the Wronged Man—dribbled money to them with which to pay for rent and food. My mother learned (a cynical necessity) how to charm money from him, how to play, for keeps, that infinitely subtle, infinitely complex game of being a child to alienated parents, mediating, playing one off against the other.

* * *

My mother and father lived in Bucks County for a time while my father worked as a reporter for the *Philadelphia Inquirer,* and then when I was three, in the middle of World War II, they moved to Washington, to Benning Road, that last housing project on cleared, bald lots before the woodsy netherlands of Maryland set in. From there, barely twenty years old, my mother began her (fairly impressive) assault on Washington.

Whatever the deficits of her formal education, my mother at twenty had read more books, more literature, than most men ingest in a lifetime. She had started on Shakespeare and then on the nineteenth century at home in Sewickley (Scott, Dickens, Browning, Austen, Thackeray, and so on) and as a teenaged married woman plunged into the twentieth century and the books being written by her older brothers and sisters: Fitzgerald, Hemingway, Edmund

Wilson, Malcolm Cowley, Faulkner, Lewis, Dorothy Parker, and the lesser breeds, including all the then hopeful and fashionable Marxist types of the thirties, who ultimately seduced her, for a time, into joining the American Communist Party. When she left the party after the Moscow trials, the party branded this small, passionate adolescent as follows: "Enemy of the People?" The question mark was placed there either in deference to her age or to the fact that it was still America and fates were still provisional and dogma needed the hint of diffidence.

Now she plunged into wartime Washington.

16

It has grown cold. The air feels as if it will break and shatter into small sharp pieces. The temperature has fallen to fifteen degrees below zero.

There is a faint sliver moon with a blurring of snow nimbus. The animals are burrowed deep. The night air is just the medium, thin and ruthless, to transmit inaudible high-frequency shiverings and keenings. They transmit along tight shining wires: numb helplessness and waiting, a vibration, a void, the nearest thing the world has, this time of dead winter (sunless, sapless, the world made of gray deadwood and iron) to death itself.

Halfway up the quarter-mile steep drive to Keith's house, the car's wheels begin to spin. The track is plowed and sanded, but the front-wheel drive has found the ice beneath, and cannot grip.

Bundled in fur hats, I in parka, Susan in her coat of coyote fur that Gary made from animals he trapped (a coat she does not wear in the city lest animal rights people spit at her in the street), we leave the car and begin to trudge the rest of the way up to the house, which we see in the distance above us, through the leafless trees. The house is a sleekly modern Bauhaus design, set down on a Connecticut ridge, and in the cold darkness it shines like a crystal, gives off a radiant warmth and light. I see Keith's figure passing a window—warm inside, and oblivious to us in the dark cold below.

The sound of our boots on brittle snow as we ascend.

We struggle up and I find the icy air I gulp and gulp is not enough. I stop and wait an instant, inhaling air like dry ice in my lungs, but cannot get enough still, think to myself all will be well if I can make it to the crystal house above us, but as I try to do that, to climb more, my heart struggles more and more, the lungs pump, I feel an adrenal panic rising. Susan's voice grows more urgent ("What's the matter? Oh, Lanny, what's the matter?") and I angrily wave her off.

Why angry? I feel death all around. This is the season.

I cannot breathe. Death presses like a vise, squeezing the margins until they threaten to meet in the center, and if they do, the meaning, the text, life, vanishes in the dark blank.

To stop and rest is impossible, but to go on up the hill may be putting more on the heart than it will tolerate.

The home like a crystal on a dark night is familiar to me from long ago. I am outside. I approach the house. Never come to it, quite.

Sometimes the house is dark, and I come just at dusk and find myself barred: doors locked, windows dark, the night closing in and getting colder.

But here in Connecticut coming up the ridge, the cold is already down in the death zones. I tell myself all will be well if I can make it to the hospitable crystal and touch it until it opens and admits me. But I also think, again, that I am going to die here.

I am a fish gasping on a beach of absolute cold, and I shall perish out of my medium.

Maybe life isn't serious. It probably isn't. Therefore . . . what?

Fatalism as relaxation. Humor. Acceptance.

Theoretically. But death is a little too close now. I am not Buddhist enough to take it calmly.

The look on my father's face the night before the by-pass operation that began his long miserable slide into death. His eyes looked the way that I feel now: fear, questioning, all anxious interrogation of the moment. All front gone.

But struggle up, struggle up all the while, the crystal getting closer in the negative night, the cold like an X ray.

Lungs labor, heart labors, I go up the snow stiff legged like Frankenstein's boxy monster—a brittle slogging, Susan in the coyote coat tugging grimly. We swim toward the light against this undertow of sharpblackdeathdeathdeath.

And then: burst into the crystal, into the light, into perfect normality and time again—our friend Keith at the door, rush-rush in out of the cold *Whew!* Door-slam against it and death as well—welcoming.

"Greetings!" says Keith, heartily beaming, his famous eyebrows making their bristling salutes.

The fire is going in the Bauhaus, the logs perfectly clean cut, with flame flowing over them so smoothly and steadily that I think for an instant it is a gas fire, the wood seems so bone-clean and the flame so . . . unconsuming, as if it were an interior decorator's trick to simulate fire but leave no ash and make no smoke.

Drinks. Sit. My lungs are still, a little, secret-heaving,

but I can talk as if normal. The moment of death-cold passes, but returns from time to time during the rest of the evening, and never more so than later, after eleven, when it is time to go. But at least the car lies downhill now. I could almost slide down to it on the ice.

But as we sit now in front of the Bauhaus fire, we talk about the book that Keith is researching, about writers and editors we know.

And, cozy in the crystal that keeps us from the dark and wind that razors down from the top of the world, we talk about the Cold.

It is the coldest cold in a hundred years; it is a metaphysical freeze.

The cold leads me and Susan to the love-and-jealousy-and-survival drama of our house and barn cats, which we serve up to Keith as if it were Shakespeare.

That night before we left the farm, I heard the cats in the barn (Leon and Sylvia, probably, unless another wanderer got in) engaged in a life-or-death fight. Yowls and screeches, claws and chain saws and concealed knives.

I listened to the opera with interest because the stranger cat we now call Leon knows how to break into our house. He has done it, when we were away in New York for a few days. He shed his fur all over couches and chairs, he left his indelible territory-marking male scent-spray in every room, and on the corner of our bed, just where I lay my head when I roll on my side to sleep. I think he understood that last detail perfectly: He smelled it out. He wanted to put his stinking aggression right up my nose.

Leon is an enormous and elegantly beautiful gray cat with an outlaw personality and a remarkable guerrilla intelligence. I think of him as a sort of dangerous pimp. He broke into the house through the little swinging cat door in the basement, the one Bruce uses.

Now, Bruce is Leon's antithesis in every aspect except size. Bruce is a big gray-and-white with a sweet nature and character of almost mystical mildness, the absentminded professor in a thirties comedy. For months we watched as Bruce cringed and fled whenever Sylvia, tiny and wild and jittery-neurotic about territory, decided Bruce had infringed. I watched her once chase Bruce halfway up the birch tree by the pond. Bruce then tried a heavy backflip to earth again, but Sylvia caught him in midair and sank a claw deeply into his nose, where even in free fall she held it until they crashed to earth and Bruce disentangled himself from the fur-and-fury bundle as a cannonball disentangles itself from the cannon.

But Bruce of late (. . . *the wedding guest here beat his breast, for he heard the loud bassoon;* Keith glazed) had grown macho and fearsome. He had fallen in love—with Sylvia's budding daughter Frankie. (We at first thought Frankie was a male and named her Franklin Delano Pussycat, in honor of Hyde Park, over on the other side of Dutchess County; when we found she was a female, we changed it to Frankie.) Frankie is mostly white, with gray-striped tail and, on either side, at the rib-cage level, two neat markings like quotation marks.

She is a lovely, skittish little cat. How amazing that her just-budding prize of sex should stir such howling violence. Bruce and Leon fight murderously for her. When we returned from New York we found, just inside the cat door in the basement, an apocalyptic scene of matted fur and blood stains on the floor. And all through the house, from room to room, we discovered that Leon had left his scent.

We assumed that Leon had departed after this apocalypse. We congratulated Bruce on defending the house. We piled firewood against the cat door.

But Bruce and Frankie inside the basement never slept, and their eyes looked terrified, besieged.

(Electricity fired out of Keith's eyebrows and he put a log on the Bauhaus fire and yellow flame licked it in a smooth and aerodynamic flow.)

Then betimes, we began to suspect that Leon was still within the house somewhere, the saturnine dybbuk of the place, hiding the way a killer or a sickness hides in the dark. We listened in the middle of the night. We heard those deep lion growls that male cats make when competing for mates, the yowl that begins a long way off and builds, that begins I guess in the gonads in Egypt thirty thousand years ago and makes its way up to the throat.

When we came to the basement we found Leon after a long search with a flashlight—hiding in a dusty corner behind stacked storm doors. I could not reach him. He was unbudgeable by conventional means. Viet Cong. He stared back at my flashlight with a focused self-possession. We stared at one another for long moments. Leon was huge, a beautiful gangster of a cat with a saturnine what-are-you-going-to-do-about-it face.

Then, ridiculously, I began getting angry. There was no way to reach Leon. I sprayed him with one of Justin's water guns, which troubled him not at all. I sprayed him as in an impotence dream when you hold a gun of some kind and find when you pull the trigger nothing comes out. You have failed to deliver.

Finally in a donnybrook of noise and overturned packing boxes and cat-yowling—my heart beating faster and faster, a middle-aged man with two infarct chevrons on his sleeve storming around a basement in pursuit of a barn cat—I maneuvered Leon fast-forward to the open basement door, sluiced him in a blur of fur, and out he shot into the icy night.

It took me fifteen minutes to calm down.

I blocked the cat door with firewood. The other cats cowered in the pipes behind the furnace for the rest of the night.

(The wedding guest here rose and went to see to the chicken.)

I did not tell Keith that I had decided to shoot Leon, to kill him with a .22 rifle.

The following night (after I had gotten Leon out of the basement), when the temperature was ten below zero, I shined a light toward the barn, down in the distance, and saw that my flashlight was answered by two unblinking luminescent eyes—Leon's.

The barn is large and full of hiding places. I could never find Leon if I chased him inside. However: Standing by the house with a rifle and a flashlight, I could flash him like a deer. I would aim between his shining eyes.

Now when I reflected for a moment, it seemed to me not only shaming but absurd that I would wish to shoot a cat. What kind of perverse gun-monster would do that?

Still, he was an intruder, I thought by way of rationale; he was tearing up the house, disturbing the other animals. Further, he was untrappable. I could not transplant him to some other part of the country, not without a major safari to get him. Better with one well-aimed night shot. I might even do it when Susan (who was appalled when I suggested it) was away for the evening. Then Leon would simply disappear, and in a week or two, Susan could remark, "I wonder what became of Leon. . . . I don't see him around anymore." And I (cat-killer, villain) would look up from my book and say, "Yes, strange. I haven't seen him either."

* * *

What a peculiar year. In the summer after my heart attack, a vast blanket of heat lay upon the country, day after day, the temperature above 100 degrees for weeks at a time, and then such torrential rains that the Mississippi River flooded for more than half of its length, the worst flood in a century.

Now we were in the photographic negative of the year: What had been record heat now became this terrible metaphysical cold, the worst in years. Now we went days and days below zero, the air like shining razor fragments.

I dreamed that I attended my own funeral. It was held in Geneva, New York, with the entire staff of *Time* magazine in attendance. The CEO of the company, a dream version that I conjured from a diplomat I used to know—a fidgety scarecrow with white hair and nervous eyes—delivered a weepy but defensive eulogy whose main point was that the company would forge on, despite this terrible loss, which some quitters and weaklings in the corporation said was insurmountable.

* * *

Why do I want to kill the dark gray cat?

Why: He challenged me—another tom—to do it. He marked my territory (my bed!) and dared me.

He is gleaming, cocksure, and saturnine. Mack the Knife. A fine animal: Though living wild, he provides sleekly for himself—his body full and strong, his longish coat shining almost as if it had been expensively shampooed. He never came to the house to ingratiate himself as the other barn cats did, finding eventually that it was a feeding station. Leon moved fast and stayed at a considerable distance. I can tell from the way he moves when exposed in the open (and therefore possibly under some human or animal predator gaze) that he has a cunning survivor's self-awareness. When we were struggling with one another in the dusty basement, I the human giant blundering and thundering through the packing boxes, sawing the air with my Maglite beam as if it were a sword of Jedi, Leon was blurringly fast and yet entirely self-possessed. He never panicked. Even when I managed to plant a foot on him and hold it there, calling for Susan to bring a box, he stayed still and stared at me and waited. His eyes were (I thought) quite comprehending, and a little sad. But when I lifted my foot pressure minutely for a moment to turn and grasp the box, he felt his chance perfectly and exploded away on a perfect escape vector. The tomcat as wily Odysseus.

What an outrage. I felt like three layers of fool: (1) a grown man who would get so absorbed in feuding with a cat; (2) a grown man who would be outwitted thus; (3) a man who would consider taking a rifle to an innocent creature that was trying to survive in the wild in bitter cold, a cat I had absurdly anthropomorphized as a strutty street pimp, as Mack the Knife, or worse, had demonized: the Dark Cat.

He is out of sight now. I hear him sometimes at night. He is evidently not always so self-possessed (or merely terrified into immobility), for I hear fierce, violent howling.

This is, do not forget, coyote turf. Coyotes love to eat cats, when they can catch them. I have never seen the coyotes venture inside the barn. The closest they have come (when I have seen them) has been when they have gathered under the full moon just below our windows and made music, their dancing fountains of coyote-howls, pumping leaps of sound rising, subsiding, intermingling.

But maybe they also come around on the dark nights, and do not make a sound.

If that is the case, then Leon comes by his cunning honestly.

And I am just another coyote in the middle of the night.

On the other hand, I have a rifle. A shotgun as well, although I was put off the thought of the shotgun by a mental image of what Leon would look like if hit by a blast from the twenty-gauge: little left but dark gray fur and a livid mess of the internals. A .22, on the other hand, would make a minimal hole. Why, Leon could be stuffed and mounted. I could have the entire Leon, majestic in the front hall, like the lion in the lobby of the Muthaiga Club in Nairobi.

Get a life.

On the other hand, being a coyote myself with a tendency to have heart attacks, I remained lingeringly curious about why Leon had aroused such an intense reaction in me.

Leon was a sort of high-speed raccoon nuisance, but I had credited him with a certain demonic intelligence. He tripped intruder alarms, my adrenal reflexes. My body read him as a danger even if my mind accepted him as a night-prowling pussycat. Adrenaline fired, I lost my temper well before the mind could saunter into the picture and speak reasonably. And the anger lingers now, a rage reaction that has left a hardening residue in my heart.

I feel as if the metaphor (hardening residue in the heart) has gone into my body and become actual. An idiot business like a rage at a cat is exactly some insidious inconsequence that comes into the house, the heart, and burns it down.

These things have no intelligent sense of proportion.

I am approaching a serious point. These stranger emotions (anger, mostly) destroy the heart and overwhelm the conscious, seeing self. A residual animal impulse fires up from its dark pen, somewhere in the limbic system, which has no sense of fitness or priorities, and for a time, all is chaos in the better (higher) neighborhood. Eventually, the rage subsides but it leaves its mark, its stain. It marks the heart—whether the rage is suppressed or expressed.

Clearly, I need a higher practice.

Susan has been studying Buddhism. We have discussed it now and then. I have never approached Buddhism formally. I am marginally distressed by its trendiness; Buddhism has become popular among actors and reformed drug-addict rock musicians.

Still: morning.

It snows in a fine steady snow-drizzle. The two- and three-foot fall of a week ago had deep track patterns: The new fall has covered them now. I look out the window to the barn and see the cats have not been out yet. The page from here to there is clean and smooth.

What an internal constriction anger is, a closing of the heart.

I think I understand young Leon perfectly well (again, *semblable, frère*). Dutchess County—snowfall, farm fields—does not necessarily make me peaceful. I have sometimes ridden the New York City subway system for hours and used it as an office to write in, being absolutely serene and collected while rattling underground from Manhattan out to the farther boroughs and back again, eyeing from time to time the newcomers on the car who might be dangerous.

In crisis I am calm, as when I had my heart attacks, but tend to go paradoxically nuts when the surroundings are most serene and the issues trivial.

Perhaps my basement battle with Leon made the cat calm and self-possessed, as riding the infernal subway calms me somehow. I think of Malcolm Muggeridge's story of meeting Graham Greene on a London street in the middle of a bombing raid during the Blitz. Muggeridge saw on

Greene's face a look of beautitude, and judged that Greene
was at last where he had always hoped to be: in hell.

I think sometimes that like Greene, I suffer from a
tropism toward misery. Or, to dig a little deeper, perhaps
what seems the leaning toward pain and self-affliction is in
reality a frustrated appetite for danger, an occluded, overdo-
mesticated masculinity.

The male's anger, in domestic and civilized circumstances, is the heat of a powerful engine idling, stuck in
traffic. The anger is the engine boiling. Male energy must
not be allowed to turn inward against itself—and yet when
it turns outward, it so often expresses itself as violence. But,
kept inward, the violence explodes like dynamite going off
under steel-mesh blankets at a construction site: a muffled
whump! The blocked heart cracks.

* * *

What an admirable cat is Leon: top cat of the barn,
Ché Guevara among the coyotes. I am the evil empire in
the smug white house, aiming a rifle through a window at
night, the crosshairs fixed on the spot between the shining
eyes.

The aftermath of anger is shame, remorse. The red gas
dissipates, like an idea fading, like a fantasy to kill someone. It does not stain the snow.

I imagined shooting the dark gray cat, but have no
further thought of it now.

The dark thought left my mind and slipped through
the windows and now has a wild animal life of its own outside among the other thought-creatures with fur and teeth
and claws—creation over which top-creature Leon reigns
and over which he tyrannizes and howls at night. I shake

out the unspent cartridge and stack the rifle in the corner of the bedroom, and sigh at myself for an idiot.

Then shine the Maglite at the barn again. Leon's eyes are still shining there in the black cold.

* * *

Molecules come to a dead stop. Color has vanished. The sky has turned to iron; day is heavy.

The world is abstracted out of itself.

But the cold at night, when the sky clears, is not now heavy so much as transparently, lucidly empty. The night becomes the thinnest, thinnest ringing in my ears, the high vibration of an invisible wire pulled tight through the universe and touched once.

My heart, strong, dogged—strong as a healthy dog— does not hear it, but pounds on.

* * *

After my second heart attack, I decided to set myself some great physical challenge, some large, difficult physical task. I read Geoffrey Wolff's account of his middle-aged assault on the Matterhorn. I wanted to do something like that—sail around the world, go down the Mississippi or the Congo River, motorcycle across the Steppes. I wanted some large project—something daunting and real, not mere thinking and imagining and twiddling fingers over keyboards.

But weeks passed and then months, and I have not yet found the adventure. Money must be made.

Perhaps this bitter winter in upstate New York is my project, or my preparation for it.

The windows now are frosted to opacity—a pleasant,

minutely crystaled and luminous effect. The wind has come up, blowing in from the northwest and whirlpooling around the bowl-shaped farm. The wind makes the house sing an eerie music, chill and soprano and wraithlike. It is an old house, the original portion built before 1800, and it has cracks and chinks, through which this polar breath plays: The house is a woodwind.

The house leaks heat in a profligate way. It has warm flows and chill spots, like a spring-fed pond. The cordwood lies buried in snow. I root in the frozen mound to find logs and haul them inside to toss upon the fire to steam and crack until they dry enough to catch.

Every trip to town must be planned carefully. The roads are now the driest powdering of snow upon a hard-enameled ice. Blown snow rises in turbulence into crystal air. We have cut a path from the house to the road. I let the four-wheel-drive Jeep run half an hour before I set off.

The world has grown sharp. From the eaves, stalactites hang, long, long and thinnish ice-teeth like those in the mouth of some extinct flesh-ripper eons ago. Trees rise out of snow and rocks like dark gray metal bristles, jabbing. Air cuts. Ice cuts.

Ten below. The Jeep won't start. It grinds weakly but will not turn again.

The firewood is fixed in ice outside the kitchen.

The dead of the year. My brain has gone into some suspension. I have sunk deeper than lethargy, down into a sort of spiritual death, an extinction of intellectual fire and passion. When I see the deer on the road at night, they stop in the middle of the glazed blacktop: Their motionless blank-shine eyes give back my headlights. I pull the car to rest, the only motion is the high-frequency shiver of their weak-looking spindly shanks, like high-urgency muscle spasms. And then (to use a term I heard a baseball sportscaster employ) they nonchalant away—a slow hump up the plow-thrown snowbank and into the leafless metal woods.

Shortness of breath, shortness of days, shortness of life. January.

* * *

I flee down from Dutchess County between winter storms to New York City. There was an earthquake the other day in Los Angeles—6.5 on the scale. Today on CNN I watched the Ohio River in a thaw-flood, washing houses away, crushing off rocks in a thick flow of grinding brown ice-chunky river water.

New York City is winter-dirty. In the subways, the homeless sleep in the cars in their upright fetal posture, as if they had gone to sleep with a terrible stomachache. They smell of flesh unwashed and some accidental fecal moment, so that the others in the cars (the settled folk, the jobbed, the homed) crowd to one end and leave the woebegone fetus-sleepers to the best seats, like babies abandoned long ago and grown up filthy-wild, and still in need of changing.

I have disturbing premonitions. I think my body has instincts within it like those animals that can feel earthquake coming: I sense something of the toxic slither inside now, and must think it away and think it away each time, and each time it returns. I feel that when it comes again, for the third time in my life, that will be all: term of office expired.

Death premonitions have to be managed, organized, subdued, harnessed. Am I merely so attuned to the year's dead nadir that I feel my own death in the surrounding suspended life? Maybe. Perhaps I am thus trying to poeticize my way out of danger, turn chest trouble into metaphor. Metaphor after all is harmless. A cunning defense. Will it work? Death does not know how to read; death is a crude, illiterate realist.

When it comes, it comes like the Ohio River through the heart, grinding away the home with ice chunks.

* * *

I think about Richard Nixon. He moves like a dark gray animal through the edges of memory. My mother hated Richard Nixon, whom she knew when both of them were young in Washington in the days after the Second World War. They sat together at a dinner party or two. She told him at the famous dinner at the Shoreham that he should get out of politics because he did not understand human beings. That, I suppose, was putting it mildly, but also putting it wrong, because he did understand people, very shrewdly understood them, and used the understanding. But he did have circuits missing.

I think of him ruefully because I, a generation younger than he, am sitting here listening to my heart, and Nixon sails on, in persistence, in triumph even—book after book, elder statesman. He beat the bastards. (It would be later than this, after the bitter winter, that he would die and be buried in his defiant, smudged greatness.)

I call Carl Bernstein, old president-breaker and companion of my youth, and ask his advice on this point and that one, the two of us being each other's confessor and corner man from time to time. Carl soldiers on too.

* * *

The heart is so seldom clear. For a time after I almost died, I kept a kind of wonder and indignation. I felt as if I had been newly washed.

But that metaphysical freshness has faded. Illness and the presence of death take the mind into the dimension of the sacred for a time. Then gravity returns the soul to the daily, to the ordinary and unaware.

The dog, Fred, still a puppy, stares out at bluejays feeding on the bright snow, and emits an inner howl of interest and frustration, nose against the glass. The sun through the window strikes Fred's honey-red coat.

Nearby Death does take the mind into the sacred—or anyway into a different kind of sight.

Perhaps what we need to see through the window is death, for seeing that, we are able to see, beside it and around it, everything else. If death comes close, the ordinary cracks and falls away.

Death enforces the miracle of life.

But the transaction has so much weather, such storms, such effects of darkness and light, of anger and clarity.

Now the ice begins to melt, and drips from the eaves and down the long sharp icicles, that through the windows are white translucent witches' fingers, or witches' teeth dripping a pure distillate of cold.

17

Carl the President Killer had his fiftieth birthday party the other night—on Valentine's Day—in his loft on Hudson Street down in the district of New York's meat market. The streets were deserted. A north wind sluiced through them. The snow from the big storm was heaped on either side of the streets, six feet high in places. Cars vanished into their parking places, ensnowed in soft white burial mounds. The black street that had been scraped clear became enameled ice.

Carl's loft was large and warm, lit with votive candles everywhere and extravagantly decorated with flowers. Carl assembled close friends, including some of the rich and famous, to celebrate the birthday.

I stood for a long time talking belly to belly with Norman Mailer. Now seventy-one years old, still davanning minutely from the waist in that tuning-fork quivering-rocking motion that used to suggest barely restrained aggression, Mailer's competitiveness had mellowed, I thought, to a kind of resigned philosophical kvetchiness. His body, with its stiff, thick energy in the trunk with the necklessness and the big head, had come more and more to resemble that of that Tasmanian Devil. But his manners seemed to have gone in the other direction. He had become a pleasant man.

Mailer did not know me. He did not seem to recognize my name as that of a *Time* reviewer some years before who had given a nasty review to *The Executioner's Song.* Nor did he remember that I was the character who had written an essay for *Time* climbing all over him for his performance in the case of Jack Abbott (a prison writer whom Mailer befriended and helped win parole for, who on his release from jail almost immediately murdered a waiter who would not let him use the restaurant men's room late one night).

I did not bring up any of this. Out of thin air as we talked at Carl's party, Mailer said, "Well, it is my theory that the world is made up ninety-nine percent by people who are either killers or suicides. . . ."

I thought it was an arresting—possibly unoriginal— idea.

Which was Mailer? Killer, surely. He certainly thought of himself as a killer. He had fantasies of killing (in *The American Dream* and other books), he sponsored the killer Jack Abbott for parole. Why do famous writers like to have killers for mascots? I had wondered about that—about Bill Buckley's period sponsoring Edgar Smith, or William Styron's convict in Connecticut, who escaped from prison just days before he was due to be released and went across the state line into Massachusetts to rape and terrorize a housewife there in front of her children.

I have sometimes thought that authors' affection for killers represented their nostalgia for real life. Or maybe the mascot killer is a kind of raffish and seignorial good luck charm, a brute Sancho Panza on a leash. Perhaps it is an assertion of the writer's masculinity, and the compartment of danger that he carries, for all the blank bullets of sublimation that he fires harmlessly onto paper: the woman-work of wordiness. A samurai self-conception, really, though the Japanese ideal of poet-warrior (chrysanthemum and sword, the knight and artist interchangeable) was more elegant than the somewhat Freudian Mailer-Abbott model, which bespoke, to me, a roiled and ambiguous—and therefore violently assertive—masculinity. The samurai had integrated the artist and warrior in such a way that one function became an expression of the other, a part of the other, an alternate mood almost. And this was ceremonially done: It had the finish of ritual, the rich lamination.

But the Famous American Writer leading his killer dog seemed a stunt, like a movie star walking into the Ritz with a leopard on a leash: a self-aggrandizement and romantic self-conception. If writers were honest with themselves, their convict-mascots would be bad check artists.

Later in the evening, it came time for Carl's friends to give toasts and speeches. I looked around the room, at Carl, who inspires such love in his friends, a man complicated in his vulnerabilities. Bob Woodward gave a graceful talk, and Richard Cohen was very funny, and Abe Rosenthal gave a witty mock-exasperated account (maybe not so mock) of his days as managing editor of the *New York Times,* being outgunned by Woodward and Bernstein on the Watergate story. Shirley MacLaine gave a speech that began: "Who would have thought a tough journalist would lead with his heart?"

Which Carl did, boyish and headlong, with a lovable genius for folly. His son Jacob said, "Dad taught me it was all right to fuck up," and we all chuckled in a complex, affectionate way, knowing the statement had many layers.

Carl, in any case, was not a killer, surely. He was too sweet natured. If he had demons, they were not the homicidal kind. But he was not a suicide either, not by any means. He was, for one thing, far too lovable to women to want to kill himself.

* * *

Which was I?

Norman Mailer, wrapped in a double-breasted blazer that fit him as tightly as a straitjacket, rocked back and forth in front of me, beside Carl's kitchen table, framed by votive candles. He was talking about Lee Harvey Oswald now, about having spent six months in Minsk trying to track Oswald there. Was Oswald a killer in Mailer's sense, as opposed to a suicide? Or just a weird globe-trotting American patsy who packed a lot into a short life?

I did not ask Mailer these things. His book, when it came, would disclose what he had found. I was bored by Oswald anyway, or by the assassination, that Rubik's Cube of American paranoia. It was an old puzzle anyway. I seemed to detect that Mailer was tired of the subject as well, though he was obliged, at age seventy-one now, to heat himself up to the subject again every day. I admired Mailer's bounce and energy, after so many years of slamming around and contending. He worked hard, and knew how to take care of himself. No suicide there, not a whisper of it.

But I struck myself as a mixed case. If imagining myself as a variation on some great-author model, I would rue-fully cite Hemingway, would point to some trace of his lifelong buried anger if not his more attractive exuberances. All of his adult life (the chosen part) was devoted to proving himself a killer, and ended with the irrefutable evidence that he was also, ultimately, a suicide.

I seemed to be operating in the opposite direction. I had two heart attacks to prove I am a sort of suicide. The anger installed long ago in my heart, as if in a lead-lined chamber, would explode from time to time and, being so brutally contained, injure no one but myself.

But after so much self-damaging, I thought that I detected myself now changing. Every boy needs to be tested by his wars. Perhaps mine were cardiac, and having survived them, the rites of passage, I had proved something, if only to myself—especially to myself; there was no need to prove anything to anyone else. I had gone into the field and met my worst enemy—that is, myself, or the death in myself—and had survived it.

That did not make me a killer, though. That seemed less a way out of the internal suicide-killer conflict than becoming a mystic—opting toward a third way.

I thought sometimes that Carl worked fitfully in that direction, and that the results were sometimes admirable. And yet in his earlier years as a journalist, Carl indeed possessed a killer instinct; in his case the killing would be regicide by journalism. Death by digging. Death by ink.

In some shadowy way, I thought it was an Oedipal gesture, but one deflected from the son's usual victim (the father) and even turned upside down: Carl *(causa pietatis)* slaying his father's tormentor, Richard Nixon, who was standing in, however, (in Carl's mind) for Carl's father, who was the real object of Carl's hostile passion.

It was Nixon's suicide in some sense, as well, that long, slow death in 1974.

Why did Nixon, that famous political hitman, remorseless Dick, dark knight of American realism, collaborate (as if drugged, as if dreaming) in his own ruination? How did it happen that the Crisismeister went so passive? Did not burn the tapes? Lay on the front porch of the White House with his jugular exposed?

It had been so many years (more than forty) since I was

a Senate page boy and sat on the steps of the rostrum of the U.S. Senate chamber in the summer of 1953 and, looking behind my left shoulder, saw, just a few feet away from me, the new vice president, Richard Nixon, sitting in the presiding officer's chair, following the debate with that look of self-conscious earnestness, a sort of glowering piety (determined to be a man among men, determined to please Mother, edgily alert for any disrespect that might be aimed his way).

I was working on the Democratic side of the Senate that summer. I wore navy blue trousers and white dress shirt and black necktie. My boss was Bobby Baker, Majority Leader Lyndon Johnson's protégé—North Carolina country boy later indicted for obscure chicaneries. If they could have bottled Bobby, he would have been linament and vitality tonic they might have sold from town to town from the back of a wagon.

* * *

My father, then an associate editor for the *Saturday Evening Post* in Washington, knew a senator from Michigan (a one-termer named Potter, who had returned from the war crippled and walked stiffly, scissoring on two Plexiglas canes that had batteries inside and could light up in the dark like magic wands). Potter's regular page boy had asthma and could not endure miserable Washington once the summer set in, so Potter put me on the payroll for a couple of summers as soon as school let out.

They were all just starting out in those days: glamorous John Kennedy, voluble young Hubert Humphrey, dark-drunk Joe McCarthy, the postwar generation of men on the make. As a Senate page boy, I felt that I had become an errand boy on Olympus.

18

Now, after the deep freeze on the farm, being so confined—staring out at unplowed roads, healing up glumly, introspective in the upstate icebox—I wanted to be in a place that would be new and foreign to me.

I had spent enough time with dark cats in the basement. I wanted warm air, colors, and sunlight. I wanted the hard metal grays to melt into bright, vivid liquids. Wanted escape.

I had a chance to go to the Caribbean, which I knew only superficially from one or two vacations, years ago. A German magazine, *Geo,* asked me to write a long article, not about the island resorts but rather about Caribbean history, economics, politics, race. The assignment was ideal. My article would be published in German; I would escape even more thoroughly, slipping out of my very language.

It is good to apprentice the mind to a story larger than one's own. That is the reason I like to go off on magazine

assignments: delok in trenchcoat, wandering outside myself, hovering over others' lives.

You have to be there—see, hear, feel things: unmediated information. It is good to be out in the midst of the
nasty and the modestly dangerous, even if the glimpse of
evil is merely what the delok dines out on. Journalists—
self-important voyeurs, ever inadequate in their own troubled eyes—are haunted by the suspicion that they are not
much good at real life. They prowl the world looking for it.

Or else:

I wonder if I like to go to some of these stories (Sarajevo, Gaza, for example) out of an unconscious nostalgia for
the dysfunctional drama—an old, buried expectation of
wreckage grown into a kind of need for it. The journalist in
search of dysfunctional history would, so to speak, profes-
sionalize his private inclinations, seek them on a bigger
scale. The objective correlative of a private inclination to
misery—and the memory of it from long ago—might be
the messy history of an entire people (Palestinians, Bosnian
Muslims, Jews, for example).

* * *

Glamour and the objective story, the sensibility pro-
fessionalized: In an introduction to his translation of
Goethe's *Italian Journey,* W. H. Auden wrote: "A journey is
one of the archetypical symbols. It is impossible to take a
train or an aeroplane without having a fantasy of oneself as a
Quest Hero setting off in search of an enchanted princess or
the Waters of Life."

Auden thought that Goethe's Italian journey—aban-
doning Weimar, the hard cold, and going south, more or
less incognito—was such a quest. But the trip served a
practical purpose. Goethe wanted to shake off the sorrows

of young Werther, to get rid of the weight and shadow of self, and to plunge into a new world that would demand alert observation and objectivity. He broke away in order to improve what he called the "elasticity of my mind." He disciplined himself to record minute details of the passing weather, the condition and history of the soil his carriage bounced across as it headed south, the course and tilt of the rivers.

I had no fantasy of mystic quest. I do believe, though, that there is a redemptive transparency in things clearly and precisely seen, clearly and precisely recorded.

If an unusually introspective man finds his alertness driven inward physically by a heart attack (a coup at home in the heart of the palace, an old friend's betrayal), it becomes indispensable, eventually, to force the attention out again into some new orbit of the objective. The man must retrain Goethe's "elasticity."

What's needed is even a small kind of suicide, enacted for the sake of self-transcendence. Self-obliteration, and out of it, renewal. Thaw out the heavy Teuton, stuck long past Christmas in the winter dusk and ice.

* * *

The wings iced up as the plane taxied toward takeoff at La Guardia. They became too heavy to lift—crusty, enameled, passing down the runway through hardening white air, into a glacial dimension.

The pilot in panic backthrust the engines, skidded the plane to a stop, well past the end of the runway, teetering. The airliner, a 727, cracked matter-of-factly in two, breaking its tail section, as if the plane had been made of dry brittle ice, like the air.

The winter had taken on an apocalyptic quality. The

afternoon the plane froze over, we came down to New York from Dutchess County, choosing the weather carefully, working (by car and train) between storms, and took a flight the next morning out of Kennedy. We changed at Miami to an American Eagle flight and by lunchtime we had landed at George Town on Exuma, in the Bahamas. I was still wearing snow boots when we passed through the customs shed.

Now, balm in the air, cotton-ball clouds. The roads our taxi picks its way along from the airport are pocked and eaten, like Kenya roads, a thin coating of crumbly black-gray asphalt upon the bed coral of the island, the road alley-ing through sceneless mangrove. Rodney the taxi driver recites singsong the news since we were here last, last March. Susan's family, creatures of habit, have been coming here for twenty-two years. The roads ministry has been digging the trench for the waterpipe all the way out to the airport, Rodney reports. The roads are improved from last year, and have become almost drivable.

* * *

Fat Albert, the drug-traffic surveillance blimp, hangs in the sky, a sort of bloated angel tethered at several thousand feet, floating above Exuma, watching electronically every boat and every small plane coming and going, like an AWACS. *Fat Albert* has worked. Exuma and Little Exuma used to be busy drug-staging stations for cocaine coming up from Colombia and destined for Florida and American consumers beyond. Hotel waiters would suddenly be rich. Local characters would walk around with cartoon-big cylinders of dollars in their trouser pockets. Now and then a murder in the mangroves, some poor local boy who got in over his head or double-crossed his partners. In a hotel up the island, since out of business, the owner, it is said, was assassinated, his brains splattered on the walls of one of his rooms.

* * *

It is regatta week, and almost 400 boats are anchored in the George Town harbor off the Government House and the Peace and Plenty Hotel. Here are the usual scruffy yachties, with their alarming ultraviolet skinburns, their beards and sun-etched laughlines and golden straw hair, and an air about them of dreamy fecklessness. Sometimes their teeth are bad, rotting in their mouths, because they gave up dentists when they left the North. Most of them have disconnected themselves from the days of the week, as they have mostly disconnected themselves from the land, which they tie up to intermittently for supplies and drunks.

I am stunned to be out of the dead winter, but uneasy about it, as if I have not earned the release. Too quick. A change of channels. How can any metaphysics of season survive when the scene change can be done like that, unstruggled for? An obscurely shaming anticlimax in this too-easy escape from a winter so deep frozen and awful.

I sit on the balcony outside our room at Peace and Plenty. The sewage discharge system is not quite working, and when the wind goes down we smell the fecal effluent. Trouble in paradise.

Around George Town there hangs a Third World atmosphere: the wild chickens that live in the roadside brush, the roosters that crow at all hours of night and day, the broken roads, the town's mascot imbecile who directs traffic from beside the road and using a straw broom sweeps the asphalt with that intensity of the retarded—the urgent business of his inner world. Exuma is an old shoe, a torn shoe—no good for formal occasions but comfortable.

Susan and I ride the fifteen-minute ferry across the harbor to Stocking Island, to spend the morning on the beautiful and empty beach on the Atlantic side.

In bright, calm sunshine, the sea before me is a recession of whites-to-blues as the water deepens. The sky, for all the sunshine and clarity, conceals some ominous haze far off—a weather darkness I would watch if I were sailing, for it might have the power to storm. But we have had enough of ominous weather up north. We are months off from hurricane season.

We cross laser-lighted ripple-netted tidal shallows and emerge at the sea-monster rock: Beyond its gray mass, we make out in the sand the wreckage of a drug smuggler's single-engine plane that crashed into the beach in 1981, and after that night began vanishing, subsiding into the beach and reappearing from time to time, as if the wings were trying to lift through the impossible weight of sand and water and find the upper air again. Now when we come to it, only the wingtips show, and the ocean dreamily hammers them with its reassertions of its heaviness and falling, its roll and collapse, time after time after time until, watching it, the plane reminds me of the Jesuit retreat sermons I heard as an adolescent at Gonzaga High School in Washington—so similar to the sermons James Joyce recorded (the Jesuits had developed a reliable central core of material, like a politician's all-purpose campaign speech, with metaphors and stage effects well polished), wherein eternity could be understood by the dove's wings flying around the earth again and again and brushing the planet minutely so that we must conceive timelessness to be the time it would take those little dove's wings to wear the planet earth to nothing, brushing it with the feathers. And that would be only the beginning of the first second of eternity in the Jesuit retreat master's awe-saturated spiritual campaign trope. The drug smuggler's sand-mired wingtips made me think in such terms. Until the plane could fight free and rise again, we would be mired in time.

Fat Albert, the drug-busters' white blimp, watches all of this from its kite-tethering in the heavens above us: can see us at this moment watching the smuggler's wingtips, could read the labels, I am sure, on our bathing suits. Albert, the motionless all-seeing, has his eye upon the sparrow: the optic of the law.

The deeper water deepens to almost-purple; its light rises and bounces off the clouds, so that the very air between sea and cloud becomes empurpled. Layers of colors from beach: deep lemon green and sand-scrub dune grass, beige-white sand, ripple-web shallows at low tide, turquoises, aquas, then layering out in light blues to darker blue to darker, and the deeps. Cotton-ball sky undershadowed, underblued.

*   *   *

I am moved, each time I come to Exuma, by the tenuousness of life here, the sense of life shallowly encamped on strands of coral barely greened. The roots here have nowhere down to go, and so they clutch the hard surfaces of the rocks. The people are bright splashes; they have valiantly good manners, and a merriness that is a form of grace, considering the history, and considering the future, neither of which looks good.

In any case it is always startling to come crashing down out of the uncivilized North. (I even come to believe for a moment that the charlatan Leonard Jeffries is right when he talks about the Ice People and the Sun People, and sense that the harsh, barging approach of hideously white strangers—myself—savors of an alien, disgusting something, skin like death, ships of doom.) Well, anyway, we could say good morning first, make eye contact and pleasantry before the business, before the *bring-me-coffee.*

The average sugar plantation in the Caribbean lasted forty years before the soil was exhausted, and then the Europeans moved on to the next island. Sugar and spice. What amazing mayhem in the world the Europeans' appetite for something special for the mouth, a restlessness of the palate, brought about. Black misery the price of the white delicious. White cannibalism itself, vacuuming the earth for treats like krill: Great whites feeding, the imperial Caucasian browse.

The two-stroke offal-pump putters behind me, feeding the fish in the harbor. The yachties rock abed in the fresh afterdawn breeze, blowing from the fair-weather direction, northeast. Their dinghies bobble behind them like toddlers trailing Mom.

I woke from a dream that left me (in the dream) sobbing in uncontrollable, inconsolable grief. I had taken Justin to a boarding school in Bozeman, Montana, because he wanted to go there, and as I was about to leave him, faced with some enormous loss, I fell into a wild, hopeless, heaving grief—like the abandoned child's grief, a kind of nullification.

An aftergrief lingers in my mind as I look out at the sailboats, a sight that soothes me beyond all others, except, in a different way, the sight of new books.

The hotel boat leaves the dock to ferry guests to Stocking Island. Aboard is a group of drinking, braying women vacationing in gang cluster, whose laughter like that of the coyotes in Dutchess is infectious, leaping and hooting, flame licking and feeding upon itself: dental brays, the women's teeth all bared in their hilarity like horses rearing back in their partytime uproar. The boat recedes, and with it, above the engine noise, their whinnying out across the shadow-and-light dancing harbor water, mast-tips doing merry circles in the air as the waves down below prompt them.

Across the harbor is the salt marker atop the highest hill on Stocking Island, an obelisk that told ships passing by that they might put in here for salt. Justin and I climbed the hill last year among the scrubby vegetation.

When we drive southeast from George Town, the road becomes a pockmarked rutted track between monotonous mangrove—as same-same as a Maine road running between pines on either side. The roads are deeply pitted; the real problem is that they are paved. If they had been left unpaved the dirt-coral would have settled to its own levels and been passable. But the asphalt pits horrendously, and exaggerates the problem. Crews in dump trucks work the roads with shovels and temporary sand-coral fill, which lasts until the next strong rain. Forlorn the upcountry sense of abandonment, the ghosts of plantations long ago, goats on a tether, the shallow soil. We pass Rolletown, named for an original British colonist, Lord Rolle, who gave his name to half the black slaves on the islands.

* * *

The massacre at the mosque at Hebron has followed us here. It has enflamed again the arguments that we have about Israel and the Palestinians. Susan, being an Arabist, takes the Palestinian side, and I defend Israel.

As we leave George Town, we pass on the road the gesticulating brain-damaged man directing traffic. He holds his right forearm in front of him, with fist clenched, in a stylized nineteenth-century gesture that makes him look like Stephen A. Douglas in debate, or Daniel Webster. His face seems given over to some abstract passion, his face twisted in intellectual intensity. I think this is a mockery somehow of the arguments that Susan and I have as we pass, debating Hebron, the right-wing doctor who burst into the mosque and opened fire with an assault rifle, killing forty or fifty Arabs at their prayers. I do not of course defend him or the Israeli settlements on the West Bank or the settlers' sometime fanaticism. But do defend Israel, and the idea of Israel. I have a long memory of Israel's founding and all that went before it: I have a profound preoccupation with the Holocaust. Susan wonders why. She has surprised me by asking that, surprised me because to me the Holocaust possesses a certain self-evident centrality and weight. I have lived so long with the Holocaust as a baseline of evil, as a dark presence in my moral calculations, an ur-myth of what people are capable of, even the most civilized, that it has been permanently installed in my imagination. I do not question its importance.

Susan, being younger, has no such preoccupation, and having spent years studying Arabic and absorbing a very different perspective on the formation of Israel. Why am I so obsessed with the Holocaust, and therefore with its role in the origin of modern Israel? I was born three weeks after Hitler marched into Poland. The Holocaust was underway as I was learning to walk. As I said my first words.

* * *

Elie was in Auschwitz when I was on Benning Road in Washington. My mother and father did not know about the concentration camps then, of course. Later, when they did, the movies and photographs (cordwood corpses, waxy stick-boned arms and legs, the unbearable nakedness and impassive objectivity of human life-disposal) formed the conscience of a time, formed mine, certainly—melted the raw elements of the mind, as if in some terrible new fire, and left it, when it cooled, reconfigured. It was impossible to have seen those images and not feel the foundations of all civilization crack and shatter. Impossible to know what happened to the European Jews who survived—the DP camps, the doors slammed in their faces, the international cold shoulder—without cheering for the foundation of Israel. Impossible for me not to retain much of that passionate sympathy even now, even when I listen to the Palestinians' stories and understand them, and sympathize with them as well. When I am in Israel or in Gaza or the West Bank, I have sometimes felt an acute right brain–left brain internal quarrel, sensing myself in the presence of the irreconcilable.

* * *

Leave the hatred to those who need it. Come to Exuma's blackland coppice: mahogany, horseflesh, mastic and cedar, the gum elemi, reddish-brown bark like a peeling sunburn, the wild figs, of great height, the strangler fig, the Bahama strongbark, the wild coffee, the satinleaf, with underside rust-colored down, or pigeon plum, sea grape, blolly, orchids, bromeliads—the lovely gardens of the Bahama fowl snake. Come to whiteland coppice: braziletto, haulback, cat's claw, dildo cactus, Turk's cap, the New World.

I lose myself in books about the local botany and history. It is the hour of magic evening light, golden, slanting, paradisal. I look out over the water and imagine how black slaves, the true man groves, blew west from Africa in the white man's pods and seeded the limestone here—lilty transplants, bright-eyed, easy now and valiantly courteous.

The evening makes me feel peaceful, jaunty: tip of the hat, bright flowers and bees!

Mom's van, full of cakes and breads, breezes past the giant ficus tree where the Bahama ladies sell their baskets and slides betimes to her roadside vending spot near Sam Gray's Enterprises, Mom debouching. "Praise the Lord! Praise the Lord!" she cries to the air, to the ficus—her son Alston, the maître d' from Peace and Plenty of an evening, beside her now all bright and singsong smily. If there are hatreds here I cannot feel them.

A centipede on the kitchen floor. A scorpion in the shoe. I deliver a learned talk at dinner in the hotel about how a wire from a car battery, if applied to a scorpion sting or snakebite, will break down the poison and render the wound harmless, but I am met with skepticism. It is true. I know Africans who have used it on mamba bites: A miracle, one man rested for a few hours and then got up and worked for the rest of the afternoon. Resurrection by car battery, a sort of Frankenstein jolt of juice and life rekindles itself.

Here on the island, I dream about my father in the afternoon: One day he appears to be conflated with Mikhail Gorbachev (whom he physically resembles, both men formal, grave, with civilized eyes, in well-cut dark suits), and in the dream I am asked to transcribe their conversation on an electric typewriter, but cannot, for the initial capital G key sticks on the electric typewriter I am using, and makes the entire machine heave in a stutter: G-G-G-G-G-G-G. I am back to cub reporter somehow, at the *Washington Star*, where I started out as a journalist years ago, and feel the humiliation of that retrogression, as if everything between then and now had been wasted and useless. The room in which I sleep is hothouse airless, and I wake covered in sweat.

It occurs to me that in the dream I was trying to bring my father back with the typewriter (the conceit of writerly creation), but the machine jammed, and so he never made a full visual appearance—I conjured only the inference of him through Gorbachev, his sleek public exterior, his Russkie-commie doppelgänger.

I wished to resurrect my father by transcribing him. But the key stutter-jammed, the machine like my father's breathing toward the end, the urgency and apnia-catch of the breath, so that only the first noise of the word would emerge—*G-G-G-G-G-G-G*—while all the while his eyes were full and wild like a rearing horse's rising up and away against the held reins, a panic of near death: The horse had seen the snake beneath its hooves.

There is some atmosphere of that poison here, of ultra-violets spurty through fang and pincer and whiplash stinger, the venoms from secret sacs secreted and bringing thus bright blossoms and spinnakers of pain—pain in its vivid differentiations, pain striped and spectrum-ed and hued like tropical fish.

Christine said that people die here of diabetes and high blood pressure—some of the same, I thought, that got my father—but do not die of heart disease and cancer. Christine said this dogmatically, her Bahama lilt turned to a Nazi categorical *Gauleiter* bark as she picked her van ever-so-easy across the shelled acne-scape of the Exuma roads. It was the Queen's Highway, as it happened, going north from George Town, past the new airport, through pine and mangrove scrub and Lord Rolle's "generation lands" toward Farmer's Hill and beyond that to Barre Terre. The Queen's Highway is a grand name for a miserable track.

Christine, of indeterminate age but surely seventy or

more, was born in Farmer's Hill. Her mother died when
Christine was six, and she never knew her father. She moved
in with a sister, but could not get along with the sister's
husband (I caught, I thought, a whiff of some abuse in that
house long ago) and at the age of fourteen, Christine moved
out and began to live on her own. "It hard," Christine remembers, her small, bright face clouding at the memory for
an instant. "I live on cocoplum . . . and nutting hot to
drink . . . never."

I am a little haunty with my father's unexpected appearance in the afternoon. Some atmosphere of Christine's
voodoo, perhaps. My father appeared in the fevery air. Made
sense, his coming here: My father would have been at home
at such a latitude of mind and civility; he had something of
the style, something of the same mental weather as Exuma,
the amiable trades, lazy without being sinister. His style savored a little of the Bahamian manners—a folk version of
the courtly—a friendly satire of the formal.

This island, bright and fragile, was abused and abandoned long ago. The crime was something like rape, a violent penetration, an intimate taking, then casting off and
brutally striding away: white men hitching up their trousers.

In the aftermath of 1834 when slavery was outlawed
in the British colonies and the planters packed and sailed
away, they left only their names attached to their former
slaves. Lord Rolle, who never even came to the islands but
sent his sons, bequeathed a name that every other black on
the Exumas seems to have now.

The whites left little else. Their houses were never
grand, were more like cottages than manor houses, for the
whites lived here only fitfully, reluctantly, preferring Nas-
sau. There is a forlorn legend, still believed but false, that
when Lord Rolle abandoned his lands, he declared in his
will they should be left in perpetuity to his former slaves

and their descendants. It is not true. His lordship's will stated that such holdings should be sold in order to buy the family more lands in Devon, back home, where they belonged.

* * *

On the ferryboat to Stocking Island, Sherman finds a place for herself where no one else could sit, folded under the windscreen, above the captain's instrument panel. She talks to herself for a time, play-acting some solitary fantasy. Then she grows still, her face hardens, though it remains intensely alive with her troubled intelligence.

Sherman, I guess, is ten or eleven years old. Her parents are not along for the trip to Stocking Island this morning. They have hired a Bahamian girl to keep an eye on Sherman. The parents are southerners, Georgians, I guess by their accent, who drink much of the day, with a forlorn singlemindedness. The mother, in her early thirties, is an ex-belle, wan, thinnish, with slackening flesh. She has something of Zelda Fitzgerald about her, a former coquettish freshness hanging in her vicinity like a taunting ghost, watching the process of ruin hastening over the flesh.

The woman smokes almost incessantly. Her addictions keep her busy in a humiliatingly urgent way; I have watched her try to light a cigarette in a wind while sitting on a beach—cowling herself in a towel, working frantically, unsuccessfully to torch the cigarette, almost setting fire to the towel wind-whipped around her pinkening earlobes and neck. She lighted it at last, smoke billowing out from under and wisping away in the sunshine wind. And then she set about the concoction of her morning drink.

It was 10:30 A.M. Mama Zelda and her husband had come across on the ferry, bearing a freezer chest with ice and juices, and a separate padded bag for the vodka. Each, mother and father, carried a sixteen-ounce thermal mug with mouthpiece top to suck the drink through.

Now Mother Zelda, dangling her lighted cigarette, began her drink—unlidded the mug and charged it with fresh ice; added a splash of cranberry juice, then withdrew the brown-bagged vodka from its padded case, and poured and poured until the mug was filled, which she relidded. Whereupon, her cigarette long ashed now in the wind and dangling from her mouth, she settled again upon the powdery sand, beneath her tattered palm.

Her husband, several feet away, does not smoke. He brunches on an iced beer, with something else much harder in his thermal mug, which he sips for variation. He is a red-eyed, lost-looking man, with full mustache (a mistake, probably) and receding chin and a snubby nose, down which his heavy, gold-rimmed glasses slide: He habitually and distractedly pushes them back up with his forefinger, a gesture invariably accompanied by a rapid wince.

Between Scott and Zelda I see little communication of any kind, although each maintains an animal awareness of the other's presence, a woozy unlooking symbiosis of the kind you see between eighteen-month-olds set down together upon their diapers on the nursery floor: "Parallel play," the child development people call it.

Each tends to his/her drink, keeps it full. Zelda reads sometimes, from large beach-fare paperbacks. Scott receives fax messages through the hotel office. He reads them with his mouth open and his nose wrinkled, like a little boy, or a nerd about to sneeze.

Scott and Zelda make me angry, mostly on Sherman's behalf. Sherman is a skinny, stringy-washed-blond little girl with pale blue Scotch-Irish eyes. When I see her—her little brat riots, her tempests of attention-seeking followed by blank-out sadnesses, long melancholy stares into space—I rewitness something I saw a long time ago.

Toxic deposits in the memory, wastes that leak into the heart and ruin it: There is such a thing as a communicable incapacity to love.

It is not the breaking of the heart itself and the sadness that hangs like an aura about the story of the breaking. The meaning is something worse, without the redeeming glamour or bittersweetness. Your heart simply silts up, until it becomes an isolation chamber. Within, the heart churns up its own Patagonian weather, squally, struggling against the wind, fighting off shipwreck. Joyless striving.

I thought poor Sherman, wild, shirtless tomboy, was being delivered up to all that, launched toward Patagonia, drink by drink, as I watched on the Exuma beach. Watched from a distance. The gin-clear waters of the Bahamas indeed! The poisons lapped gently at Scott and Zelda in the ultraviolet sunshine, and lapped its acids at the little girl.

That night I would get lashingly angry at Susan, over nothing, at the dinner table with her parents in the hotel dining room—a shot of rage that frightened me because it was out before I was aware of it, before I could censor it. Rage with a life of its own.

I did not speak to the little girl Sherman—my neoself, my reincarnation—in part because it occurred to me (the vicious nineties being what they are) that it might look like the dirty-old-man approaching: How else interpret this middle-aged man's intense interest in the girl? The reality would be invisible: the peculiar identification I felt with her, the surrogate father's indignation and the child's heartbreak that I felt for her, indignation and heartbreak commingled.

I sat on the beach in my bathing suit, suddenly aware of the livid scar down my right leg, from groin to ankle, where the surgeons had stripped a vein to make tubing for the latest bypass. I shifted my legs closer together to hide the scar. The other leg's seventeen-year-old scar, the twin, is visible still but somewhat faded: You have to look a little to see it. The marks of a bite from a long time ago. And I could imagine Sherman (odd that a southern couple would give their daughter the name of the South's despoiler) with her forty-years-hence legs cut like mine, scarred like mine.

I saw the instant of the child's soul being bitten: not trauma recollected in some therapy later or falsified or embellished by self-pity, but the clear event itself, the moment.

Here we were on the bright beach of the New World. Bloodshot Columbus and his crew have capsized on the sand. They deliver up Old World diseases: reeking drunkenness under the palms, grown-ups' uncleanness.

A venereal pollution: "Syph," we would call it in junior high, the child's idea of adult corruption; the risqué forbidden fucking disease that made your dick burn, and you peed pus.

The real disease was rage. It would kill off whole neighborhoods of heart muscle. The transaction in the end would be precisely literal. The heart will stop pumping because of what I have seen here in the vivid, corrupt sandbox. Virulent lovelessness.

I have a mind to murder Scott and Zelda on the beach, and drag their bodies into the gin-clear waters and let the browsing sharks and crabs and other nibblers of the harbor finish them off and leave them on the bottom sand like the dolphin carcasses we see by the dock where the ferry comes.

Funny there is so little forgiveness in me for the pair, for Scott and Zelda. But the child's imagination (and mine is childish to the infantile when I go back into this time travel) is absolutist and unforgiving. Children gamble for high stakes, are infinitely more at risk than their elders, and therefore cannot enter into the higher and subtler orbits of forgiveness and understanding. Yet in another way, children are more forgiving and understanding, in a reflexive way, unpremeditated, than anyone older. The child of this type—my type or Sherman's—bestows abundant grants of the benefit of the doubt, knowing no better and being generous anyway, and being, more than that, in danger and deep behind the lines and at the mercy of strangers in a peculiar world that children are unequipped to sort out as old survivors do. We sail upon the turbulences of the given, and only later, when it is too late, see what the sail has cost us.

I love children, of course—my own and others. I say "of course," but loving children is not of course by any means. Damaged children, it may be, love children more (I mean wholesomely, I do not mean perversely), more when grown themselves because they return to the childhood again in a kind of wonder to see if its breaking can be undone. It can, though only in the next generation, not in oneself. I think that lovelessness has a barnacled permanence. It is the sea monster I sense in myself, in the depths, an intimate strangeness, the dragon at the core, the heartlessness that sits upon the sanctum's throne, the reptile of indifference. I fear it because it is so alien within me, it has such dark, matter-of-fact powers to coil itself around my chest, the insides of my life, and strangle it there.

* * *

The colors of the surface are layered in their magnificent recession out from here (beige, aquamarines, turquoises) to the distant cobalts of the deep sea softly heaving. I watch Sherman's mother decay on the beach thirty feet away from me. The sight for a moment softens my anger. I feel stricken for her, sad for her. The sight of her dying moves me: bright Sherman flying skinny-legged in the distance, spraying sand, and her mother here on the near-beach, nearer the water, lost.

Why is it difficult to love? The heart cannot be forced to do it. Is love an inclination of the character? A matter of temperament? A grace, a matter of luck? Something that must be worked at and worked at and worked at? A conscious labor? I must think so, hope so. The rage that kills love kills the heart. I have felt it happen.

19

Sunday morning. I eat the Miami hotel's health break-fast of fruit and yogurt. Then, having been thus virtuous, think about whether to smoke one of the cigars I bought last night at the newsstand (Macanudo and Partegas), as if proximity to so much fine Cuban tobacco, just across the Straits of Florida, made its delicious, dreamily curling rich smoke irresistible, virtually inevitable. I have not smoked a cigar since my heart attack.

I order a pot of coffee and cut the Macanudo's tip with my thumbnail and torch it up with a flare of capitulating guilt and pleasure and blow the white-blue smoke toward Key Biscayne.

This is my first trip alone to foreign countries since the heart attack. I leave tomorrow night for Santo Domingo, then for Grenada and Barbados.

I have no anxiety. The luxurious pleasure of travel spreads before me—the weightlessness of being alone, one of the great joys. I never feel lonely when traveling.

Last night I walked out of the hotel, the Inter-Continental, among tall office buildings and banks, a high wind blowing off the ocean, and found an automatic teller machine. The machine was outdoors, part of the bank's sidewalk wall. I tapped in the code to withdraw $500 from my checking account, heard twenty-five twenty-dollar bills counted mechanically into the cash tray.

When I opened the cash drawer to withdraw the bills, the sucking wind went in before my fingers and began blowing bills wildly around the small cash airlock. I closed it, but two or three bills escaped and swirled to the sidewalk, I retrieved them, barely, and then crumple-clutched the money in the drawer in fistfuls every which way and stuffed it into my pockets.

A homeless man on the empty street watched all this from a distance—a very black thin and snaggle-toothed man I glanced at from time to time—and when the comedy was finished, he rushed up to me as I started away and asked for money. I gave him three quarters from my pocket, but he could not bear it; he was in a trance of money hunger, having seen so many bills dancing in the air, a wind-funnel of twenties, escaping my fingertips. He had only to catch some, like leaves—deciduous white man shedding money. So, having given him the three miserable coins, I accelerated my pace on the empty street, for I saw the imploring heat in his eye.

He followed, not close, but dreaming of the money still, his body tensed in a sort of supplication, beseeching, and expressing as well a real indignation: *What the fuck! All that money, bills blowing around, and I can't even have one of them? I get the loose change, quarters from your pocket?*

I knew he was not dangerous on the empty street, for he was slight of build, and stick limbed. Unless, of course,

he was crazy and had some fury in him, in which case bets
were off.

By now I was half a block from the Inter-Continental,
which rose in its slabby chain-hotel opulence, and I reentered the orbit of its protection, its platoons of doormen
and valet parkers, its liveries and noisy wind-flapped flags.

As I walked I could feel my homeless man's deflation
and defeat. He slowed his pace, as if the force field of the
hotel held him off. My privilege. His exclusion. I felt in my
trouser pocket for the plastic card that was the electronic
key to my room, went up the steps to the marble garden
lobby, and felt there as I reentered the pebble-in-the-shoe of
guilt (no more than that), and turned to see that my companion had slid obliquely off (as if to say he had not been
following me at all) and shuffled, without looking back, toward a park with a tiny Ferris wheel.

One of the powerful memories—an image, an emotional configuration—has to do with exclusion, a winter
dusk, a house that I wish I could enter but cannot. I look at
it with an empty longing. Wonderful word, *longing*: desire
made aching by the sheer long distance from its object, and
darkened by a hopelessness.

The pebble in my conscience grew larger. I should
have given the man money. Surprised him with a twenty-
dollar bill at least, and sent him off in a little daze of appetite momentarily gratified.

Once on a Christmas morning in New York, when I
was alone and miserable in the eighties, I set off for the subway stations with my pockets full of dollar bills to give to
homeless people.

I went to the IRT station at Eighty-sixth and Lexing-
ton: no homeless. They had mysteriously vanished. I rode
the subway to Grand Central, and began exploring the
labyrinth, the subway and train corridors where normally

the homeless are evident everywhere. I was in a mood of misery projected into Dickensian fellow-feeling and alms-giving, but all the objects of my charity had disappeared. I suppose they had gone to soup kitchens. I do not know: They were gone. After an hour's search, I began to feel ashamed of myself and imagined that they had repudiated my easy sentimental gesture, done the only dignified thing and withdrawn themselves. Gray New York Christmas, cold and iron, even its moment of charity misbegotten.

I found a teenaged black girl begging on Second Avenue and gave her twenty dollars, which she greeted with a small, bright surge of surprise. Someone had thrown her out (boyfriend, stepfather, mother).

* * *

Brilliant Goethe rolling south, out of Weimar, toward Verona, sewing his manuscript pages together neatly, carrying two small pistols concealed in his pockets. Entry in his *Journey* for 21 September (which is my birthday) in 1786:

> Today I paid a visit to Dr. Turra, who for five years devoted himself passionately to the study of botany, compiled a herbarium of Italian flora and laid out a botanical garden for the late bishop. Now all this is over. His medical practice has crowded out the study of natural history, worms have eaten the herbarium, the Bishop is dead, and the botanical garden has been planted with useful cabbages and garlic.

I felt as if my heart had become the garden, gone now to cabbages and garlic, and its bishop dead.

Follow your bliss. A Public Television shaman's fruit-juice rhetoric.

Find your bliss first. It is not so easy.

The past crowds up behind me all the time. Is it the enemy of bliss, or the key to bliss? Surely not the key.

Perhaps the past is the lock, and once it has been unlocked, then the gate will swing wide and I will look within: If all were well, the past would be arranged like an Arab courtyard, secret and hidden from the street, but within, all ordered, clear, grace-filled, courteous: the secret heart.

But the past is more mirage than garden—a hallucination that is half the time sinister. The past is not my bliss, but writing it up is my apprenticeship to bliss. A way of earning a better version of it. Or a future. Revisiting Christmases past like Scrooge, reassembling—and therefore repossessing—life on intelligible terms. Telling stories cleanses and recleanses the tale, until it shapes down to its irreducible self.

The girl Sherman in the Bahamas merges with myself in Key West (same beach, heat, limestone, coral, alcohol, sun) many years ago in time's narrative elasticity. Time has a perfect reproductive memory.

The image of the wheel returns in my mind; time wheeling back upon itself, repeating, reconnecting to what had been lost, and I think again of Emerson's "The eye is the first circle."

Bad weather, Patagonian squalls: poor Sherman. I used to watch her useless fuddled father make his rounds of the hotel in his dense interior fog, bloodshot, watched him with a kind of hatred and with perfect recognition.

One afternoon in a drunken exuberance of fatherhood, he hoisted Sherman onto his shoulders in the hotel lobby and very nearly inserted her head into a ceiling fan above him. He never saw the danger.

I admonish myself to give up judging, this harshness.

I have spent three days in the Miami hotel, hardly leaving the room, resting, watching CNN, reading, writing, staring out at the boat channel.

I watch tugs working freighters through the buoys, and sailboats pushing in, slow motion, from the open water. Boats are the most pleasing sight, the most soothing, boats under sail, white-puffing on their sweet splashy vectors, blue-slicing waters on a pleasing heel, fresh, clean, escaping.

Across the channel from the hotel, two white cruise ships lie at anchor, sleek and inviting in some way, but also institutional. This morning as I watched them, I imagined being caught in a stateroom, claustrophobic, way belowdecks, and I opted out of the cruise before it ever started. I could not breathe, I felt the companionway fill with people and smoke, a sinking suffocation, and so drew my mind abruptly away and back out into open water again, with the small boats glistening up the channel.

I watched this from a kind of high, cool cave, the recessed picture window of my room on the fifteenth floor. CNN went on and on on the television, the farflung, fragmented, electronic world. The sun in the morning when I woke up came up over the Atlantic and then the yachts slid across the shimmer. I spoke to no one for three days, except for telephone calls now and then. A pleasant troglodyting. I concentrate upon the center of the wheel, center of the circle. I imagine that the center of time is still.

* * *

Breaking my retreat at last, I took a taxi to the campus of Florida International University and spent an hour with a professor named Anthony Maingot, an expert on the Caribbean, a refreshing man who impatiently waved away all thought of what the Caribbean poet Derek Walcott called (Maingot quoting him) "the historiography of the oppressed and the historiography of remorse"—meaning, I take it, the interminable clichés of the victimed and genocided.

Maingot's breezy dismissals relieved me a little of the weekend's reading guilt, going back again through the conquest and slavery and greed. Time to move on, said the professor, it is a new world.

I thought, thinking of myself, *Indeed! Indeed!*

And he orated on about the asymmetries of power between the Caribbean islands and the United States, and allowed that they were a good thing, an opportunity for the little islands to work around the big continental power, to hustle for advantage. It seemed to me as he talked that I saw the rhetoric of old suffering and guilt vaporize and blow off.

I had been reading a Jamaican named Rex Nettleford, a black teacher and artistic director at the theater company in Kingston, very bombastic and filled with the grandeur of the sufferings of his people, reminding me of much American black-anger rhetoric, grievance-cherishing, hurt-caressing, self-defeating. And here came Maingot with his Hernando de Soto message of making things work and not taking the past too seriously (*Oh, never do that,* I told myself); it is, among other things, too boring. The past, you see, is curiously archaic, almost as if it belonged to a different artistic medium, a theater, an art form that cannot work anymore, in which the posturing and language come to seem bogus: One can see the past's makeup, its false beard, its fundamental insincerity.

Get real, Maingot said: work to do, problems to solve, things to figure out.

Surely it is part of a heart cure to think like this, to

give over the art forms of old grievances, the proscenium of childhood trauma.

* * *

The plane, to illustrate Maingot's point, is sailing along 30,000 feet above the waters that Columbus first came dawn-slicing through, 500 years ago, in the caravels of white man's doom, the fatal ships. We windplane over clouds, a metal capsule full of Afro-mestizo-Europo genes, the Dominicans smelling as they do, the men, of heavy hair oils sweet-musky, a beautiful mestizo woman in the seat in front of me having half-crinkled hair and wispy dark face hair and lovely eyes.

Columbus enslaved what he discovered, and yet half a millennium later, here they are, eating the American Airlines microwaved chicken, and forwarding their Rolexes to a new time zone.

New Worlds pile on top of new worlds. Each age ironizes the last, and leaves it orating in period costume to an empty house. Some such fate for Rex Nettleford, I think. Through the very ventilation system of the plane there gusts an overpowering smell of some deodorizing powder.

* * *

The Dominican Republic: We left Santo Domingo at seven in the morning and drove three hours, heading north by northeast, first through the *cordillera* (a mountain range of three or four thousand feet, beautiful green country with peaks the shape of shark's teeth), and then across the Cibao, the rich farming region of bananas and plantains and then tobacco, cocoa, beef, and beyond those *latifundia,* a vast flat of rice wetlands, and on to a town called Cotuí, where we hoped to intercept the presidential campaign of Francisco Peña Gomez, the (comparatively) youngish, leftish candidate of the PLD (pronounced *peh-eleh-deh*).

We stopped at the public square in Cotuí at the party headquarters and found we were off by a day. Peña Gomez would come tomorrow.

The headquarters was a dark, bare room with posters on the plaster walls and two dozen straight-backed chairs pushed every-which-way askew. The headquarters was empty when we walked in, but soon a local leader hurried in, and then another, and then ten or fifteen more party workers. The word spread quickly that we had come. We shook hands all around, I muttering something half-English half-Spanish, Cyrus Veeser, my translator, explaining me quickly as *"periodista norteamericano."* We thanked the men and shook hands all around again—I am always surprised by the softness of the hands, even of the campesinos, and the limpness of their shakes, like Masai saying *"sopa"* (hello), with a soft single downplump of the hand—and decided to drive on to Nagua, where *El Doctor,* the president, Joaquín Balaguer, would have a rally.

The day was bright and hot, and as we approached Nagua the traffic thickened. By the roadside, people stood waving red banners (red is the color of the *Reformistas,* those of the Balaguer party).

We fell into a kind of caravan, a fast-moving parade, with the *Reformistas partidarios,* who drove an amazingly (not so amazingly, given the corrupt cash-on-hand) expensive procession of Japanese four-wheel-drive jeeps (Nissans, Toyotas, Mitsubishis, all of them shiny and showroom new) with enormous red banners streaming from their windows—an impressive battle display, the banners in wind-whipped sunbright glory, and many arms stabbing out from the windows, the forefinger pointing upward in the salute of the *reformistas.*

They were answered from the roadsides by other faithful insistently jabbing forefingers and sometimes by a *Peña Gomista* defiantly replying with a thumbs-up, which is the PLD salute. This sort of exchange has been leading to violence of late, and so last week the Catholic Church helped to negotiate a compact between the parties that they would stay away from each other's political demonstrations. It seemed to be working today: We saw no violence.

In Nagua, the roadside crowds grew denser. Peña Gomez supporters stared from their doorways, their housefronts often decorated with a poster photo of Peña Gomez—his amiable black face, his unmistakably African features—and beneath it, the party's message: VOTA BLANCA. Meaning "Vote White," the party's color, if not the candidate's.

Peña Gomez's color, his race, are of strange urgency here, and of a rather confusing significance. On the one hand, Dominicans are undeniably racist. The great majority of them are mulattos, a broad category of complexion that ranges from the lightest *café con leche* to a distinctive darker hue that is a sort of underempurplement of skin, an eggplant coloration down deep, but lightened closer to the surface. It is offensive to dwell on skin color so, but important to explain the Dominican psychology, I take it, which abhors the Haitians and the African heritage even though that heritage is evident in almost every face.

So here is Peña Gomez, deeply popular Dominican pol and yet born in Haiti, orphaned and adopted by Dominicans. And worse: suspected of wishing to consolidate Haiti and the Dominican Republic into one country again, a vision that horrifies Dominicans because it recalls the Haitian invasion and occupation of 1822–1844. If you remind a

Dominican that that invasion also freed the Dominican slaves being held by the Spanish masters, the Dominican concedes the point, as if it were unimportant: "Yeah, well. . . ."

When I asked one intellectual if Dominicans share a residual Caribbean anger at having been the victims of conquest and enslavement, he interrupted me: "But they do not think they are victims! They feel they are masters! It is the Haitians whom they consider to be slaves!"

On the loudspeaker as we approached the rally, we heard the hyperventilating warm-up man shouting, "No to Haiti! Don't share the government with Haiti! Don't let Peña Gomez move the government to Port-au-Prince!" The warm-up man referred to Peña Gomez as "that black man"—"What will that black man do?"—and at that I looked at the very dark people in the crowd to see if they perhaps were offended. They evidently were not.

A rumor has gotten started—I am not sure where— that the United States wants Peña Gomez to be elected president, so that Peña Gomez can open the Dominican Republic's borders to Haitian refugees and thereby relieve Americans of their moral dilemma and embarrassment about what to do about the Haitians washing up on the shores of Florida.

Another rumor has it that Peña Gomez is being financed heavily by narco-traffickers. The stories say that Peña Gomez is more corrupt even than Balaguer, and that his regime would therefore be an even greater disgrace and regression.

Actually, almost everyone agrees that Balaguer is not himself corrupt; my own reading is that he would have no interest in the usual payoffs (money, houses, luxuries) because, if I am right, he wants only power: He lives by that and nothing else. He is a García Marquez variation on Lyndon Johnson, with additional commentary by Joseph Stalin.

Balaguer is one of those political creatures—political monsters with no other life or interest or instinct than power and its manipulation. He has ordered murders, one hears (death squads in the 1970s finishing off some of his leftist enemies; no one knows the count, but hundreds, surely). He has been a force in Dominican politics for so many years (sixty maybe, or more) that he has achieved a mythic, semidivine (or vaguely diabolic) stature: He is part of the Dominican Shinto, a native deity, dispensing favors, abundances, and wrath as well.

Balaguer is totally blind now, eighty-seven years old. The stories of his peculiar twilight reign have an element of magic realism. He is said to have all letters and memos and other correspondence read to him, separately, by three or four people, so that he can be sure he is not deceived.

He had seven sisters, all younger than he, and a mother on whom he doted. Six of his sisters have died: He ordained that none should be buried until forty-eight hours after death: He was said to be terrified of burying them alive. He seems to have had some residual guilty fear that his father was not really dead when Balaguer buried him. I imagine Balaguer's fantasy of the old man waking in the blackness of his coffin and pounding hopelessly on the lid to be let out. Can Balaguer hear the pounding in his sleep? Or feel the ultimate claustrophobe's terror?

Something in him is surely haunted. Alexei, an Eastern European journalist who has lived in the Caribbean and Latin America for years, and who has known Balaguer since the days when Balaguer was a lieutenant to Trujillo, says it is Trujillo who haunts him. Alexei says that there were times when Balaguer was the titular president and Trujillo was the "strongman," the *caudillo,* that Trujillo and Balaguer would step in from a balcony where they had been waving to the assembled masses, and Trujillo would slap Balaguer hard on the face.

Alexei peers at me with his eloquently squinting Gypsy's eyes and says, "What haunts Balaguer is Trujillo, always. When Trujillo died, Balaguer destroyed all the houses where Trujillo lived, or let them fall into ruin. Balaguer is competing with a ghost. He always wants to be Trujillo."

Alexei and I sit in the coffee shop of the Gran Hotel Lina, a hotel where Trujillo's cook used to run the kitchen, but which has evidently fallen on problematic times: The hotel has a 1950s feeling, something threadbare in the decor, and Alexei, who has known all of the Latin American leaders and even trained some of them, bursts with stories, turns surreal, or magic realist, as he tells them. His accent is sometimes difficult to follow. He tells of Balaguer's children.

Balaguer never married, but he has evidently fathered an indeterminate number of children. He favored peasant women, and would sleep with them one time only, or for a very brief time. Apparently many children were born of these liaisons. Balaguer offered parsimonious support for some of the children, but otherwise would not acknowledge them. Alexei says that he was standing in Balaguer's outer office one day when he saw a thirteen-year-old girl running out of the *caudillo*'s office in tears. Alexei asked an aide what had happened. The girl had come to Balaguer and asked him for support to go to school. He gave her RD$300—about $25.

Balaguer loved his sisters and his mother. He visited his mother's grave every Sunday for many years. Alexei is full of stories. He says that Peña Gomez has married Evita—a horrible woman whose ambition is going to destroy a good man, Peña Gomez, who is not terribly intelligent but has a good heart.

In Nagua, we park our van on a side street and make our way through the red-flag-waving crowds toward the dusty baseball stadium. Merengue blares from two immense systems of speakers that are two black cones of sound amplifiers—hives of noise, pounding the galloping-horse sex beat of merengue, a pulsing wave of eroticism that gives the dusty country air a bright, lubricious candor.

We pass under the small grandstand behind home plate, and the cinder-block box of a men's urinal emits a choking wave of urine-stink. Everywhere are soldiers with guns—pistols with that hanging important weight, the swinging dick of male menace. Or else the assault rifle in various forms, the little burping Uzi (a mark of rank) or the heavier long-barreled M-1 or Kalashnikov, but the atmosphere is festive nonetheless, bright with the driving music, and a rising sense of excitement.

We push toward the security line that surrounds the presidential pavilion, shouting, *"Prensa! Prensa!"* and the people cheerfully clear the way, more or less; but then the crowd grows thicker and the soldiers push back, a swaying crush sets in, and I become aware just then that there is a very active gerbil in my right trouser pocket, a busy, furtive animal.

I look and see just behind me a large man seeming to watch the crowd abstractedly, while his left hand explores my pocket and his right hand is sunk in Cyrus's. I grab the pickpocket's wrist and start to yell, and he hair-triggers a burst of wonderful indignation (a bit too rehearsed and histrionic), and the gerbil leaps out of the pocket and he withdraws into the crowd as if a powerful undertow has taken him, his face all the while screwed up in an expression of indignant, even litigious display. How can I not be impressed?

I clutch my wallet. He has gotten nothing from my trouser pocket (a dry hole) and press forward—*Prensa! Prensa!*—through the soldiers' line, which opens up for us with surprising hospitality.

Now we take our places among the palace press corps, inside the security zone. The pavilion where the president will speak is a surprisingly small tin-roofed affair erected in the middle of center field. The temperature here is welcomingly cool, out of the sun. Facing us, at the front of the lean-to pavilion, is the head table, a sort of dais at ground level. There the waiting dignitaries chat: local party workers in red *Reformista* baseball caps (*BALAGUER ES MI MEJOR AMIGO* or *BALAGUER TRABAJANDA PARA TI*) several generals in full banana-republic regalia, gold-braided and beribboned, wearing the steep-peaked military hats with vinyl gold-leafed visors that crown the Hispanic autocrat uniform.

Off to one side stands the priest who will deliver the benediction: He wears white vestments and a stole adorned with stylized blue Columbus caravels and the dates 1492–1992. That touch surprises me, even though I know that the Dominicans are officially proud of their connection to Columbus and that Balaguer spent a great deal of money celebrating the 500th anniversary of a landfall that elsewhere in the Caribbean savors of evil memory and the beginning of everything that went wrong in the world.

We sit at the rear of the pavilion, among the palace press corps, behind their television cameras. The palace press corps is notoriously underpaid and corrupt. Balaguer's government treats the docile hacks to free cars and even houses in order to ensure sweetheart publicity and press-conference questions that come sailing right over the plate every time. Apart from that, the reporters seem remarkably like the White House press corps. They have the air of anxious privilege, like protected children being a little naughty among themselves, but knowing the limits.

Now the merengue music gives place on the loudspeakers to a carny-barking emcee, shouting and hyperventilating and rolling his *r*s in a satire of hucksterism and enthusiasm and rhetorical high style.

A way off in the sky we hear a helicopter flapping, and the crowd, knowing what it means, begins cheering. Several *partidarios* flourish hand-held amplifiers that harshly honk incomprehensible Caliban gutterals.

The chopper *whackwhackwhacks* into view, a camouflaged military craft. It is not *El Doctor*'s. It is the escort, and presently settles fluttering very near us, kicking up the dust, impressing the campesinos. Then—*deus ex machina*—the white presidential helicopter appears in the hot blue sky, circles the field once—the crowd faces all turned skyward now, curious, cheering—and descends to land behind the pavilion.

I feel a strain of violence in the air, amid the excitement—my own fantasies of assassination attempts, of bombs going off. The pavilion looks a little like the one in which Anwar Sadat was sitting to review the military parade when he was killed in a storm of bullets from his own troops, and I visualize now an enemy of *El Doctor* opening up: see the bodies all around me, the press corps flattening, the dignitaries on the dais blasted, the people behind me screaming and overtopping one another to get away—the "Nagua Baton Twirlers" who have been performing will emit terrible high girlwails.

As I conjure all this in my imagination, two very tall, beefy, very black men, Haitian surely in their origin, station themselves directly in front of me, putting themselves between me and the dais. They behave like Secret Service men—that impassive menace—and yet they are dressed shabbily. Cyrus allows that these men are lead-catchers, and it is true that they have placed themselves in a direct line of fire from the crowd.

The lead-catchers eye me for a long moment, and question my identification, but when they are finally reassured that I am *periodista norteamericano, a* New York, they drift into a reverie of inattention, they stare at their shoes, or admire women in the crowd.

El Doctor at last appears at a door behind the dais: a tiny old man surrounded by a dozen larger men—generals, party men, local officials. Balaguer wears thick bottle-bottom glasses, behind which his eyes swim sightlessly. He starts to make his way to the red and gold throne fifteen feet from the door, but cannot seem to advance. He shuffles and rocks back and forth as if walking into a high wind, and takes an eternity to come to the throne and table, an embarrassment even in the midst of the cheering and shouting—which emanates from a crowd that mostly cannot see him anyway but merely infers his presence from the focused stir in the pavilion.

El Doctor wears a black suit, white dress shirt, and black necktie—a tie that I am certain he did not tie for himself, the knot being off-center and unfirmly noosed. *El Doctor* lists noticeably to his right, and his eyes are fixed on some interior middle distance as he is steered by the elbow toward the throne—which looks much like the one Trujillo used to use. I wonder now if it is the same one. At last he finds it. The band plays the national anthem, the *himno nacional,* in tinny blare, and when it ends, *El Doctor* subsides into his throne—only to be forced to rise again for the priest's interminable invocation—a high voice-cracking performance that artfully confuses God *(El Señor)* with *El*

Doctor as the source of all good and bounty. Personal God, personal *presidente,* little distinction between them.

When at last the priest is finished—flushed and proud of himself, then coming to the dais to wring *El Doctor*'s hand and speak to him too many long seconds (I see the generals getting impatient with this ambush of the presidential ear)—the Caliban megaphone behind me honks a noise of inarticulate and somehow despairing petition, ardent and false and condemned, all at once, a disturbing noise.

Speeches. At a podium set up to one side of the dais, locals thank *El Doctor* for his munificence. *El Doctor* pays no attention.

Instead, he does business now in earnest, like a godfather. Petitioners seriatim come to whisper in his ear; one sits at his right ear and *El Doctor* leans and listens, then renders his verdict, and (like a priest in a two-sided confessional) leans to the left and listens to the new petitioner there and gives his verdict—so on, an aged, sightless pendulum back and forth, working his way lucidly, attentively, through a considerable crowd of business. An efficient and impressive performance, while in the foreground of ceremony and noise, the official bombast proceeds.

When the petitions have been heard, and when *El Doctor* has presented deeds to several dozen new government-sponsored apartments to house some lucky country folk, then the frail, shuffling dictator will vanish into his advisers again and reappear aboard a glass-enclosed popemobile, a strange hybrid of phone booth and haywagon, and will be slowly driven through the town in enormous and gleeful caravan.

El Doctor, tiny in his funeral suit, blind as a bat, is borne like a religious relic through the streets of Nagua— Trujillo's apprentice in all things, including murder. When

I look at his face in repose, it seems to express a metaphysical weariness: I think he is kept going only on sheer will, for the energies of the body have undoubtedly departed. He has the stare of a nursing-home catatonic: eyes fixed and mouth profoundly downturned.

Suffering and power: a crucifixion of old age. God is a personal God. Balaguer is an authoritarian martyr, a monster of absolutist sacrifice: Is it the dream of pure will whereby politics ascends to the divine? And what strange purity there is now in blind old age that sheds everything human except the will, the pure energy of brains that has only to listen to the whispered fugitive words and with the least of gestures (nod, murmur) bestow largesse, or condemn—dispose, change utterly.

El Doctor rocks in the popemobile above the garbage-littered streets. The peasants in from ricefield and tobacco field jab the air with forefingers, honk and blare, and dance in place, knees and groins all syncopated. Caribbean intellectuals talk about the music that makes for the common Caribbean identity: They say that just hearing merengue sets their blood in motion, dancing. I wonder what effect the music (which stirs even me, a tuneless northern iceman) has upon Balaguer when he hears it (and he hears it all right—there is nothing wrong with his ears). Does it tickle some residual blood-and-dance reflex in *El Doctor* and make him wish to leave the display case of sanctification where he rides in order to pulse with the peasant girls again?

His face behind the glass is as still as an icon. We are stuck in the caravan traffic now. I watch as the *Balaguer Movil,* as it is labeled, sways off like a motorized palanquin and is swallowed by the peasant crowds. People tell me that everyone around Balaguer is corrupt but *El Doctor* himself is not. It is a question whether old age and near-death amount to a final purity or an ultimate corruption. I am making an

evil pun upon corruption. Balaguer feels the death coming
that will make him totally corrupt, in the mortal way.

* * *

In a barrio called *La Ciénaga,* down by the Ozama
River (jumbled shacks put together on dysentery flood-
lands), I asked, with hidden motives, what I would do to
get treatment if I were to have a heart attack there. I was
talking to a Jesuit, Padre Cela, about the health and sanitation of the barrio. Padre Cela told me he would have to try
to find a motorbike to take me to a hospital somewhere.
There are no ambulances, and the people certainly do not
have cars.

I do not feel vulnerable exactly, though I have a
numbness in the left pectoral that troubles me: It certainly
does not feel cardiac, but rather like a numbness brought on
by a severing of the nerves in surgery, but I cannot be certain, and therefore practice a kind of resignation—a
quelling of the self-importance—not only that of the *periodista norteamericano* (not much arrogance there anyway) but
the metaphysical self-importance, the egoism of thinking
that one's death matters. Which, of course, it does not.

I sit in a beautiful evening light in another barrio, *La
Zorza,* talking with the Mothers' Club, especially with a
white-haired woman named Fresa, vigorous and intelligent,
who is organizing the women of the barrio into a kind of
health-awareness club (not, God knows, a health club in the
North American sense, all Evian water and Nautilus machines), and looking out the barred, glassless window, I see
a boy on a tin rooftop across the street. He is framed against
the last light of the sun, a sweet light, and is absorbedly
flying a kite, playing with the kite string as if he were
pulling a fishing line against the modest evening breeze.

Fresa's voice bubbles on. Malnutrition? *O sí.* Rice and beans, plantain prepared this way and that, bananas. Chicken when and if it can be had. But malnutrition still? They get diarrhea a lot. They suffer chronic fevers because of the infections down there in the river bottom. Odd that the prime riverfront land should be so undesirable and sick-infested. Tourism will come and drive the barrio squatters out, however. *El Doctor* has pronounced the barrio to be an eyesore. He wants to install hotels and a marina, and trans-plant the people to someplace far away—that is to say, to drive them away and let them go where they will, back to the *campo* where they came from. Father Cela and the oth-ers, Fresa among them, are fighting this uprooting of the rootless, but the government in any case gives nothing to the people to encourage them to stay, and so they must build their own schools and lobby to have water piped in.

* * *

Talking to Fresa, I keep an eye on the parade of people passing the window. I see two girls in midadolescence: One has a deformed face, the left eye enormous and bulging and surrounded by drooping flesh. The other is animated, talk-ing gaily. The girl with the deformed face walks beside her, listening. I try to read her face, which in its deformity is strangely powerful, and filled, I think, with an immense sadness, a kind of monster's gravitas. I detect a bitter intel-ligence. I search to understand the relationship between the two girls. Are they friends? Are they sisters? Could they even be twins? I think of Milan Kundera's conceit (in *The Unbearable Lightness of Being*) that being is divided between heaviness and lightness. And here in the Santo Domingo barrio, the two walk together, Lightness chattering away about something (boyfriends?) and Heaviness profoundly silent. Metaphysical twins.

We travel to lose ego, I suppose. To scrape the ego like the bottom of a boat and make the water run more sleekly past the hull. Or else to perform another sort of bypass on the heart, and make the blood flow more easily through it, the sympathies cleaner and clearer, the humility refurbished. I had a journalist friend once—a woman of melodramatic moral passion—who took her vacations in places like Bangladesh. No Club Med for Gloria.

Years ago, John Kenneth Galbraith, writing under the pseudonymn of McLandress, invented a funny little item of faux sociology called the McLandress Coefficient, which, he said, calculated the length of time that any given public figure could go without thinking about himself. Richard Nixon, as I recall, had a McLandress of about four minutes. My own McLandress for years has been lamentably low (though higher than Nixon's maybe). But travel like Gloria's or Graham Greene's—attentive, solitary travel outside the First World—sends the McLandress up into hours, days.

Travel is also the sovereign remedy for anger—sheer motion ventilating the mind, driving out the poisons that accumulate when one is stagnant. I travel as a form of hiding, an invisibility. The world proceeds as if I did not exist, except as a seeing eye. It is pleasant to float here and there inside a transparent membrane of unimportance.

* * *

I could not take my eyes off Balaguer. Sightless, he surmised everything. He survives by surmising perfectly, sensing, registering all, feeling the minutest vibration of his web. But he will not have surmised me, my eyes upon him, although of course I am of no significance to him anyway.

He sat upon the dais like an ancient irradiating crystal, with mystic powers. Well, Balaguer's powers are not so mystic: How he retains them in such extremities of old age is mystic enough. I watch him with my diseased heart, but I cannot learn anything from him. His secret is perhaps the ordinary one, a hidden equilibrium, will working lucky and cagy in a high wind, air foils, opportunism, reflexes. He will be defeated in the end.

But I thought Balaguer was also driven by something profoundly, traumatically autobiographical—not Rosebud, not a Freudian scene, but rather something to do with pride and slight on a Caribbean island (Prospero's, originally), small enough to be a universe unto itself and therefore small enough to nourish a young man's ambitions to be absolutely powerful, *El Señor.* Or anyway, *caudillo.* I grew up in a different galaxy, the United States, conceived among the shining Misters of the North, white lords consumer. We do not aspire to be God anymore. Now and then someone tries to be Satan.

A speculation: All the black bodies vacuumed out of Africa in the slave trade (from east to west, the bottom side of the triangle of the trade). And now running north, there is another line, this one white: drugs vectoring irresistibly north where they will find their way minutely into the North American veins, bloodstreams, brains, and make a ruin there as surely as the slave trade left its ruin on these islands.

Here everyone speaks of the *narcotraficantes* who use their profits to corrupt every transaction of life even more thoroughly than it had been corrupted before—the little bites *(mordida)* becoming big big bites, the entire judiciary system chewed up, for example—the drug trade evolving as the submerged body of politics (the croc beneath the river's surface), the presidency an adjunct of Colombian dream vegetables and the brisk mercantilism—*imperialismo norteamericano*—itself corrupted, fat in the arteries, shot in the nerves.

The Third World enters the American bloodstream on needles. The Golden Door indeed. The wretched longing.

I drove in downtown Santo Domingo with Bernardo Vega, the intellectual par excellence of the Dominican Republic, author, historian, former chairman of the Central Bank, scion of one of the oldest families on the island. We drove in his BMW sedan toward a Spanish restaurant called Don Pepe, the most expensive place in town.

Don Bernardo is irritated at me for having kept him waiting twenty minutes (I don't blame him). He is the whitest, or the pinkest, man I have seen in months, a tall, handsome patrician with intelligent eyes and commanding presence, and without any trace of any blood except a northern aristo-distillate of European mastery, obviously a bloodline that has been carefully protected on this island for centuries. Don Bernardo wears a gold watch whose bracelet is an unusual clasp of thin gold bands—smart for a hot climate where cloth or leather bands would get sweat-soaked and eventually rot on the wrist. Not Don Bernardo's band, though it gives him a certain Las Vegas flavor, offset by his buttondown white shirt and slouchy though well-tailored trousers.

Don Bernardo stops at a traffic light. The BMW's air conditioning functions well, and he talks ironically through the sound of cool blowing air. Suddenly at his side window appears a very dark-skinned dwarf, a woman with face lumped like a coconut. With fingers short and fat as little cigars she taps on Don Bernardo's window. He considers, finds a coin, brings down his window just enough, and drops it in her hand.

Don Bernardo is the biggest and most beautiful creature in the small pond, a fish of great privilege, smooth and pink. Balaguer has spent a lifetime mucking and bottomfeeding, or anyway, consuming the bottom-feeders, keeping them down on the bottom. Don Bernardo swims brilliantly in the upper layers where the light shines, and he gives off glints of sheen and subtle colors and privilege—smooth pampered boy, even in middle age. He makes me feel like a peasant.

* * *

And in the morning I drive down the Avenue Guzmán toward the sea. The city, like all Third World cities, is now built of a cheap cement that cannot last more than a few years—cement shacks. The old *zona colonial* looks picturesque and tiny, dwarfed by the immense granery across the Ozama River. But the colonial houses were built five hundred years ago, and are the only noble buildings anywhere.

Colonial: *Cristobal Colón—Colón*-i-al: *Columbusism.* The worldwide word and all it meant was born exactly here.

I pass the naval base just where the river meets the sea. It is early morning, and a Dominican sailor, in white swabbie uniform, stands guard alone over the beach: the mystified waiting of life! His face. A crippled dog (hind leg crushed long ago and somehow mended) humps along the Caribbean. A bus in a black cloud of its own diesel. Then, behold, beside the sea, an exercise class of Dominicans, fat people dressed in bright jogging suits, touching their toes in unison.

Bless the day! Bless the morning light! Spray shoots up dreamily when a wave smacks the jagged limestone seawall. The congregated palm-tree trunks are graceful as gi-

raffe necks, giraffes that in this case have extravagant hair-
dos, floppy toppings of fronds.

The anger dissipates in a pure acceptance: self-
important even to think the individual particle of a life, the
molecule emitting energy and light and violence, making
its minute stir here is, at the same time, the center of Emerson's circle, a divinity—so that through the morning as
through the barrio in the evening light (the kite-flying boy,
the girl with the drooping monstrous eyelid) there shines
such suffusing divinity, and the very garbage almost glis-
tens like Don Bernardo's smooth pink face and brainy eyes.

What do I do now? My heart feels sometimes as if it
wants to tighten again, and this time die. I telephone the
States and the connection fires through instantly—so hand-
somely is the Third World wired—and Susan's voice flows
back through the wires, having bounced off satellites, a
stream of articulation like instantaneous invisible skywrit-
ing, wisping words words words, full of their exact actual
colors. We cannot make out the digital fragmentation that
has occurred, or the reassembly, so artful is the techno-sleight
by which she whispers in my ear here, far away.

* * *

My father makes appearances in different forms sometimes. A little of him persists in Balaguer, a trace: something
in the mouth downturned, the eyes in their old-age woe,
that remind me of him before he had his final stroke and
went into that long twilight and finally died.

Balaguer is Agamemnon, *anax androne, defensor fidei,
maistro corruptionis,* mortal impersonation of God. Grand
deathfulness. Cunning survivor. Some say Balaguer is most
like Salazar of Portugal in his last years, except that
Salazar's men in the end were entertaining him with elabo-

rate alternate realities, ruses to make him think he was presiding at state meetings, signing papers, running things as
he always had (who knows?), signing death warrants—
when it was all a charade. Balaguer is on his guard. He is a
parable of will tenacious beyond its natural means. The
arrow, at the end of its trajectory, wills itself to sail on, as I
have sometimes dreamed myself just above gravity, about to
touch ground but somehow by an act of will floating up
again and not exactly soaring but never quite brushing
earth, either.

An old man, playing hide-and-seek with his closest
advisers and servants: Do they try to conceal themselves
from him in the same room? Can he hear them breathing?
Smell them, even? Does he sit long moments in still concentration, listening, waiting? How bitter it must be to
play that game, waiting endless hours at the end of eighty-
seven years, when the fund of time is exhausted, merely to
catch some cunning servant or treacherous crony cheating.

What sleep? After a lifetime of the exhaustions of
sheer alertness—the exertion growing more urgent with
the years—what can he have but half-hour dozes, filled
with fantasies that would slide in and out of the solid world
and float away into shadows, murking off, into dreams of
his sisters, his father's coffin, the men he shot—Trujillo's
bloody uniform as the *caudillo* rises from the dead to belittle
Joaquín and slap him hard across the face and send him into
the interior *campo* to harvest rice knee-deep in the fields,
with black black Haitians.

Then wake and think about an actuality just as alive
with nightmare. What makes a man want to live?

20

The harbor of St. George's, Grenada, used to be the vent of a volcano. It is so deep that the director of tourism thinks it has never been plumbed; unlikely, I guess, but deep enough in any case to accommodate enormous cruise ships in a snug space. The white apparitions rest enigmatically in the harbor like mother ships of the Empire come to an outpost on the edge of the galaxy. The harborside (the *carenage*) is picturesque, like Annapolis with Afro-Caribbean decor. Narrow streets rise from the harbor steeply. They are sun blinded this morning.

Oh woe, the chest is feeling clutchy today, as I ascend the shadeless tropical street, thinking about the scene in *Suddenly Last Summer* when the local boys do something awful to Sebastian. What do they do exactly? Cut off his member, I think. Or what?

Something in any case about dropping dead in a place like this is a primal fear—being far from home, far from help. The health clinic for Grenadians, over on the other

side beyond the harbor, looks primitive enough. The water
is shut off for hours a day all over the island (it is the dry
season). I wouldn't bet on the doctor washing his hands before he slashes open my chest to massage the heart—which
would be an even more dangerous procedure than cutting
off my cock.

I am not feeling well this morning.

Somewhere over in the interior of the island there is a
cinder-block wall painted crudely in English: THANK YOU
AMERICANS FOR LIBERATING US. But beside this greeting I
see an Eighty-second Airborne insignia painted; and the
driver tells me that the Americans, when they were here,
painted the thank-you on the wall—not wishing to leave
much to the locals, I suppose, who could be counted upon
to be ungrateful anyway. The driver says it was the Americans who brought cocaine and crack to the island when they
invaded, so the people are feeling a little rueful about Uncle
Sugar.

Tight-chested and woeful today: I can feel the heart in
its ambush mode, and feel myself angry and afraid, and
everlastingly weary of thinking about the ambush.

How much I am like Balaguer in his blind darkness,
for the heart, like *El Doctor,* beats on in darkness, blindness,
anxiously listening, straining to hear the footsteps and the
breathing of the assassin.

So here I am, kvetching through the spice island of
Reagania, tanning myself among the Afro-serfs. The heart
does feel funny, though. It is so difficult to decode its
moods. I have become ungraciously fatalistic, a snarling
self-pitier of the minor American clerisy, the scribbler tribe.

Some of the trees up in the rain-forest mountains here
have been trained by the wind into postures of a sort of
Japanese crippling, stunted and picturesque, Caribbean
bonsai on the north slopes. Grenada looks like Hawaii

Africanized: volcanic rain forest and beaches, island popu-
lated by Africans and their shambas, the huts and litter and
physical postures of the people perfectly consonant with
West Africa.

Except that everywhere, on streets, in fields, on hills,
in stadiums, in formal games and improvised, the boys are
playing cricket. Cricket, everyone tells me, is the only
thing that everyone agrees upon without the slightest trouble.

But one should not be appeased by either the cricket
or the spices on the air. This is a revolutionary country
where, for a time, they called one another comrade, though
today they have grown sheepish about the eagerness and
náiveté with which they went commie and threw even
friends into the prison on the ridge. They tortured one another for a little while at the beginning of the revolution, in
1979. By the time Leslie Pierre, the newspaper editor
(*Grenada Voice*), got into the People's Jug they had stopped
that and gone to mere small-minded bureaucratic harass-
ment, like telling his wife she could only bring two oranges
a month to the jail, not four.

The Americans came in and spanked the revolutionar-
ies, hard, for all of that, but the lesson was undignified, an
affront to the people, commie or not, and so today, although
they have learned to shut up about politics to foreigners
and promote the place as a tourist spot, that does not mean
they have to like it. Their welcome is grudgingly busi-
nesslike at best—no Bahamian big smile here. Well, if I
had to be nice to Germans all day, the best I could manage
would be a curt formality myself. What do we expect?

Still, Frank Thomas has me about to invest in a bar he
is trying to take over in the native quarter of Grand Anse.
Frank was my driver yesterday in a Ministry of Tourism van
touring the island, and as we talked he told me he needed

$2,000 in order to take over the bar, which has two pool ta-
bles and a counter for dispensing booze.

That is about $800 American. I thought at first he
was running a scam on me that he tries with likely Americans whenever he can—an ambitious scam at that, trying to
get $800 at a crack. Then it occurred to me that he would
surely not try to bilk a writer who comes under the protection of the Ministry of Tourism, which he is working for,
for such a con would be bound to backfire in a major way.
Anyway, I like him.

So I calculate that he is legitimate in his story, although some of the details are difficult to understand (the
present owner is tired and wants someone to take over the
place; Frank's girlfriend could run the bar during the day
when he is working at the ministry). I guess I will not invest after all. I was hallucinating a good deed—and also
having my own private club to come to in Grenada. I could
become the Rick Blaine of the Windward Islands.

Frank and I visited the club after our drive around the
island. It is a plain but pleasant iron-roofed shed, the main
business of the place obviously being pool (twenty-five
cents a game) during the day. One of the tables has a nasty
gouge in the felt, and so the boys playing eight-ball artfully
arrange to play almost the entire game at the other end of
the table—the gouge has been incorporated into the skill of
the game.

The air is heavy with a rainstorm that wants to fall, a
saturated heat, through which an American plays boogie-
woogie on the hotel's grand piano in the midafternoon,
hitting wrong notes now and then that collapse in a heap.

About death, which still spooks around in the sunshine, I am wearily agnostic. My heart has made me a little
old dictator: I am Balaguer, most of all in my isolation, the

heart beating in the dark, and the paranoid waiting for death.

The palm fronds feel the rain coming now. They rustle and wag in the anticipating wind. The wind lifts some of the weight from the air.

Up in the mountains now and then, you smell the spices, especially the nutmeg, which bursts upon you for an instant like a lovely little gift, borne on the air. The people here like to describe themselves as friendly, very friendly, but they are not, particularly; it is rather their island itself that is friendly, and bestows charming natural graces. The people have a cloud in them, not nastiness exactly. But they surely are not very sweet or generous or polite.

Frank has never left the island, he tells me. He is a man of about thirty. The island is twenty-one miles long and twelve miles wide. I could not endure the insularity. The whites who have washed up here are hideous to look at. They look especially bad in this sunshine, among these colors, their flesh turning horrible livid hues. Maybe the ice people should stick to the ice.

Balaguer has a *caudillo* double here: Eric Gairy, leader of the revolt against the British plantocracy years ago, in 1951, when he was barely thirty years old. Now, in the way of the region, Gairy has grown old and corrupt and certain of his divinity—and nearly blind, like Balaguer, vision gone to glaucoma.

It was against Gairy's government that the Maurice Bishop revolution rose in 1979, an exuberant, naïve adventure that lasted until 1983, when the hardest-lining Marxo-Leninized zealots murdered Bishop and eleven of his ministers, lining them up against a wall at Fort George, overlooking the harbor (beautiful view), and giving them the old people's what-for. Maurice Bishop, a charmer and glad-hander of tropical good humor, had not realized quite how hard and dangerous the game in Grenada might become, although he should have known.

Everyone I talk to about the period tells me that the Bishop men, including the ones who killed him, were "drunk with power," or "intoxicated by ideology," as if to say that their behavior, which included cutting off the testicles of some of their countrymen in the Richmond Hill dungeon, was the result of a kind of trance, a wild doctrine frenzy, and therefore obscurely excusable—how could they have known better? They were nice guys, a decent and friendly bunch, but once they were overtaken by ideology and power, they went nuts.

I heard this from a sheepish Castroite revolutionary doctor named Terry Marryshow, a sullen, guilty, defiant Marxist, sort of, still, who told me in his airless office in the middle of the afternoon, with the test matches on the snowy TV from Guyana, that the People wanted the Program of the Revolution, but that things somehow got out of hand . . . and well, mistakes were made.

I started getting angry and arguing with him, but then I saw that actually, he was, in a sense, sort of right, and Grenada was not my country—I was a guest. And anyway, it would be useless, and rubbing it in, to argue the idiocy of Marxism while the poor man was still sitting in its smoking messy wreckage, sobbing over his dream. Dr. Marryshow looked at me with a whipped-dog expression. At least he was in Cuba studying medicine in 1983, when the intoxicated thugs executed Bishop.

I heard the same words ("intoxicated with ideology, drunk with power") from Winston Whyte, a former member of parliament who was thrown in jail as a counterrevolutionary in 1979 and stayed there for four years.

Winston Whyte is a tall, large man of majestic carriage. His complexion is lighter than those of most Grenadians—

a dark *café au lait*—and his eyes are light green-brown. His voice is deep, and he has the deep official laugh of the public man, his laugh being more a ceremony than a spontaneity.

We were to have had dinner at my hotel at 7:30. I waited for him in the lobby until 8:15, and then gave up and went to the dining room alone, assuming that my contact had gotten the wrong night or that Whyte had simply forgotten.

When I was halfway through my dinner, Whyte appeared at my table, full of apologies. He said that he had been up in St. Patrick's parish in the north of the island for a St. Patrick's Week celebration (the Grenadians take St. Patrick's Day very seriously), and an overenthusiastic young man had crashed into the back of his car and made a serious mess of it.

Whyte and I talked for two hours in the dining room, and then arranged to meet the next morning at eight, so that he could drive me around the island and show me the place. We wandered around Grenada for four hours, Whyte driving his Toyota Grenadian style: Grenadian drivers thread themselves along the narrow, winding, and left-driving roads with a kind of reckless precision, and they have a way of buzzing dangerously close to pedestrians, as if polishing the car on the seat of someone's pants in passing. I imagined dozens of people a year being killed in this way, but apparently they are not. (The worst traffic accident in recent memory occurred on the northbound west coast road, when a sixty-ton rock, loosened by rains, rolled down a hillside and crushed a bus containing nine people, killing all instantly: a one-in-a-million shot, said Winston.)

Grenada is a small island, and yet Grenadians distinguish between "north people," like Winston, and south people—those who live and work around St. George's and

Grand Anse, where the tourists are concentrated. North people, says Winston, tend to be clannish in the rural way. South people are more a mix, presumably more cosmopolitan.

Grenada is a green and jewelly island that might be improved by a First World sanitation department. The people tend to drop their trash where it suits them and the result, as usual, is a casual spoilation—trash and garbage permitted to fall where it likes, since it is as much a part of nature as coconut shells or fish carcasses or dead cats, all part of the give-and-take. At one bend in the road, inland at the foot of a steep volcanic slope, is a large, deep, noisome landfill, which is the island's major concession, I gather, to the idea of tidying up. Along the road outside of St. Patrick's, Winston braked the car and shouted to a tall, thin man in a baseball hat, who, recognizing Winston, broke into a bright grin. This, Winston told me, was "Kitty Hawk," who had been jailed in the cell next to his for a couple of years. Winston remembered the last morning of their imprisonment, when in their dungeon cells they heard eruptions of gunfire and bombs above them. They did not know what the guns meant. They had been told earlier that Maurice Bishop and his ministers had been executed, but that was all.

When the gunfire and bombs began, the prison guards fled, and so Winston and the other prisoners were left alone, locked in, to listen to the explosions and wonder what they meant. Leslie Pierre, the editor of the *Grenada Voice,* was in the cell with Winston, and Winston said Leslie was very brave. "You don't want a man in a situation like that to start breaking up and blubbering," said Winston.

Kitty Hawk had been trained in Cuba as an antiaircraft gunner. He had supported the revolution in its early days, but when the thugs began getting thuglike and arresting Grenadians, Kitty Hawk complained, and ended up in jail with Winston and the others.

Now Kitty Hawk listened to the gunfire. He knew the sound of AK-47s, the assault rifles that the revolutionary army used. These gunshots sounded higher-pitched and faster than AKs. Kitty Hawk thought for a moment and then yelled down the corridor of dungeon cells, "I think they Americans."

Winston told me that he survived in jail by turning inward. He had various tricks. An officer of the guard smuggled to him a ballpoint-pen refill, and with it Winston drew faces on the wall, with which he held conversations. He wrote poetry on toilet paper. Spiritual things. He came to believe that only the spirit can protect a man in such circumstances. "You cannot look outward when you are there," he said. "You must look inward. You will be amazed what strength you can find there. You either find the strength or you go crazy."

I thought that my father must have played internal mental prison games when he was in the dungeon. It is surely solitary confinement and an equally terrible loneliness, even worse perhaps, since it is more surely death row. Winston and the others for a time had a camaraderie—and their standards of machismo to measure up to, their codes.

I have wondered what it is like to die by politics, and whether preferable in some way—a higher fate, if that is a consideration to the one fated to die. I do not know.

The Americans came down out of the sky, blazing away in blazing sun, shooting up the resort-gone-communist. *Deus ex machina* again, and Winston and all the others were saved.

Actually, Winston and a few of his friends had an early salvation. Bernard Diederich, a stringer for *Time* magazine and old hand at the Caribbean and Latin America, had made his way by small boat to Grenada, and talked his way through the revolutionary soldiers, shouting hardy Marxist slogans and calling everyone comrade. And then he showed up at the jail, confronted whatever revolutionary officer of the guard remained there, and demanded that the journalists be liberated. Winston, a sometime radio journalist, qualified, and walked out of jail, with Diederich, for the first time in four years.

Winston told me that the revolution engaged in torture eventually as a matter of course. I am amazed at people in so small a place turning upon one another so savagely—amazed as well that when the story was over, the jailed and the jailers were able to walk the same streets and even to greet one another.

Winston said they tried to get him to make a radio broadcast in which he supported the revolution. They had learned a trick from the Chinese or the Cubans. They used little massage hammers to tap lightly lightly lightly on the body here and there, a pleasant effect at first. But after half an hour, the tapping began to produce shooting nerve shocks, stabs of electricity through the system. "I have never felt worse pain in my life—amazing. You thought at first they were trying to do something nice."

They meet on the street: the ex-prisoners, who number 3,112, and the jailers. They cannot help it, the island is so small. They are pleasant to one another, it seems. Whether this is denial or forgiveness I cannot tell.

But Winston is surely right about the Americans. They, it seems, wanted to get in quickly and get out as soon as possible, and did not go through the process, or did not allow the process that might have sorted out and settled the mess, and satisfied some sense of justice.

They did not, for example, permit the jailers and murderers of the revolution to be tried for treason, as they should have been. The Americans wanted everything to be nice again and go back to normal, be patched over.

But the sore festers, the communists have started putting up their red-dot flags again at intersections up north, and everyone now talks with a certain nostalgia about the tragedy of Maurice Bishop's death and certain charms the revolution may have had that are lost now in these suspended, unsatisfactory days after the Americans, with their enormous wealth and their short attention span, went away, abandoned the island, and left it uneasily, guiltily, strangely stewing in the unresolved outcome of the revolution.

Winston is angry at the American insensitivity—a word he uses repeatedly. He is hurt. On the other hand, he says that prison mellowed him—perhaps mellowed him too much, cost him something of his fire, his edge, his will to win. He wants to be prime minister, but cannot challenge Gairy, who has something of the same constituency. Whyte fears he himself has gone soft. And at ten-thirty in the morning, we stop at a house overlooking the beautiful volcanic islands ranging north from Grenada, a house owned by a retired pilot. And Winston accepts a scotch and water from him, "a small libation," as he unexpectedly says, sounding for an instant like W. C. Fields.

21

The wolfish mulatto Rastaman talked about Jesus all the way in from the airport. He had a beautiful skin, a golden color, and extravagantly dreadlocked and gathered Afro-hair that was nonetheless shot through with gold as well. His profile was sharp and animal: high cheekbones, sharp woodland nose, and his eyes were a gray-green that held the light the way that certain gemstones do, as if they had been invested centuries ago with a light that could not escape but remained there, metastable, hovering in the stone like a soul.

The Rastaman's eyes were like that. But he was at some pains to tell me he was not a Rastaman at all: rather, a follower of Jesus, though of no organized church. He claimed them all, all Christian worships.

Barbados is a clockwork of an island compared to the others, a blackface version of the whitest Englishness, Westminster in government and law, a civil society that is as cricket-crazy as Grenada but crisp and provident and mature in sanitation and orderliness in ways some other Caribbean islands have barely begun to explore.

For all that, the evident pride among the people, the more-British-than-British Anglicism, this sceptered isle of starched sun people has an underboil of race and racial indignation. The talk now is that the whites of the island own too much of it, too many of the businesses, and that they are an arrogant ruling class, domineering, arrogant, undemocratic.

The mulatto driver who brought me in from the airport expatiated on this theme all the way to the hotel on the south coast, pausing now and then to explain that he did not allow this arrogance of the white ruling class to ruin his day, which was always a delight now that he was back in Barbados. He had seen New York, he had worked in London: They only made him appreciate what he had right here, in Paradise, where the weather is always the same—no seasons: *beau-tee-ful, mon.* Justin has come down from New York to spend a few days of his spring vacation with me. The hotel we find ourselves in is a perfect surprise for our purposes: a large family resort spread over several acres with pools and beach and lots of kids down from the States and from Canada and Europe, so that Justin is pleased, and so am I, happier than I have been in a long time, a pure lift.

We spend hours on the beach, the surf boiling in from Venezuela, churning sand and sea vegetables and coral bits in to shore and scaring me a little with its power. There are all kinds of warning signs as you come onto the sand: NO LIFEGUARD, DON'T GO IN OVER YOUR DEPTH. Treacherous currents are at work even when the water seems calm.

The power of the sea always impresses me when I feel it around me—the moon-power pulling. The force startles me—something I had half-forgotten. I interpose myself between Justin and the rollers booming: He respects the sea's power as well and stays well within the white surf line, never going out to try to catch them as they curl to break but rather riding in on the boil. It is ride enough. The waves carry him and his Boogie board fast up the sand and leave him high and gasping as they recede.

Peaceful evening now. Justin is on the balcony of the hotel room, reading with a Walkman plugged into his ears.

I have become endlessly conscious of race and think about it all the time as I walk around Barbados. I have been reading so much of the slave history and with it, a Penguin book of Caribbean verse. The business of slavery and race permeates everything, even the crisp linen Britishism here— the Brit-fetish.

Still, Barbados fell upon an admirable secret piece of luck. The Britishism conferred upon the descendants of slaves an indispensable thing, the thing precisely that slavery had deprived them of: dignity. With the British dignity, which the Barbadians absorbed and eventually came to cherish and take pride in, there came an entire universe of ceremony, tradition, majesty even: They made the tradition sufficiently their own not to make too much of an issue over the fact that it belonged indeed to the white men who had been precisely the source of misery and slavery.

And yet now, my wolf-mulatto with the golden hair, buccaneer for Jesus at the moment, expresses the undercurrent anger that is evidently cracking through the postimperial veneer: race again, privilege again, the old crimes of which the Britishized ritual of the island has been such a colorful denial. But I suspect the British manners now internalized in the African descendants will prevail over the anger. My guess is that Barbadian pride at being so superior to other West Indian and Caribbean islands will quiet black anger at Barbadian whites. For a public display of anger would expose Barbadians as being no better after all—and a great deal more pretentious—than other slave-descended islanders. So I guess a certain vanity will keep Barbados and its people from racial disorder, which is, after all, bad form.

* * *

A mint green translucent lizard crosses the scallop-shell light fixture on the wall of the balcony, like an exquisite reptile on the face of the moon. A ceiling fan beats the humid, warm air.

Surely the ceiling fan is the most civilized invention to come to the tropics. It touches some memory in me, a nostalgia for Key West in the forties when I was a child there. The fan makes palpable air pulse, more palpable in the stirring but nonetheless welcome, for something has made something happen, which is enough to be a genius of the tropics.

I harbor a small cult memory of the ceiling fan, and love it as a relic of some sacred (to me) time. The beating of the fan and the pulsing of the Caribbean this afternoon make something of the same pulse in the soul, a stirring and revolving: flavorsome memories, the sea bright and salty and the fanned air segmented and sensual, seeming to breathe in some erotic, female way.

The sea comes in carrying great loads of greenery, torn, I suppose, from somewhere up the coast—big-leafed seaweed. Your swimming trunks wind up full of this kelpish, kaley vegetation: The jock is full of salad from rolling in the surf.

I coax Justin out of the waves finally, after hours there that have left our hands and fingers shriveled. We shower in warm spigot water at the edge of the beach to get the sand off. He is still fairly white despite the murdering sun: Since he is such a pale Caucasian by nature, we slather him triple-thick with forty-five-factor sunblock before he ventures under the rays. Now only an underlayer of pink is starting. My own face, despite some block, is lobsterish.

The birds here are unafraid. Dowager doves approach and go about their business, poking and foraging, ladies of the garden club, without glancing aside at me, three feet away. Magnificent symmetrically stemmed traveler palms make giant fans. Condensed milk in the coffee, a thick, vaguely rotten sweetness.

Perhaps the birds are merely the usual bright resort crumb-hunters, bold as vervet monkeys to snatch from the tourists. The doves parade around me on the grass, on a browse, their heads at each step stitching the air like a slow sewing machine.

Are there poisonous spiders or snakes? My guess is that they have been gardened out of the place long ago. There is, of course, the sepsis of race and the ultraviolet rays of the sun. But against each, it is possible to wear protection, seek a civilized shade, be prudent. It is not true that the hate, the evil of history, must fester down below until at last it rises and explodes into violence and death and annihilation. Given enough time, perhaps even I could find such principles of prudence in myself—the resources of a civilized adult.

The holocaust of slavery is never far, even in "Little England." Roxanne Gibbs, the president of the newspaper *The Nation,* is a breezy New Woman, born in Guyana, career female brisk enough for New York or London. She looks like a black anchorwoman at a local American television station, the sort who would make banter with the weatherman about all that rain.

The Barbadians—*Bajans*—it may be, do not dwell

upon the slave days, but when I bring up the subject she matter-of-factly makes this point: "You know, the Jews spend millions of dollars publicizing the Holocaust, and they never let you forget it for a moment. They are always saying, 'Never Again!' and 'Never forget!' But when blacks mention slavery, we are immediately accused of being racists."

The blacks in Barbados say that the whites are exclusive, and keep to themselves. But, as Delisle Worrell, the (black) deputy director of the Central Bank, tells me, "The blacks never invite the whites to come to their homes. As the overwhelming majority, the blacks should take some initiative in that social direction. But each side sticks to itself, and each side blames the other for exclusivity."

Five percent of the population is white. And this minority controls about 20 percent of the capital assets of Barbados. The way it happens: Black folklore believes it is considerably more than that, believes in fact that the little coterie of whites (like the Elders of Zion, no doubt) controls the economy entirely, which is of course nonsense.

The interesting thing to me is that these minority whites, many of them millionaires many times over, it is true, are the descendants of the indentured white servants who began on Barbados two hundred years ago, living in the undesirable jungle-scrub center of the island—ascendant white trash. It is also interesting that, according to Worrell, the old sugar operations that were the heart of the "plantocracy" have mostly gone bankrupt.

Eventually, of course, the outrage of the Past is abstracted out of itself, though vividly enough, becoming a story, an object, an alienated thing.

And it requires an effort of imagination to reconnect to it, though from time to time, the past revisits unbidden, arrives like a drunken father in the middle of the night, when you may not have seen him for years and years. It's him, all right, but horrifyingly disintegrated and wild, himself (the past, the grief) and unrecognizable as well. Huck's Pap!

So I surmise the past of the plantations returns in that way. It is something very near the surface, summoned, I am sure, by a word, a tone of voice, a facial expression, a triggering, something in the corner of the eye, the condescension of a true half turn—the black detonations of memory.

I wish that I understood forgiveness. I suppose I do not entirely believe in it, either in a historical or a physical sense. Neither history nor the human body is that advertant or masterful. Neither can command an onset of grace, can say, "I have understood, or perhaps not understood, but anyway, I forgive." I suspect that both a wronged race and a heart susceptible to attack have to be tricked somehow into a new habit that will be the equivalent of forgiveness—will have its therapeutic effect without being theologically pure, for few of us are capable of such saintliness or such blessings.

On the other hand, what is it but grace that keeps us from being eaten to death, from the inside, by hatred? What abundances of street-level daily, hourly forgiveness are required to sustain a black forbearance? Or is it merely forgetfulness—distraction, the habit of one's own life?

The memory of violence, we know, is a blighting thing, a killer of environmental scope, like Dutch elm disease or acid rain. The memory of humiliation works something like the same effect, though with a different corrosive. At the same time violence is always a humiliation, and humiliation a kind of violence: self-same transfixing blow to the skull. Submission and dependency institutionalize the blow, make it permanent.

Now in a tourist enclave the blacks, ex–field hands,

tend the white folks at table and poolside and wash the linens, and who can object to that? Good money, surely, better than the alternative.

The deputy director of the Central Bank takes me to lunch at an elegant seaside hotel restaurant, just above a beautiful surf that breaks so loudly and delightfully I can hardly hear his disquisitions, which rise and fall in a Barbadian lilt that is curiously enghosted by a Scottish burr.

Dr. Delisle Worrell is a small and scholarly man. He has just introduced me to something called "melts," which are flying-fish roe, sautéed and served on toast, and explained that the dolphin here is quite good ("It is sometimes called mahimahi elsewhere").

Dr. Worrell says, "I believe that things evolve. Things change."

We have been talking about the anger of Barbadians who think a white ruling class excludes them. Worrell means: Once we were slaves here, now we have a prospering middle class. The old plantocracy is bankrupt mostly, it is true some powerful white families control a lot of money (though it really is only 20 percent of the economy) and blacks are every day becoming wealthier, better educated, and more in control of their island. Which is to say: Things evolve. And below the surface of his text I hear the message that it is immature and rather stupid, though understandable enough, to institutionalize the grievances of long ago—counterproductive, the economist implies, to worship the angers.

(My heart muscle, that valiant long-suffering dogface, soldiering away in the worst of conditions, looks up and nods agreement.)

Or here is Dr. Henry Fraser, a white Barbadian married to a black woman; he is the head of the island's Heritage Trust, professor of medicine at the University of the

West Indies, internist and pharmacologist at Queen Eliza-
beth Hospital, father of a handsome *café au lait* child whose
picture I see framed in the doctor's office.

Things evolve. The poor whites are millionaires. The
slaves have air conditioning and Japanese cars. My primitive raving ape's heart has million-dollar surgeon's tubing,
stainless sluiceways, a Chunnel to connect my Dover and
Calais.

The things-change principle has given me a second
chance and then a third chance, a fact that may even teach
me gratitude.

The United States is a vast, complex, overbearing
presence above the islands. The people have such elaborate
ties to the United States now, have so many relatives working and living there, so many remittance checks pouring
the Yankee dollar south by gravity feed, that grievance and
hostility are intertwined now with inextricable dependence.
The islanders own a significant piece of America and its future, and yet they chafe and snarl under the Yankee domi-
nations—real and sometimes imagined. They use the word
insensitivity often when talking to an American; the United
States and its leaders are "insensitive" to the Caribbean, to
its people and cultures. Insensitivity means, essentially, that
Americans pay far too little attention to the islands, except,
as in the case of Grenada, or Cuba, when American strategic
interests are judged to be involved, in which cases the
Americans mobilize their attention for a little while. And
then they drift off, the great American power and money
dreamily floating away, like Toad of Toad Hall finding a
new enthusiasm.

But of course a man might argue that the attention of
American money is the only attention that matters. Might
argue further that the American insensitivity—a sort of
big-money obliviousness—is precisely what permits

Caribbean peoples to gain far more from Americans than they could ever acquire from a scrupulously polite but vigilant big neighbor. After all, the Caribbeans, by the millions, have literally entered into the very American bloodstream: into the American cities, families, future. From America each month, immense infusions.

Well, the Caribbeans see it that way, and do not see it. Any subservience is resentful, bruised. The present dependence is constructed upon the fantastically bitter ground of slavery, a Holocaust and *ne plus ultra*. The centuries of slavery make the Palestinian *nakba* seem a minor interlude, though in its damage to the heart, of course (which is the lastingly important thing), it was not.

Every so often life takes a bite out of you. The bite hurts. Something is lost that is impossible to get back.

But there is compensation. The experience of the loss teaches something, if you pay attention. And everything that it has to teach is lesson and preparation for the Big Bite. Which comes later.

So it is fatuous to speak of recovery. As if what had been done could in time be undone. There is the famous swaggering Hemingway line about how the bones, when they mend, are stronger in the broken places. I doubt that, and suspect that they are, maybe, crazier in the broken places. You break your heart, you stay a little cracked.

But there is a sweeter sense of it. Justin is now sleeping in the roll-away bed they brought to our room, and the ceiling fan propellers soundlessly. I sit on the balcony and a dove-sized bird colored an astonishing dark dark pink lands here with button-bead eyes. Doves coo.

Justin awakened me at four in the morning to say that his ear hurt. We decided eventually it was not an ear infection but probably water that got in there when we were rolling in the surf yesterday before we came back to the room to change and then went to play eight-ball on the game-room pool table before dinner and the amiably bogus firestick limbo performances, from which we eventually retreated across the hotel grounds, followed by the Canadian grizzly bear in Bermuda shorts who had drunk too much to make sense or walk straight, and who would pause long seconds among the palms, swaying in the wind of his drunkenness and oblivious as a coconut.

Justin wakes to tell me, "Hey, Dad, I had a dream and in it you were doing all sorts of cool things. I mean acting cool." I understand the insult well enough and reply, "No kidding. I had a dream that you were actually smart. I had another dream that you had friends."

Justin: "Amazing. Well, in my dream, you weren't short and fat anymore. And you knew how to write."

A Barbadian woman brings a pot of coffee to the door. She wears a deep blue dress of surprisingly formal cut, and against her very black skin the color makes a tropical-electric effect, like one of those stunning flowers whose colors laser into a deeper layer of the retina, or one of those reef fish of such vividness and exactitude they seem a fancier order of creation.

* * *

I suspect that time's schedule of recovery is longer than the individual life, and that each holocaust and *nakba* (from an individual violent childhood, for example, to the attempted extinction of a race) requires more time to mend than an individual can give to the mending. So we must hope, I suppose, for the slower eventual workings of grace.

* * *

In Harrison's Cave in the middle of the island, Justin and I descend in an electric tramcar into the limestone coral, a precise Barbadian tourist spiel uncoiling, the tour guide using a flashlight to signal the hidden wall-lights on and off—the tunnel to our rear vanishing in darkness, that immediately in front coming on with stage lights.

All around is the sound of splashing, echoing water, which permeates the filtering rocks and flows with an astonishing clarity over the sinuous arabesques of ridge formations.

But now, as we enter an enormous illuminated chamber, it dawns upon the entire tour-tram simultaneously that they have gone underground into the secret genital capital of the world. The stalagmites rising from the floors of the grottoes form an astonishing forest of erect penises—all sizes, all shapes—but so unmistakably, hilariously phallic that this chamber and the other rooms of the cave seem a dick-shrine of some kind, cocks rising out of the cave floor with a blind groping urgency, some still half-flaccid, stubby, others fully there and ready, foregathered for some fertility work, some ceremony of phallicism.

The lady tour guide chirps on through the limestone tunnels about the limestone formations and the speliologists. I am touched at the ecclesiastical comparisons shot through her text: One little cave is called "the altar"; a great hall of vigorously alert hard-ons was dubbed "the cathedral."

Do the others in the tram react as I? It would have taken a supernatural gift for denial to miss this assemblage of subterranean pornography. And then I began to see the cavern's complementary genital theme—the vaginal tunnels, rendered pretty fiercely *dentata* by the stalactites needling from the ceilings.

This cavern was so vividly correct in its detail work—

swollen veins on the limestone penises, for example—that the entire scene underground there came to seem a secret chamber of the brain where sexual images generate, a well-spring and warehouse of dark, shining, dripping, out-of-time lurking in a curatorial womb of earth.

I was tempted to make raucous remarks to Justin in the midst of this, but thought on balance, as a father, that the imagery of such graphic arousal might be disturbing to a twelve-year-old. I let it pass. That he did not make the raucous remarks himself was touching evidence of his remaining boyishness in these matters.

When we left the cave, we pressed on to the Atlantic coast of the island, and sweeping down out of Scottish hills (they call the district "Scotland" and it looks that way until you come up close to the palms and bananas), we saw an expanse of wild beach under a slow-motion assault of combers. Resting upon the beach sand, like Easter Island heads, were enormous dark gray coral boulders. Their bottom margins had been eaten away by the action of the waves. Some of the giant rocks stood upon mere stems (comparatively) like primeval rock toadstools. They hinted at some enigmatic meaning.

As with the absurd subterranean galleries, the giant rocks suggested that they had been carved thus, and placed there, facing the Atlantic (all the way to Africa from here, going east on a sightline). The boulders predated the seventeenth-century settlements and the first slaveships, and thus would have greeted both with the same gravid power and silence.

They looked like gods to me, all right; not hostile necessarily, but strong. The Bajan Shinto. Would they have frightened the arriving planter class? Impressed them? Would the slaves have seen the rock gods at all? When did the slaves come up on deck to see the land they had been kidnapped to? If they were brought up for air and saw the god-boulders, did they recognize them, and think they were a promise of some kind? Or maybe only a warning?

The sugarcane is seven feet tall. The Bajans harvest it with machetes and haul it to a refinery where it gets chopped and boiled until it comes out raw crystal, like the sweet coarse sand that sits before me now in a stainless bowl.

* * *

It is evening, and a thousand bats are out, wild-flying against the sunset—chaotic, erratic flap-and-dip flight, darting and indecipherable, somewhere between a joyous puppy-frisking exuberance (sunset celebration, maybe) and a lunacy (it is indeed full moon tonight, though it is not yet in sight). What astonishes me is the bats' speed, and the total silence of their screwball dogfighting.

I have been thinking about the ice fellas who drink themselves to death in the tropics. The temptation seems strong here. They yield to an undertow, go with it, slide out to sea.

I begin to understand Hemingway more sympathetically than I have before. He would have been better off if he had started drinking again, seriously, as he had done all his adult life. Taking that away from him may have killed him—that and the electric-shock treatments, and most of all the knowledge that his mind had gone and he simply could not write anymore, or think anymore. He tried to walk into the propeller of the small plane when they stopped to refuel on the way back to Ketchum, Idaho. I made some subliminal connection the night Sherman's father nearly stuck her head into the hotel's ceiling fan.

Hemingway fondled the shotgun several times in the

house, and someone had to take it gently away from him. It is a form of darkness; William Styron called it *Darkness Visible.* I disbelieved Styron's book in some sense, for he wrote that when he broke spontaneously out of his depression, he had a dream about young girls dancing. Reading that, for the first time in his book, my reliable detector began to ring and ring, its sirens wailed, its red lights flashed.

How literary a depression, down in the dumps with giants today. The mint green lizard ventures forth, slim and translucent; his alert and purposeful little perfection makes me feel by comparison a slovenly and overextended, overelaborate malfunctioning item, like a Soviet limousine, a giant *nomenklatura* Zil, a drunken Slavic stab at precision. I remove my wristwatch and press my index fingertip to my wrist. There it is: The animal is still pumping, quietly, in the dark.

22

Justin and I flew up from Barbados—hot bright sun, calypso colors, as they call them—and landed, at night, in a cold New York drizzle, the winter still hanging on, like a Stalinist regime.

At the end of March, the farm was patched with snow, the ponds were covered with ice so tenacious that it would take days of warm sun, the temperature in the fifties and sixties, before it melted. The ice had been two feet thick, and now, with the coming of spring (a labor so long and difficult I felt as if my trip to the Caribbean—my own solution—had been a kind of a cesarean section), turned to a minutely honeycombed mush.

Easter has come at last. The light has the sweet thinness of early spring, an iron-whisk gray touched with the lightest rumor of budding, a promise of green.

On the old pond, the shallower one, the ice has receded halfway across, and when I peer into the water on the melted side, through a transparent membrane of skim ice, I see the dense mess (mud, weeds, the soup still icy cold) that will, when warmed a little, come alive with its thousand intricate systems of life: fish, snakes, all the busy, intense creatures.

I stand on the bank in the parsimonious light, my feet sinking into the squish (subsiding snows have left the earth saturated) and watching the pond bottom, the first motion of the season: A salamander skitters, dark against the mud.

The deer scats have begun to change from their winter to their summer consistency, have grown blacker and more pellety. The saturated field grasses blow bedraggled with wet, and down on the lower levels, toward the stream bed, they lie in heavy tussocks, swampy. The peeper frogs sing in what must be sheer delight, and over the peeping, make a chatty-clattering rackety noise I take to be a mating sound. The first birds—bluebirds, jays—are calling, and overhead the two resident hawks, husband and wife, work the air currents, one of them now motionless above me except for slight lateral adjustments.

Justin and I set off for an hour's drive before our Easter dinner. We descend into the Harlem Valley and then veer off eastward onto Route 41, through the farm country toward South Amenia and the Connecticut border.

The air is chilly, and the midafternoon holds the lovely purity of early spring—redemption light.

Justin and I are happy, talking. The cows in the fields around us hang muzzles to the first early grazing; their lips can touch the ground after so many months of blizzard.

As we approach the bridge over the Ten Mile River, we see flashing lights and a rescue-squad truck. I decide that the farmhouse beyond the bridge has had a fire, although I cannot see smoke.

But as we cross the bridge, a half dozen people are

running frantically, with a purposeful panic. Their hectic eyes scan the swift brown water below the bridge.

I park the Jeep at the other end of the bridge. We run back toward the river and see, for the first time, black skid marks leaving the highway approaching the bridge, see a small tree smashed down, the grass beside the skid marks littered with long-necked beer bottles that have flown out of a cardboard carton, which in turn has flown out of something else; the skid marks end on a little rise ten yards from the river, and the eye follows the trajectory the hurtling car would have taken, and reckons the spot in the trackless little river where the car would have vanished.

I say to Justin, "Oh, honey, I think this is going to be bad," using a baby endearment he is too old for, I want to shield him from it.

Nonetheless we stay.

Rescue squad workers and police come screaming in from both directions and leave their vehicles at haphazard angles.

A heavy rescue truck starts down across grass toward the river bank, and immediately (like an animal burrowing) digs itself into the ground well below its wheel hubs and subsides heavily there, big tires churning up wet black soil, the driver's face contorted in his ignominy.

The rescue workers think that two people, possibly three, are trapped in the car, which is invisible beneath the muddy soiled surface of the river.

The rescuers, working fast, improvising, back a tow truck to the edge of the middle of the bridge, and one alarmingly fat man (red-faced from exertion and, I think, possibly from drinking) flaps into the icy water from the near bank and, diving, manages to attach a cable to the drowned car. They winch the car's back end up partway. It emerges from the water like a great dead fish.

The car is bright red—a Saab convertible.

More men dive into the water. I think surely they will get hypothermia, turn blue. One of them goes underwater and comes up screaming that he needs a fucking knife to cut the fucking seat belt off the guy.

It takes long moments to find a knife. I finger the lockback deer knife in my pocket, but I think I am too far away to offer it. (Or do I watch all this with a journalist's uninvolvement, as if it were a drama above which I hover, invisible and detached?)

When the body comes out, a man's, it has been in the water for half an hour. It looks lifeless and where the shirt is pulled up from the fat belly, the flesh is bloaty bluish, and the head lolls. I cannot see the eyes.

The rescuers pound CPR until six of them come jouncing quickstep down the grass hill, past the beached-whale rescue truck, carrying a plastic stretcher that looks like a child's sled, and they horse the fat limp body on, and the six of them jounce hurryhurry back up the hill past Justin and me and the other onlookers to an ambulance, which swallows the man as the whale swallowed Jonah (whale all white with flashing lights and red crosses) and wails away toward the Sharon Hospital.

Then the rescue turns toward the other body or bodies below the surface. They cut another body loose, this one a woman. Pound CPR upon her, but seem less eager this time with a stretcher, as if they know that she is gone. But they bring blankets and wrap her in them.

I say to Justin, "Maybe the water was so cold it froze her fast enough to save her. You know those cases where a kid falls into a skating pond and stays down an hour and they bring him back to life?"

(And something of that kind happened. The woman was revived, we found out later. Only to die not long after that. All of those moments—half an hour or more—she had been under. An air pocket in the car, perhaps? But what, then, had killed her?)

I censure myself for keeping Justin there to watch all of this, but I did so for half-good reasons that were only slightly contaminated by my own morbid curiosity (which was of course matched by Justin's).

The beer bottles beside the skid marks at the place where the car left the earth and flew into the river seemed to me such a succinctly indelible lesson about drunk driving that I could not resist allowing the image to sink into Justin's mind. I had driven enough while drunk when I was younger to wince at the thought of how little inattention it would have taken (that familiar boozy looseness, that veering of the eyeballs, the hilarity with numb gaps in it) to have done just this and been down there in the Ten Mile River. It happened so flash-quick: hilarity then death.

The impact of hitting the tree must have sucked all the beer bottles out of the car and onto the grass, like an airlock effect—such a neat extraction and display of the evidence, as if they had signed a last-second legal form explaining their deaths and exonerating all except the selfsame drinkers bubbling to the bottom there.

The elaborate ceremonies of fathers and sons and cars: My father, if he had been drinking, drove with a sort of blazing deftness, far too fast through heavy traffic, but with the drinker's fluency of motion, his reflexes still just good enough to connect eye to hand with an unmediated elegance. Once when he lived in Yonkers during the sixties and I was home from college, he drove us out South Broadway from the city.

He had been drinking at Hurley's bar in Rockefeller Center after his work. I met him there and watched him sluice down a couple of double vodkas in his rapid, easeful way, his eyes dancing with a bad-boy merriment as he did it, glass upended. Then on South Broadway he hurtled weaving through the traffic at fifty or sixty miles per hour: alcohol in his blood firing directly off the spark plugs.

It was an impressive and horrifying thing to watch him drive when drunk—impressive because he was so good at it, could shave so close and not hit, could speed so seamlessly. But my younger brothers and sisters told me that there were times, later on, when he tried it (a harrowing drive back from Newark Airport once in the late seventies, after his second wife had died) and was virtually out of control, bouncing off the median curb.

I do not think he did this often. He was not a habitual drunk or drunken driver. But it may have been a blessing he did not kill someone.

The red Saab hung, half in the Ten Mile River, from the hook of the tow truck, and the bodies came out, first one and then the second. The rescue men thought a third body might have been thrown out of the car and might have drifted down the swift river. Now firemen walked far down the river, looking. From the bank, Justin and I could see, snagged on a tree branch in the water, a denim jacket that the rescue men had peeled off the first body when it came out of the car.

My father came to me again in a dream. He showed me again the same humiliating house, the one I have dreamed about a thousand times, his house surely, falling apart, squalid, this one with rooms connected by gangplanks nailed together perilously and bouncing as one walked across them.

In one part of the house, a filling station had once been located; the gas pumps were now yanked out and left holes in the concrete floor like those in the gum when teeth are pulled. Calvin Trillin, the *New Yorker* magazine writer,

came to the house—it was a Sunday—along with an elaborate cricket team that he had assembled, recruited among
New York writers. They played cricket with great ceremony in a courtyard in the middle of my father's falling-
down house, and commented now and then, under their
breath, upon the shabby condition of the place. I stood to
one side of the cricket game with an intense sense of humiliation, although in the dream, dreaming, I congratulated
myself on understanding the rules of cricket for the first
time.

Death elides with humiliation. Why not? What is
more embarrassing than the disintegration of death? Humiliation is a sort of intermediate death, a rehearsal for it.
When I was four years old, some soldiers speeding out Benning Road in Washington one morning flew out of control
and hit the tree across the street a terrible blow (which left
a vivid scar on the tree) and now they lay dead on the grass,
their bodies covered with blankets. The air smelled of acrid
acids, the internal car fluids, death.

And now these in the red Saab: To be fogbound in the
bright Easter light—flying in such a capsule of violence
and sinking into dark water to die—seemed a harsh parable, and I was moved by its clarity.

23

It is reluctantly turning spring, early April now. The ground is sodden and squishy with snowmelt, the lower fields of the farm a virtual swamp, the earth saturated and the hay grass standing in tussocks, like little islands. Its color is a bleached-out straw, yet here and there, a little higher up the hill, I see a scattering of emerald, the first green flame. It should be a rich summer, later on, with such an abundance of water-soak.

No point in following the grief, I conclude, after everything. Grief makes you sick, the grief of the past, and pursuing it too long, obsessively, turns the disease chronic, disabling.

How cagily I raised the subject with my mother when we drove up from Washington to the farm. I nudged her memory toward it, I lured it, dropping small baits of suggestion in her path until I had her deep in the forest again, in the 1920s and '30s, at which point in the journey her memory became autonomous and proceeded without me: She was at home, for better or for worse.

She found her way to her mother's house and its sad story—how her mother, "on the rebound," had married that much much older man, Tom Vickers, a middle-aged well-to-do Pittsburgh steel broker, and had gone to live in the big house in Sewickley. And how her mind—of itself, or, who knows, under the assaults of Tom's brutalities—began to wander, go out of focus, become strange.

My mother remembered how beautifully her mother, Hildegard, used to fix my mother's hair before school every morning: And there came a morning when my mother was nine when her mother, tying a ribbon in the little girl's hair, seemed suddenly, subtly changed, seemed someone else, seemed to have taken leave somehow. The little girl, my mother, was mutely shocked, and registered the moment, and never forgot it.

My mother came home from school one day to the mansion and found a delivery man, sitting at his ease with her mother on the patio, the man lounging with a proprietary air. My mother, a fierce little girl, chased him off. For my mother had become the adult and her mother had become the child.

The old man, born just after the Civil War, a Victorian and martinet, a bully of rectitude, was oblivious for a long time. How could he have imagined what his vague and almost otherworldly wife, so artistic and impractical, was up to during the days when he was downtown among the mighty, brokering steel?

It was the Great Depression, of course. The crash in 1929 had hurt Tom Vickers to some extent, but it was only as the Depression spread and sank deeper and deeper into the country that he began to feel its effect, as factories closed and the demand for steel fell and fell.

When he learned of his wife's wanderings, he threw
her out of the house. He banished her, always in the family
the prototype of Lear in his dudgeon. And he demanded
that my mother renounce her mother, Hildegard, and never
speak to her again. My mother, at the age of twelve or thirteen, refused to do that, and so she went into banishment
with Hildegard.

First, they checked into an expensive hotel in downtown Pittsburgh. They stayed at the hotel for a week, signing the room-service checks for their food. They began to
worry about the size of the bill, and, instructing the front
desk to send the bill to Tom (a little scene about that), they
moved to a cheaper hotel.

At last the bill in the second hotel grew alarmingly
large. Mother and daughter found a taxi, and told the driver
they needed a boardinghouse, not too squalid. The driver
found them one. And when they moved in, they found that
the man living in the room across the hall from them was
their ex-gardener.

So the banishment began. Tom Vickers gave them ten
dollars a week to live on. My mother learned that if she
went to his office and behaved in a suitably daughterly and
dutiful and fawning way ("Oh, Daddy"), the old man would
give her money.

Hildegard retreated by degrees into the paranoid
schizophrenia that took her finally to her last refuge, a state
mental hospital called Maywood.

My mother's face (now we were driving through
southern Jersey countryside, cows, barns, a thin and hopeful
early April light) crumbled for a moment:

"The police found her once walking at dusk along a
railroad track. She had an idea she needed to go to Baltimore, and she was walking along the tracks toward Baltimore."

Then there was a legal hearing, instigated by old Tom—"the filthy son of a bitch!"—to have Hildegard declared insane, so that Tom could take full possession of whatever property they had held jointly. For Tom by this time had decided to dispose of Hildegard and remarry.

My mother vividly recalled the hearing. She was by this time married herself—at the absurd age of fifteen, forced into the marriage by the selfsame Tom—and she was living with my father, who was twenty-one, in State College, Pennsylvania, where he worked as an AP stringer. She scraped together the bus fare to go to Pittsburgh for her mother's sanity hearing.

A nurse from the state hospital led Hildegard into the courtroom, and Hildegard, seeing Tom, came into sudden fierce focus. She shot her finger at Tom at the end of her quiveringly stiffened arm and said in a loud, clear voice, "There's the man who did it!"

Hildegard, legally insane, returned to the hospital where she would stay for the rest of her life: "Not unhappy," my mother said the nurses told her, "living in her own private world." The doctors all agreed that she was a paranoid schizophrenic, and my mother did not disagree with the diagnosis, although she said, with bitter emphasis, "She was right to be paranoid!"

My mother's memory—sometimes memory is itself a kind of paranoid schizophrenic—wandered for a couple of hours through such territory: Pennsylvania in the thirties, her parents, the trauma when her father forced my father to marry her when she was still a schoolgirl. The old bastard took them to lunch after the "ceremony" to an expensive downtown Pittsburgh restaurant. My mother went to the ladies' room and looked at herself in the mirror and turned wonderingly to the attendant and told her, "I'm married! I just got married!" (This, my mother almost sixty years

later, aping the little girl's voice.) And the woman attendant said, "Oh, no, my dear. You are just a child." My
mother wore a pleated plaid skirt and white bobby socks
and loafers. And after the lunch, Grandpa Tom packed the
happy couple aboard a Greyhound bus for State College,
and did not leave them until the bus was gone. He did not
want my mother to return to the boardinghouse or even to
pack a bag.

And so began the beginning of the life that brought
my life, and now my mother's toward the end, the other
bracket of time, and I, driving beside her in the Audi heading north ("What kind of car is this?" she asks suspiciously,
and when I say "German," she makes a face, as if after all
these years, buying a German car is a form of collaboration
with the Nazis) with my many-bypassed heart pounding
away and not so far behind her, I would guess, in that
bracketing of the other end of time.

We enter the New Jersey gaslands, sulphurously
swampy and pipe coiled, evil smelling. We pass into the
American intestinal zone, refineries flaring and hellish
against the sky. Giant fuel-cylinder farms among the wetlands and migrating birds. Chthonic stinks fill the lungs
and rise by capillary effect through the sinuses, into the
mind.

We talk about stingers—brandy and crème de men-
the—a favorite drink, long-ago poisons, from the forties.
My mother remembers the night when she invaded the
men's bar at the National Press Club in Washington. She
remembers it because she had been drinking stingers that
night with my father and some other journalists in the
"Tampax Room" of the Press Club. Farther down the hall
through leather-covered swinging doors lay the dismal twi-
lighted Men's Bar, with its polished brass plaque that iden-
tified it as such: WOMEN STAY OUT.

My mother, after several stingers, blazing indignation, marched from the Tampax Room to the Men's Bar, several men following, pleading with her not to do it, and blistered through the leather swinging doors, to the stuporous surprise of the boozehound regulars.

The Irish bartender crossed himself with humorous alarm and said, "Jesus, Mary, and Joseph!" My mother looked him in the eye and in a loud firm voice, demanded, "A stinger, please." The bartender, to his credit, went along with it. "Yes, madam." He mixed it. She drank it—hurrying the drink, gulping it in a sort of unconscious macho display, after which, her point made, she allowed a courtly older journalist to lead her back to the Tampax Room, where she savored the rest of the evening with a smile of sardonic satisfaction.

"It used to make me so goddamned mad," she says, "the things we were excluded from." She remembers the ring of men, standing at the men's bar, their heaviness, their dark booziness, their oppressive domineering air, and the image merges in her tale with the ring of men her father always surrounded himself with—"his cronies," as she says. "He hadn't a friend in the world. He had cronies, sycophants, stooges who would flatter him all the time: 'Yes, Mr. Vickers. No, Mr. Vickers.'"

The ring of stooges and cronies was there when her father forced her to marry her cousin, my father—the Victorian had found out they had slept together—standing in a supportive semicircle as witnesses in her father's Pittsburgh office, along with the private detective who had brought my father in from State College across the state, and the Presbyterian minister who performed the ceremony.

The cronies and stooges were there again in the courtroom when her father had her mother declared legally insane, and one of them came forward and stuck out his hand

in a jovial, condescending way—after the judge had put her mother away for good—and said, "Hello, Elise." She said to him, "You dirty son of a bitch!" And walked away in her aura of fury, the black-red weather system she could conjure even then.

So through the stingers the night she liberated the men's bar, she saw the same oppressive men: saw her father's male-master gravity and menace. And it enraged her.

But all men were not like that. When she became pregnant later with my older brother Hugh, she went to live with my father's father, Dr. Morrow, with his wife and seven other children in a little town called Loysberg.

Dr. Morrow was a kind, decent, gentle man with none of the bully in him, none of the heavy male brutality. His father, Albert Morrow, had been a colonel in the U.S. Cavalry. Dr. Morrow had been born out West, in Texas, on the army post at San Angelo, and as a young man had worked as a semiprofessional baseball pitcher in Florida before going to medical school, late, in his thirties. He did not marry my grandmother, Marjorie Vickers (niece of old Tom Vickers—the marriage of the cousins Hugh and Elise was a little too close to taboo) until he was in his forties. All these older men marrying younger women.

Dr. Morrow, unlike Tom Vickers, had an essential sweetness about him. When my pregnant mother came to live with him and his numerous children, he treated her as a father ought to treat a child. The family did not have much money, and often did not have quite enough to eat. Oatmeal for breakfast was the main meal of the day. Once a day the doctor would go to the grocery store for a can of soup, which, much watered, served to feed the children their midday meal. Dinner was problematic. But the doctor always saw to it that my mother had enough to eat.

And when Hughie was born, the neighbors brought

my mother what she remembers to this day as the best meal she has ever eaten: roast chicken, mashed potatoes, gravy, stuffing. "I felt guilty eating it all alone, when the other children had so little. But it was so good—the best thing I have ever eaten in my life!"

I have long sensed that the Great Depression was a far greater influence on the American character in the twentieth century than Americans know. In any case, in my own life, the years preceding my birth (in September 1939, the moment the Depression gave place to World War II) have seemed a sort of premonitory bleakness. I have felt their influence all of my life: the lingering fear, the knowledge of hunger, the stoicism and drinking, the universe that emerged from the massive failure of the American economy, a grainy, black-and-white imagery (the technology of movies appropriated to memory and atmosphere): a decade without color, but gray as a sidewalk or darker and dull, like pig-iron.

The mentality of cast-off clothing—the slush seeping up through the sole of the shoe, a flapping shoe tongue and a hole the size of a fifty-cent piece, mortification in the classroom at the torn shirtsleeve, contorting to conceal it—compacts in the deep strata, like trees pressed into coal, into an enduring shame and worthlessness. All that (in my biography anyway) comes out of the Depression.

I buy jackets and trousers at consignment shops sometimes—thrift and shame, thrift and shame: Some Dutchess County squire's cigarette burn-hole from—who knows?—years ago looks at me from above my right forearm. Classy castoffs from the Millbrook Consignment: some swell's gray flannels that fit me oddly in the bottom, the ones with the hitherto unnoticed piddle-stain just west of the fly. Other gentlemen's duds, and with them a far-off, barely perceptible vibration of shame. When I was nine or ten, my mother collected castoff tweed jackets for me from Katherine Bryan, "Sister" Barnes, who later married John O'Hara and was for years my mother's best friend and taught her some of the bad habits of the rich. It was Sister who would look at some rich middle-aged lover boy and announce in her elegant whiskey-voice, stage-whispering: "What a man! You can see his balls jiggling in his trousers all the way across the room!"

It is the way of journalists—writers in general, maybe—to make friends with the rich and powerful and feel in the transaction an unhappy sense of having become a sort of parasitic witness, a pseudofriend with some back-channel acceptability as scribe-bard-entertainer, but never, ever, the real thing—whatever the real thing may be, an illusion of some aristocracy, some hereditary ease.

The farther wisdom in this, of course, is that those in possession of the real thing are often fools, a fact that provides momentary relief, before a different sense of shame (pandering to the unworthy, abasing oneself) sets in.

None of this is worth the trouble it occasions; it is a storm in very shallow waters. Ernest Hemingway expanded on this theme with appalling dishonesty, having left his first wife, Hadley, for a modestly rich woman, Pauline Pfeiffer, then blaming (in *Snows of Kilimanjaro,* for example, and later *A Moveable Feast)* wealth for sucking him in and destroying his talent and happiness. Of course, there is a difference between marrying the rich and buying their pee-stained trousers at consignment shops.

Just before my second heart attack, I was living for a month in Washington, in Georgetown, in a lovely though oddly designed house that had once belonged to Joseph Alsop and had been rented to me by the friend of a friend, the present owner. Alsop had entertained John Kennedy there the night of the inauguration in 1961. The house, on

Dumbarton Street, is built on three sides around a garden, with a small swimming pool tucked into a corner. The overall effect is of a kind of jewel case: light and glass arranged to display a beautiful and expensive prize, a secret concealed from the outer world. The house, still and silent at midday, May sun pouring into the garden (the day before my heart attack), and throwing a subtly reflected greenish dappled light into dining room and study, onto the objects resting here and there each with its noumen of prestige (a *legion d'Honneur* that the grandfather had been awarded as ambassador to France many years ago, old books, an aerial photograph of the family's island estate in Maine).

I thought of Yeats's (the genetic fallback, evidently, bard of the family occasion) *Purgatory,* in which the tinker's child rails at him in the ruins of the manor house, and the tinker describes, "Old books, rich books, books by the ton!" The old man is fuzzy in the ruins: "I try to remember what the butler said to a drunken gamekeeper in mid-October, but I cannot. If I cannot, none living can. Where are the jokes and stories of a house, its threshold gone to patch a pigsty?"

"My God, but you had luck!" says the boy. "What education have you given me?" And his father answers, "I gave the education that befits a bastard that was got upon a tinker's daughter in a ditch!"

I was always obscurely moved by the brutality of the line; it is a brutal play. The tinker describes how he killed his father, the stable groom who married the aristocratic daughter of the house which he then ran to ruin: "I stuck him with a knife—that knife that cuts my dinner now."

I felt at times as if I had broken into the house in Georgetown. Or as if I had become invisible and could ghost from room to room. As if I could pass in front of its mirrors and not make an image in them, but merely a cold white smudge in the air, a kind of aerosol.

My own internal self-destruct—the heart attacks and the blood-clotting anger that caused them—began somehow in the 1930s, I think. The mechanism that got broken in me broke in the years before I was born. The themes of lives flow together and fuse and compound. There are times when I am sweet Dr. Morrow, or my father through Dr. Morrow, and times when I am old Tom Vickers: an overbearing bully, a martinet, a nineteenth-century ranter.

* * *

So I have felt the shadow of the period for most of my life—both the public shadow (the national trauma) and the private one, which was a sum of specific dramas like my mother's privileged childhood turned to banishment, or Dr. Morrow's sad migrations in search of a medical practice.

After Dr. Morrow died in 1938, my grandmother got a job as a librarian in Baltimore, and Uncle Chris, the oldest after my father (who was married and gone to Philadelphia to work on the paper there) found a job, and they valiantly held the family together. Then the war came and the older boys went into army or navy, went to Europe or the Pacific, and after V-J Day, came home to a different country.

By that time, my parents were young journalists on the make in Washington. My father did his navy time at the Great Lakes Naval Base on Lake Michigan, outside Chicago, as the editor of the base newspaper: He was twenty-five and known as "Pops," and as he had two children, he declined an offer to serve abroad. He spent the war in the Middle West, having adventures in the Dixieland jazz clubs of Chicago. His only memory of danger from the war, as far as I know, arose from the morning during basic training when he and a horde of other novice sailors were locked in a closed room that was gradually filled with gas, a drill to teach them to put on their gasmasks under emergency conditions.

When he told me the story, with its atmosphere of choking panic, I had a mental flicker of Auschwitz. But with an American-boy rite-of-passage happy ending, the sailors spilling out of the gas-room into bright midwestern sunshine, laughing and choking and free again.

If I am Dr. Morrow and Tom Vickers sometimes, my memory is also Hildegard, memory itself gone wandering, aimless, paranoid, precisely schizophrenic. Depression is by definition feckless. This all arises out of some depression (psychological, metaphysical depression as well as, by coincidental pun, the dark-shadowing economic depression). My father is my delok, my memory is Hildegard, my wandering, disturbed grandmother.

These myths have been simultaneously forming and eating away at my heart all these years: the time, the country, the family, the architecture they coalesce to form. Myths have such powers. I cannot disavow them, or escape them, or expel them from my heart, except by telling them as a story.

I have been reading *Walden,* the wonderful warming, flowing "Spring" toward the end of Thoreau's meditation, and after that, the conclusion: "However mean your life is, meet it and live it; do not shun it and call it hard names. . . . Love your life, poor as it is."

24

The swallows have reappeared at the farm. They leap and slide in the air above the pond, beside the barn, in the flight patterns of bats, swoopy-loopy-darting.

Reminds me mordantly of journalistic flapping. But without the feathers: like a balloon fully inflated and released in a birthday room to fly wildly like a spluttering rocket until it expires exhausted on the floor or wherever it happens to land. So much hot air.

The ice melted days ago on the pond water, which now is a grudging half-green, half-warm color, a little sinister, like clinging winter—or like the color of African rivers that have crocodiles in them, a murk of concealment. The pond water has something devouring about it, cold. It is vaguely disturbing to see the reflection of white birches on its surface, as if its ugly blank were trying to swallow the spring.

We walk in the morning up to the white rocks again, and a kestrel fires across the valley at our eye level. The cats catch field mice and voles once more, whose taking they celebrate with a high jaunty toss of the head, which has the effect of flipping the limp mouse's or vole's body over the shoulder like a necktie.

When we reach the outcropping of white rocks, and look out over the farm in the valley, the dog chews a cherry-birch branch and out flow blood-beads of wintergreen sap, a rush of spring perfume like some drifting eroticism that hovers in the air, until a breeze bears it off.

Snow-melt runs through the field grasses, through wind-felled or rotted toppled trees heaped in the woods, through the peeper frogs' bottomland, the cottontail rabbits' briary, through hornbeam roots and scattered quarry quartz, through the rich varieties of deershit and coyote scats and coon drops and other offerings that under the spring wash melt back into the earth like lava, the cylindrical or buckshot or mud-pie turd-forms dissolving into camouflage.

The dog in the golden evening light gains on a rabbit, whose focused intensity of fur, legs fully extended at each bound, flies for its life toward the safety of the briars, pure life and death in perfect distillation in the clearest drop of a moment: the red-gold hound in his hunting flurry, the rabbit skimming across the earth: pure time.

In one of the concealed fields beyond the woods, I come upon a deer's rotting carcass, the rib cage picked clean and white but the skull still covered with decomposing skin, and the deer's eyes blank and glaucous. The animal may have starved in the cold, or may have been shot last fall in hunting season and left there, then been deep frozen and only now thawed and returned to its work of decomposing.

In the evening, the peeper frogs make the sound of the stars peeping in the dark-crystal sky, and there is a sharp sliver moon. The coyotes have begun to yip and yodel, several fields away.

Fred is a high-energy hound, a vizsla. He has been released now from months of blizzard confinement and deep freeze and he runs across the fields in mad circles, his neck craned forward and hound's nose (like a fighter plane on a strafing run) grazing the terrain, in an exuberant frenzy to smell and see the world and take it in his mouth and gnaw it.

I feel the same. Or rather, I see that I ought to feel the same. But the thought precedes the instinct, which is getting it all backward. Still, my brain reaches down to feel, as if for the first time, a stirring of blood and body, a melting, a rising of the spirit like sap up from the cold, solid death below the surface, where the winter was. In the cold, it is difficult to feel, and I am inclined to think too much in any case. Repairing the heart has to do with the recovery of feeling.

It is sixty degrees by the big-dialed thermometer on the farmhouse porch. The rhododendron still droops in its woebegone way. A wind chime vibrates minutely, noise high and fine and silver-fragile. A one-engine airplane putters across the horizon.

I began this writing as a record of heart attack and a struggle to recover from it. I assumed that I could not recover until I could account for the reasons for the heart attack, and for the one that hit me seventeen years earlier.

I now begin to think that the introspection, however pseudoclinical, is useless, or anyway illusory, that it is silly to think I can understand the reasons for these implosions of mine (anger and so on). A heart attack is a mysterious event. Life does not often have reasons; heart attacks do not necessarily have explanations; death certainly does not have reasons or explanations. To expect that would be to expect justice, some Newtonian cause-and-effect. Which is not what experience teaches.

We have to be content with the simple-physical: Smoking, bad diet, stress, and heredity are the principal causes, everyone guesses. But no one understands heart attacks very well.

The greatest sin is ingratitude. There is an arrogance in the idea of "recovery," even a sort of obliviousness. Spring is the great consolation and reminder. It is recovery indeed, and I am grateful to absorb the truth that the earth will accomplish its recovery perfectly, even when I eventually go melting into the farm's camouflage.

Time has taken on an astonishing transparency. I reach through it, through its depth of field, and touch everything within it. Time has taken on a clarity and tenderness.

* * *

I tend to browse on the dark side of things. I am one of those. If there are brights and shadows, I gravitate toward the shadows. I dwell upon them. I dwell in them. It is a fault. I am sorry for it. It is a temperamental inclination.

I have a dreary tendency to expect the worst; it is a way of trying to disarm dangers by embracing them first in imagination and even exaggerating them: turning them into preemptive cartoons of disaster, even into art. It is a way of singing to catastrophes and thereby attempting to put them to sleep.

I have been writing, I think, not only to try to understand the heart attacks and anger, but, more fundamentally, to try to chase away a depression that settled on me years ago, when I was a child, a cloud I have been unable to shake or dispel. I beg indulgence. I have been singing to my in-

ternal shadows. They belong to prehistory and are inaccesi-
ble.

In the evening light of the farm in mid-April when I
walk out, every blade of grass is articulated to the eye in
perfect clarity: a wind of golden light across tousled emerald earth.

25

A year has passed since I had the heart bypass operation: I hardly think of it now. Ingratitude.

Or I think of it sidelong. I step around it quietly. I do not wish to disturb the subject, to stir it up again.

The year, I think, has amounted, among other things, to a period of mourning. I accepted my own death and even moved into it, as one moves into a new house, but I did not grow calm as a Buddhist is said to do in the neighborhood of death.

I thought the new house was a step down in the world. Death felt like the definitive version of the recurring tumbledown family dreamhouse; the dreamhouse was the model of death's disintegration.

My body, heart pump and all, had returned to health months before. Restoring a mental or spiritual atmosphere of health, of living connection with the world, was more difficult, possibly because in the past that connection had

311

been blackened and fire damaged. Anger burns out the circuitry.

There are many kinds of heart damage—for example, the flabby, gluttonous, fat-clogged decline, a glacial subsiding of the flesh, a decay that is the opposite of violence. My heart, as I have said, was not fat at all but went bad out of emotional violence.

I wish I could say I have learned a becoming calm, or have taught myself New Age–illuminated serenities. I have not.

But I have improved, I have improved. The eyes open only in blinks to unaccustomed lights.

* * *

I observe the first anniversary out of the corner of my eye, being in motion again, a new onset of restlessness, the motif of escape. I have cashed in accumulated weeks of vacation at *Time* and set off from the farm, the old Jeep Grand Wagoneer loaded up like the Joads' truck.

Susan and I are driving across the country to California: southern route out, northern route back.

We left Washington, D.C., in the midst of a heat wave, bright, suffocating, claustrophobic. As we crossed the Potomac, the sky abruptly turned an evil copper color, and then blackened and released a Shakespearean thunderstorm that chased us well into Virginia, past Culpepper. Indignant nature lashed us from the capital, across the river, into the Confederacy. The highway vanished, the storm engulfed us in black-gray water as if we had plunged into turbulent surf and we flipped and rolled there, disoriented. A blaze of lightning, and then the rain flew out of the turbulent black like showers of silver nails.

But as we passed into the Shenandoah Valley, the sky

cleared, as if nothing had happened, as if it had all been a violent fantasy, and the afternoon reverted to a motionless equatorial yellow-white and the usual compress of wet heat. The countryside exhaled steam.

We drove south-southwest, through Virginia, grazing the shaggy Great Smoky Mountains, off to our southeast, and pointed west across the interminable length of Tennessee.

Beside DeGray's Lake in Arkansas, as I carried the bags from the car toward the park lodge where we would stay that night, a bolt of lightning split the universe around me—an apocalyptic crack—and then, an aftermath of electric-smelling air, and through it, smoking leaves and twigs fluttered down, all around me, like the remnant feathers in the air after Sylvester has swallowed Tweetie Bird.

Too much motion: We had bounced day after day through the upper South, the Jeep pounding valiantly through 110-degree heat.

Then outside Dallas the country was transformed; trees changed, water changed, distances changed. The closer-jumbled, dense, well-watered deciduous greens of the East left off and the bigger, drier spaces of the West began.

* * *

We have stopped for a day's rest. I sit under a live oak tree in the Texas hill country, beside Cypress Creek outside Wimberley, a beautifully clear stream overshaded by cypress and live oak and pecan trees.

In the water below me among the limestone rocks I make out trout and long dark ferns like dreadlocks flowing with the stream. Ophelia as a Rastafarian. Farther downstream, a small waterfall.

Too much motion—half of the United States top-speeded through in only days. I must be still.

The sun on the steaming day breaks through, just now, and turns the air emerald for a moment; now vanishes behind the sodden heavy clouds. All—trees, water, air—returns to a more subdued, still shade of greens and bark-grays. The air rumbles now and then with emunctory thunder.

Then a shower: I study the precise flowing geometries of the water as it slides past the rock below me about to tumble over the five-foot fall, the water sliding smooth in perfectly formed spontaneous arcs. When I place my heel in the water and set up a countersystem of ripple-arcs, the two systems interweave with a spectacular cross-hatching pattern, not tumultuous but rather a perfect new complication of the old pattern, like two cultures interweaving to form a third culture, but nothing of the beauty of either lost in the process. Has this ever happened in the human world?

And so, in the midst of that fine-spun geometric clarity, it rains, a sweet soft rain, but with heavy drops (the air so thick with moisture). The drops strike the glassy water upstream from the falls, and form individual circles that travel out to meet the others and form their arcing interripplings. But now the rain grows heavier until the entire surface is agitated, loses the quality of glass and instead turns all excitement, like a crowd seen from a distance.

Susan pushes off from a rock onshore and swims down the creek toward the falls, breasting against the dreadlock ferns, only her head visible above the surface, springing forward with each stroke, then sliding.

When she reaches the stepping-stones that are like crenellations at the edge of the little fall, she turns and braves the dreadlock ferns again. Her ripples overwhelm the

rain-ripples, she being a larger event in the stream than
they.

Then she rises up out of the water onto a rock, and the
rain stops, and the water is presently like glass again, a
darker, minutely shimmering replication of the trees and
sky above, though through the replicated sky float islands
of scummy mosses now and then.

The shimmering in the water, in tense segmentations,
reminds me of the visual effect of an ocular migraine I had
one spring day some weeks ago. I sat on the porch at the
farm with Susan, and suddenly her face looked like a Pi-
casso—or else a George Price cartoon in the *New Yorker*.
Her eyes seemed to twist screwy in her head, as if her face
had been split into two planes. I shot my gaze back down
onto the *New York Times* I was reading and found I could
not bring the print into focus, and in the southwest quad-
rant of my vision, I saw a tense geometric shimmering, in
the shape of a boomerang, like some token of a quivering
drug-vision on a sunny day.

I thought, of course, I was having a stroke, a panic
mingled with fascination at the shimmering reality-
distortion effects. Reality was torn a little, like bright silk
ripped—a visual equivalent somehow of the mystery I en-
countered as a child on my great uncle's farm in North Carolina, where I first saw a shotgun fired, at a distance from
me, and was astonished that I saw the gun going off and
only so much later, heard the sound of it. The noiseless
muzzle-*poof* of the gun—*pausepause*—and only then, the
boom! Reality cracked open for a moment.

With my torn vision, I lay down, resting my sight but
checking it from time to time by opening my eyes to see if
the tense shimmering had passed. Interesting effect: I
watched my vision.

In time, the shimmering split halves of the world reconciled themselves again. My doctor, Bob Ascheim, later told me the experience was ocular migraine. He said he had it all the time. So much for revelations.

The water here in the Texas hill country is a miracle of these shimmerings: The glassy surface tosses off dreamy-lively articulations in patterns of such fugueing complexity and perfection of improvisation that I am awestruck by their interlacings in the radiance of the reflected sky. Below which, in another dimension, slip the trout and dreadlocks. And upon the surface the waterbug that moves by flicking upon the surface tension, the breaststroke flick of all four limbs so fast you see only a kind of minute jolt of electricity, see the result but not the stroke.

I suppose that the mind is the water (the body itself so much the salty inner ocean, 60 percent of it, anyway) and reflects the sky exactly so, and shimmers tensely exactly so with its disturbances and articulations, rainstorms, ripple-nettings, and that each life is a drop upon the radiance of the stream, the entire history of lives in the world amounting to a transient rainstorm on the beautiful creek surface.

Last night I dreamed about our farm in Dutchess County, and a hillside in which I saw nests of many turtles, holes in the hillside teeming with turtles.

In the middle of the night, Susan placed her hand upon my back and thought I was not breathing, and gave a gasp and pulled my shoulder, whereupon I stirred, breathing deeply, and she relaxed. I knew what she was up to, feeling for my breath. I said nothing, and we both went back to sleep.

A snake I cannot identify, about eight inches long, swims down the center of the creek, its head held above the surface, its length at quarter-speed twisting through the water. I give a short sharp *whoop!* and the snake stops dead in the water but does not dive; its coils pile up toward the halted head, an accordion effect, or like a train with the engine stopped and the cars behind jumbling up a little. Then proceeds. I *whoop* again—another minute train-wreck ensues, but a briefer pause before the snake sinews on untroubled to its destination on the bank downstream from me.

Now the mirror of the river surface holds a turkey buzzard crossing an interval of green-blue watery sky. I look up to actual sky and see the bird as it rides off behind the trees and then spirals back. Now there are three turkey buzzards circling. I wonder if they are merely cruising the territory, or if they have seen carrion below. (Me?)

I thought again of my father dying—the moment he died, exactly. I thought of it when I looked in a full-length mirror in the bathroom in our limestone cottage here in Texas above the creek, and the sight of my torso and legs, a body much like his, even the chest hair growing in the same patterns, brought him into my mind again for another visit—not a sad one, but a kind of middle-distance hovering in the strangely colored air of the stone cottage, whose walls have been painted grasshopper green. His body morphs into mine, or mine into his, for the perishable instant in the grasshopper light.

* * *

It is a year exactly since they cracked open my chest again. I have been wondering what, if anything, I have learned, in the time since then.

There has never been a sweeter creek than this, never a sweeter day than this. The sun turns the creek and creekside all emerald again. A large trout slips out of the dreadlocks, into a pool of green-golden light. The turkey buzzards have now ridden the breeze away and vanished.

* * *

Days later, in Canyon de Chelly, Arizona, I learn of Bill Henry's death.

I am at the lodge on the Navajo reservation, on the pay telephone calling an assistant managing editor of *Time* in New York, Jim Kelly, to discuss an article I have written. Jim comes onto the telephone distracted, his voice heavy, with an undershadow and tension.

"We just found out Bill Henry died of a heart attack in London."

Bill was only forty-four. His father and his grandfather had both died young, of heart attacks, and Bill talked about that sometimes, in a haunty way, his eyes registering the sort of minutely blank *what if? what now?* that I saw in my father's eyes before his stroke. Father and son, father dragging the son along by the invisible genetic tether, over the cliff. Bill: fearing he was running tumbling after his father, into the dark.

Bill was considerably overweight, and he worked himself harder than any writer I knew. When he died, he was in London to review some plays for *Time*. That was typical enough. He combined his job as drama critic with three or four other jobs. He took on hard news assignments for *Time*, he freelanced, he wrote books, he opened his mail while he talked on the phone and twiddled his computer. He worked too hard.

Some weeks before Bill died, I had asked to be relieved of a complicated, short-deadline cover story for *Time*, on Louis Farrakhan and the American black Muslims. I did not want to stay up night after night writing and closing the piece. I had spent the night like that too many times in the past. It struck me as risky. For me. It was the first time that I had asked to be excused from a cover story. The editors were understanding. They said they would find someone else to do it.

So, short-handed, they asked Bill Henry to write the piece. He did so, quite professionally—soldiering. The following week, I sent him a note apologizing for the fact that he got stuck with the story I felt too apprehensive to write. Bill replied with a jocular-bitter message listing the hours he had worked during that week (many, many hours), and the hours he had slept (almost none).

At the lodge at Canyon de Chelly, I put down the phone and walked out into the bright Arizona sunlight. I felt a little as I had at DeGray's Lake when the smoking twigs and leaves were fluttering down, the air electric. Shock indeed. Poor Bill was the tree that was struck this time. The lightning had come close to me, but I was left standing there among Tweetie Bird's fluttering feathers.

I fell to mourning Bill for days in a tremendous southwestern stillness, among the canyons. Or rather, in thinking about Bill's death, I thought about my own, and realized that I had spent the last year in a kind of mourning for the part of my heart that had already died.

We camped in the national parks, the campsites busy with the summer tourist trade. The great American nature was not quite suburbanized, but close: standardized campsites with charcoal grate and picnic table and a bare patch where the tent goes; the mule deer nonchalantly tame at Zion, circulating obliviously, like cats, among the tourists.

The road, the intricate American circulatory system: ingenious RV rigs of every description in lumbering disorderly caravan, trailing extra cars like dinghies, bristling on top with bungee-corded bikes and motorcycles and canoes, the stainless Art Deco bullet-shaped Airstreams being the retro aristocrats of the road, and among them a thousand variations of snubby-nosed Dodge Ram vans customized and Ford Econolines with venetian blinds in their windows, or pickup trucks with clamped-on RV cabins, and now and then superannuated hippie vehicles, Ken Kesey schoolbuses from long ago, or VW microbuses painted psychedelic, filled with black Labs and time-traveling bearded-and-tie-dyed nomads as young now precisely (a new issue of the same creature) as they were in 1968 when I first came to New Mexico to visit the communes in the Sangre de Cristo Mountains. At one commune called Morning Star, the fathers and mothers of these children took drugs and scratched the earth in some zonked abstract gesture at agriculture, symbolic cultivation; they lived on food stamps mostly. The overprivileged gone to seed. The Mexicans and the Indians hated them for their play-poverty. The Anglos and Mexicans and hippies sometimes took shots at one another, the hippies having abandoned peace and love for a feudal tribal hatred.

Another tear in American time. Motion on the road, and yet time standing oddly, disorientingly still. Travelers circled in some loop of stationary fifties or sixties, recycling the Airstreams and VW microbuses, their disparate vehicular visions of what America is all about. The weave of time and that of space disjoined, peeled off from one another in the mind.

The canyons, being deep cuts in time, mocked the lesser cycles of human generations.

Odd about the canyons: We would drive across ordinary western American desert, the vast drynesses, mesquite-shrubbed, sagebrushed, the only motion being wind and tumbleweed.

And then, before us, abruptly, out of nowhere behind a screen of scrubby pines, the earth would open and disclose itself: a majestic, enigmatic neverland, blue-hazed, the very intimacy of the world.

The greatest astonishment of the canyons, after I had studied them, was the kinetic force of their motionlessness.

The surface of the stream in Texas, a sort of recording membrane, registered each cloud's motion and passing bird's flight and waterbug.

The stone of the canyons—which were the deepest, truest tear in time—held upon its membrane, sensitive as film, a story of millions of years' dramas and dynamics.

At Canyon de Chelly, Susan walked down the trail to the bottom. I stayed perched on the rim, afraid of the climb back up. Still in a state of aftershock about Bill Henry's death (on a very low McLandress, thinking as much about myself and my own heart as about Bill, the two facts crowded uncomfortably into a small mental room together), I sat for several hours motionless on a pine-shaded rock just above the 800-foot vertical drop to the canyon's dreamlike, pastoral floor.

I fell into a trance state, staring at the rock walls on the other side: the layers exposed—the fluid striations of eons' pressures and heaves. From the canyon floor the wall came up in gently waving laminations, atilt with the earth's tossings and turnings, but then at higher altitudes began more complicated stories: whorled roundings of rock, a sort of lava-boil, and an unreadable significance of streakings, and pecked indentations like Morse code that changed their message as the angle of the climbing sun changed and sent out new dot-dash patterns.

Geologic muscularity and stillness. And down the canyon a light of gray-blue mist that will be burned off when the sun gets higher. The Navajo arrive in pickups to set up shop behind me in the parking lot, where they will spread turquoise and silver jewelry on the truckbeds and quietly quote prices all day to the Winnebagos.

As the morning advances, light and shadow on the

stone make different configurations, new messages. An ascending sun makes the sockets of the indented stone grow darker, and turns the surrounding stone a brighter, sharper shade.

The dawn's pinks wash away, and in full morning, the stone harshens toward alkali white, though never as smiting as the mountains of Moab across the Dead Sea, never that Middle Eastern blinding abstraction. I go off on a side-meditation about the theology of deserts. The rock forms and rock colors of the American Southwest, I think, encourage different thoughts of divinity from those biblical places. In the southeastern canyons, if anything, pantheism. In the Middle East landscapes, monotheism.

A raven crosses my vision at eye level. Ravens like to ride the updrafts that fluff the air at the canyon rim, and you see them up there, high-flying from the perspective of the canyon floor far below. The raven emits its cry, a rasp run through the haze. A wasp with long legs dangling like a heron manages the rim's air currents with astonishing expert steadiness, in profile to me at the edge of my shade pine, hovering over the great drop.

I feel short of breath. I become certain that in an instant, I will tumble forward from my rock and into the canyon, into the depth of geological-genital time.

Rapture of the heights, more a temptation than a phobia: the abyss-temptation. Not a fear, exactly. I fear snakes, but am not tempted by them. I simply hate snakes and recoil from them. I recoil from heights for a different reason: I fear the narcotic, swooning magnetic pull of death by falling.

I had a friend who suffered especially strong fears of tumbling. Once he came to visit me in New York during Christmas season. I undertook to find him a hotel room. Most of the hotels were full. I tried the Harvard Club, which had one room left, on the fourth floor. I announced the fact triumphantly to Jerry, who looked sheepish, mumbled and stuttered for a time, then admitted that he could not stay in any room above the second floor. The terror of the window—even a closed window—was too great. Once or twice, he said, he ended by sleeping in the bathtub, with the bathroom door shut tight. I shook my head at this, in some compassion and puzzlement.

Sitting too close to the rim of the canyon, I exert a main-force, conscious effort and throw my weight backward, toward safety, like a baby sitting in his diaper and his gravid baby fat being capsized harmlessly backward.

I twist and rise carefully to my knees and crawl away from the precipice.

I take refuge among the Navajo pickups and look at their silver for an hour, until Susan, radiant, climbs out of the trail from the canyon, up from the bottom of time.